HUMAN
and
SOCIAL STRUCTURES

MANCHESTER
1824

Manchester University Press

HUMAN AGENTS
and
SOCIAL STRUCTURES

Edited by

Peter J. Martin and **Alex Dennis**

Manchester University Press
Manchester and New York
distributed in the United States exclusively by Palgrave Macmillan

Published by Manchester University Press
Oxford Road, Manchester M13 9NR, UK
and Room 400, 175 Fifth Avenue, New York, NY 10010, USA
www.manchesteruniversitypress.co.uk

Distributed in the United States exclusively by
Palgrave Macmillan, 175 Fifth Avenue, New York,
NY 10010, USA

Distributed in Canada exclusively by
UBC Press, University of British Columbia, 2029 West Mall,
Vancouver, BC, Canada V6T 1Z2

British Library Cataloguing-in-Publication Data
A catalogue record for this book is available from the British Library

Library of Congress Cataloging-in-Publication Data applied for

ISBN 978 0 7190 7863 3 *hardback*
ISBN 978 0 7190 8172 9 *paperback*

First published 2010

Typeset by Special Edition Pre-press Services
www.special-edition.co.uk
Printed in Great Britain
by CPI Antony Rowe, Chippenham, Wiltshire

Contents

Notes on contributors   *page* vii

PART ONE – GENERAL ISSUES

1   **Introduction: the opposition of structure and agency**
     Peter J. Martin and Alex Dennis   3

2   **The structure problem in the context of structure
     and agency controversies**
     Wes Sharrock and Graham Button   17

3   **On the retreat from collective concepts in sociology**
     Peter J. Martin   34

4   **Structure and agency as the products of dynamic
     social processes: Marx and modern social theory**
     Alex Dennis   52

PART TWO – RECENT SOCIAL THEORISTS

5   **The two Habermases**
     Anthony King   71

6   **Pierre Bourdieu: from the model of reality to the
     reality of the model**
     Richard Jenkins   86

7   **The production and reproduction of social order:
     is structuration a solution?**
     Wes Sharrock   100

8   **On the reception of Foucault**
     Allison Cavanagh and Alex Dennis   117

PART THREE – AFTER THE DEBATE

9   **Beyond social structure**
     Richard Jenkins   133

10   **Two kinds of social theory: the myth and reality
     of social existence**
     Anthony King   152

     Bibliography   166

     Index   180

Notes on contributors

Peter J. Martin taught Sociology at the University of Manchester for many years. He was Head of Sociology there for three years, and from 2000 until 2003 was Dean of Undergraduate Studies in the former Faculty of Social Sciences and Law at Manchester. His major publications include *Music and the Sociological Gaze* (Manchester University Press, 2006), *Sounds and Society* (Manchester University Press, 1995) and (with Wes Sharrock and John Hughes) *Understanding Modern Sociology* (Sage, 2003) and *Understanding Classical Sociology* (2nd edn, Sage, 2003). He is now a freelance author and musician.

Alex Dennis is Lecturer in the Sociology of Deviance at the University of Salford. He is the author of *Making Decisions About People* (Ashgate, 2001) and has published articles on decision-making in complex organisations, philosophical contradictions in ethnomethodology, pragmatism and symbolic interactionism, and (with Peter J. Martin) on the concepts of power and social structure. His research interests include clinical decision-making, deviant behaviour in public spaces, and (with Greg Smith) is currently conducting an ethnographic study of the work of security guards. He provides web and email facilities for the Society for the Study of Symbolic Interaction.

Graham Button gained his Ph.D. from the University of Manchester in 1976. From 1975 until 1992 he taught at Plymouth Polytechnic (subsequently the University of Plymouth), where he was Principal Lecturer in Sociology. During 1980 and 1985 he was Visiting Faculty at the University of California (Los Angeles) and Boston University respectively. In 1992 he joined the Cambridge laboratory of Xerox's Palo Alto Research Centre as Senior Scientist, becoming Director in 1999, and in 2003 was appointed Laboratory Director of Xerox's European Research Centre in Grenoble, France. In 2005 he took up the position of Executive Dean of Faculty at Sheffield Hallam University, and is now Pro-Vice Chancellor of Arts, Computing, Engineering and Sciences.

Allison Cavanagh gained her Ph.D. in Sociology at the University of Manchester in 2003 and is a Lecturer in Communications Studies at the University of Leeds, where she is currently Programme Director for the B.A.

in Communications Studies. Her research interests include media history and new media, and her most recent work has focused on new media theory, in particular theorising power in relation to networks. She is currently working on the development of models of media participation which are sensitive to new approaches to power. Her recent publications include *Sociology in the Age of the Internet* (McGraw-Hill, 2007).

Richard Jenkins is Professor of Sociology at the University of Sheffield. Trained as an anthropologist, he has undertaken field research in Northern Ireland, England, Wales and Denmark. His empirical research interests include social identity in all of its aspects (particularly ethnicity, national identity and disability) and enchantments ancient and modern, not least religion and popular belief. Theoretically he has yet to progress much beyond symbolic interactionism (and he completely neglected to take the post-modern turn). Among his major publications are *Foundations of Sociology* (2002), *Pierre Bourdieu* (2nd edn, 2002), *Rethinking Ethnicity* (2nd edn, 2008) and *Social Identity* (3rd edn, 2008).

Anthony King was awarded his Ph.D. by the University of Salford in 1995. He began his career at Liverpool University in the same year and was appointed as a Professor of Sociology at the University of Exeter in 2007. He has published widely, including major studies of football (*The European Ritual*, Ashgate, 2003), social theory (*The Structure of Social Theory*, Routledge, 2004), and has recently competed a monograph on European military transformation, provisionally entitled *From the Rhine to the Hindu Kush*. Although diverse, his work aims to explore processes of European integration from the perspective of actual social practice.

Wes Sharrock is Professor of Sociology at the University of Manchester, where he has been since 1965. His main interests are in the philosophy of social science, philosophy of mind, sociological theory and studies of everyday conduct. His current research interests include the organisation of work in the construction of online ontologies in bioinformatics, and issues in data sharing in collaborations between social scientists and computer visualisation specialists. Amongst his recent and forthcoming publications are: 'Closet Cartesianism in discursive psychology' and (with J. Coulter) 'Against theory of mind' in I. Leudar and A. Costall (eds); *Against Theory of Mind* (Palgrave, 2009); *Studies of Work and the Workplace in HCI* (with G. Button, forthcoming); *There Is No Such Thing as Social Science* (with P. Hutchinson and R. Read; Ashgate, 2008); and *Brain, Mind and Human Behaviour in Contemporary Cognitive Science* (with J. Coulter; Edwin Mellen Press, 2008).

PART ONE

General issues

1

Introduction: the opposition of structure and agency

Peter J. Martin and Alex Dennis

Now, social science generally is still [at the] stage of being able to consider only the very large and clearly visible social structures and of trying to produce insight from these into social life in its totality. States and trade unions, priesthoods and family forms, guild and family structures, class formation and the industrial division of labour – these and similar organs and systems appear to constitute society and to fill out the domain of the science of society. In fact, however, these are already structures of a higher order, in which ... the real concrete life of sociated individuals is crystallized ... The real life of society, provided in experience, could certainly not be constructed from these large objectivized structures that constitute the traditional objects of social science. (Georg Simmel, 1997[1907]: 109–110)

There are in fact no masses; there are only ways of seeing people as masses ... we mass them, and interpret them, according to some convenient formula. Within its terms, the formula will hold. Yet it is the formula, not the mass, which it is our real business to examine. (Raymond Williams, 1990[1958]: 300)

Of all the 'turns' taken by theory, by far the most frequent one is to turn away from the world. (D. R. Watson, 1997: viii)

The quotations above should already have provided a strong sense of what this book is all about. In the opening paragraphs of the essay from which Simmel's remarks are drawn, he argued (as he did elsewhere) that 'seemingly insignificant everyday mundane interactions are constitutive for sociation, society and culture' (Frisby, 1997: 9) and contrasted 'clearly visible social structures' with the 'experience' of 'sociated individuals'. Indeed, the apparent opposition between what has been called the 'objective reality of institutions' (Berger and Luckmann, 1991[1966]: 78) and the apparently subjective experience of individual human beings has given rise to a basic tension within sociological thought. Simmel's remarks, it should be noted, are now more than a century old, yet it would seem that little progress has been made in reconciling the 'objective' and 'subjective' aspects of social life, with the concept of 'society' still seen in opposition to that of the 'individual' and social 'structure' opposed to human 'agency'. Although the contributors to this book represent a variety of sociological positions (and we have not sought to impose homogeneity upon them), one thing that they do share is the belief that this tension has generated a succession of dualistic views of social life which are fundamentally misguided and a set of binary oppositions which are ultimately irreconcilable.

It has been claimed that the origins of the 'new vocabulary of "structure and agency"' can be dated precisely, with the publication of Giddens' *Central Problems in Social Theory* in 1979 (Varela, 2007: 201). Yet, as we have already suggested, the underlying issues have a lengthy history. By the 1970s, Parsons' notions of 'system and voluntarism' were well established, so Giddens' new terms were in a sense redundant, since both oppositions referred to 'the *same* theme of social determinism and individual freedom: the problem of Durkheimian social system/structure and human voluntarism/agency' (ibid.). In the 1960s this 'problem' had been seen in terms of 'two levels of social reality' – with 'social structure or system' opposed by 'social action and interaction' (Cohen, 1968: 236). And, as Martin argues in Chapter 3, the issue is apparent in Durkheim's and Weber's early attempts to formulate distinctively sociological approaches. The result of all this is that 'two theoretical perspectives which are generally regarded as antithetical' have developed, one in which human action is held to be 'determined by macro-level social structures' and another in which the individual is seen as 'consciously deciding about and governing his or her surroundings at the micro-level' (Kirchberg, 2007: 115; see also Lukes, 1975: 19–20, n76).

Indeed, the development of these contrasting perspectives has become something of an orthodoxy for those reviewing the history of sociological thought in the twentieth century:

> when the one-dimensionality of Parsonian structural functionalism (and related objectivist positions such as structuralism, Marxism, etc.) became increasingly manifest in the late sixties, a microreaction ensued which, by the end of the seventies, had shifted the metatheoretical balance to the other extreme of one-dimensional subjectivism, represented (for pedagogical reasons) by Schütz, Blumer, Garfinkel and others. It is only when the limitations of both objectivism and subjectivism were underscored that the possibility of a synthetic micro-macro link eventually emerged in the eighties. (Vandenberghe, 1999: 48)

It will become clear below that (whatever one thinks of the above characterisation of functionalism, structuralism or Marxism) we believe the portrayal of Schütz, Blumer or Garfinkel as espousing 'extreme one-dimensional subjectivism' to be a profound misrepresentation of their works – a misrepresentation which has, however, become tediously familiar. Rather, our contention is that the issues involved are wholly misconceived if represented in terms of such dichotomies as objective versus subjective, structure versus agency, macro versus micro, holism versus individualism, and so on, and hence cannot *ever* be dealt with by trying to effect some sort of reconciliation between the opposed elements, or – for example – to identify a 'linkage' between the 'macro' and the 'micro' (Alexander and Giesen, 1987: 1ff) so as to create a Great Unified Theory for sociology. Similarly, to place analytical emphasis on *either* the individual *or* society is to miss the point: it is true, as Durkheim put it, that in an important sense society is prior to the individual – yet at the same time no one was more aware than he that the social order is above all a moral order, depending on the beliefs and normative commitments of real people (Lukes, 1975: 227; King, 2007: 211). In short, the proper focus of sociological attention must be the achievement and maintenance of what Schütz called 'the realm of intersubjectivity. The world ... experienced by the individual as shared by his [*sic*] fellow creatures, in short as a *social* world' (Schütz, 1972[1932]: 139). It is this realm, we suggest, that Blumer saw as 'human group life' (1969: 77) and which one of our contributors, Richard Jenkins, simply calls the 'human world' (2002a: 4). The reality of normal social life, as another contributor, Anthony King, puts it, is that people are 'embedded in social relations with others' (2006: 470).

The idea of social structure

Yet there are some who still wish to hold on to the idea that there must be social 'structures', independent of actual people and constraining them. Such a conception of structural effects underlies, for example, Bhaskar's 'critical realism':

> The relations into which people enter pre-exist the individuals who enter into them, and those whose activity reproduces or transforms them; *so* they are themselves structures. And it is to these structures of social relations that realism directs our attention – both as the explanatory key to understanding social events and trends and as the focus of social activity aimed at the emancipation of the exploited and oppressed. (Bhaskar, 1989: 4, emphasis added)

This extract raises a number of issues; we will take up four of these. First, what would the reproduction *or* transformation of 'structures' actually be like? Indeed, is the distinction a valid one? How would an actor or analyst know which was occurring? This would require a complete knowledge of all the consequences of a given action. Such matters are pursued further by Sharrock in Chapter 7; for the present the essential point is that *all* social activity makes a difference – change is constant, and social life must be understood in terms of process rather than 'structures'. As Becker has put it:

> There is no simple way to sum up all the changes and decide that so much

> change, but no less, is revolutionary. Nor is there any good reason to make
> the distinction so clear-cut ... We need not make these distinctions defini-
> tively, since our interest is in the growth and decay of forms of collective
> action rather than in the development of logical typologies. (Becker, 1982:
> 308–310)

Second, it does not follow that because people enter into sets of social relations that precede them, these relations therefore constitute 'structures'. No one can deny that individuals enter a world which is organised in all sorts of ways, but to call these patterns 'structures' and then to attribute causal powers to them amounts to reification, or committing the 'fallacy of misplaced concreteness' (Whitehead, 1963[1925]: 52ff).

Third, it is difficult to regard these 'structures' as the 'explanatory key to understanding social events and trends' without lapsing into some form of determinism, in which particular actions are ultimately explained as the result of general social forces.

Fourth, we are also dubious about the notion that 'critical realism' can contribute to the 'emancipation of the exploited and oppressed', and we have tried in vain to identify a single instance in which this has occurred. Lacking this, we believe the claim to be wishful thinking at best and at worst an excuse for political quiescence.

A similar 'critical realist' position has been developed by Margaret Archer. In response to the criticism (made by Anthony King) that 'appeals to autonomous structures are simply errors of description' (King, 1999: 213), Archer reiterated her view that 'we are ... talking about structural proper-ties and powers which defy reduction and are about causal influence which no re-description can eliminate from explanatory accounts' (Archer, 2000b: 466). Thus structures are held to 'exert causal influences upon subsequent interactions by shaping the situations in which later generations of people find themselves ... Like Bhaskar, Archer denies that the causal powers of macrostructures could be explained in terms of interwoven individual acts, done by individual people' (Kiniven and Piiroinen, 2006a: 226).

Archer's position, then, raises the same issues concerning reification and determinism as that of Bhaskar. In addition, like Sawyer (2001: 569), we first question the validity of proposing that patterns of social organi-sation give rise to 'emergent properties' with causal powers. Secondly, we are not persuaded that Archer's position is either useful in the conduct of empirical research or ultimately coherent. She has argued that 'realist social theory tackles the structure/agency problem from a position of *analytical* dualism ... there is never a moment at which *both* structure and agency are not jointly in play' (2000: 465). The dualism is to be regarded purely as an analytical and not a 'philosophical' one. But set against the 'reality' (ibid.: 464) which Archer claims for 'structure' – and its 'emergent properties' – this would seem to undermine the coherence of her position. 'Structures', she writes, 'are ever relational emergents and never reified entities existing without social interaction' (ibid.: 465). Just what is being claimed here?

Thirdly, we take the view that, as Kiniven and Piiroinen (2006a and b) have argued, it is not possible to produce an objective (external, exhaustive) description of social 'structures', or 'society' (or anything else, for that matter), other than through the specific assumptions, concepts and ideas of the 'observer' (for a recent wide-ranging discussion of this, see Frayn, 2006). On this view, knowledge is irredeemably perspectival, and the project of 'critical realism' is epistemologically flawed.

The present book is *not*, therefore, intended as an even-handed review of a long-running controversy about the relative merits of 'structure' and 'agency' perspectives; rather, its aim is to be an intervention which seeks to make the case that structural, system, or holistic approaches to the understanding of social life and the explanation of human action are fundamentally misconceived – as, equally, are efforts which rest on individualistic assumptions. In essence, our view is that human social life is conducted in and through patterns of collaborative interaction: sociologically, our interest is thus not in the subjectivity of individuals but in the ways in which *inter*subjectivity is achieved and maintained.

As we have already said, the contributors to this book display a variety of orientations; however, we believe that there are a least four propositions with which they would all agree:

First, that attempts to specify what is meant by the concept of structure in sociology (and the other human sciences) have led to a bewildering variety of definitions. As Rubenstein has put it, 'There is a striking degree of obscurity and confusion over a concept that is widely regarded as defining the sociological perspective ... Definitions of structure range from a concreteness that precludes generality ... to an abstractness that threatens vacuity' (Rubenstein, 2001: 2). However, for Rubenstein there is much more agreement 'on the *type* of concept sociologists are looking for. Structure is usually conceived as "external" and "objective" features of social order that are thought to have controlling power over culture and action' (ibid.: 3).

Second, that the collective concepts (such as family, state, organisation, class and so on) – which have often been seen as fundamental to sociological analysis – have often encouraged 'the temptation to reify collective aspects of human life' (Jenkins, 2002a: 4); that is, to treat them as if they were real entities, independent of the human beings who constitute them.

Third, that the explanation of human action in terms of 'structural' phenomena ultimately, and inevitably, leads to determinism, in which conduct is held to be 'caused' by factors or forces independent of real people.

Fourth, that 'structural' explanations of social life generally rest on partial, or selective, or simply misguided versions of what have come to be called 'micro-sociological' perspectives (see below, pp. 9–13). Indeed when this point is pursued, the structure-agency opposition is revealed as false, one of several misleading dualisms that have proved obstacles to the productive development of sociological thought. In the present context, our contention is that *only* if the concept of social structure (and its associated collective entities) are presupposed can the distinctions between 'structure' and 'agency', or between 'macro' and 'micro' phenomena, be sustained. Indeed, Maines has suggested that the opposition between 'macro' and 'micro' is 'a cropolitic distinction that does more harm than good for the understanding of social life' (1982: 274). (For those unfamiliar with the jargon of paleontology, 'cropolitic' may be rendered loosely – but not inaccurately – as referring to 'fossilised bullshit').

The tenacity of structural explanations

Given the highly problematic nature of the concept of social structure, it is appropriate to consider *why* 'structural' explanations have exerted such a tenacious grip on sociological thought. One important reason is the long-standing commitment to the idea of sociology as – perhaps above all else – a critique of individualistic explanations. For Durkheim, indeed, this was at the heart of sociological thinking: as Lukes has put it: 'Durkheim's central interest was in the ways in which social and cultural factors influence, indeed largely constitute, individuals (1975: 13; see also Nisbet, 1970[1966]: 7–9). Related to this is the idea that sociological concepts must be essentially collective. As Maines has put it:

> In competing for intellectual space, it was in sociology's vested interest to trade on a social factorist formulation in which group properties were seen as exerting causal influence on some form of behaviour. In its simplest expression, the dominant proposition adopted by the field was that 'social structures cause human action'. (Maines, 2001: 6)

Apart from purely intellectual reasons, we should also note the under-standable tendency for sociologists (and academics more generally) to iden-tify with perspectives which seemed to demonstrate – as Durkheim sought to do – that the ills of the world were not necessarily the result of the force of 'evil', or the machinations of malevolent individuals, but were system-atically generated by the routine workings of societies themselves. Thus, for example, Collier argues in his exposition of *Critical Realism* that this perspective can be 'transformative and potentially emancipatory' since it 'recognises that states of affairs are brought about by the workings of rela-tively enduring structures'. Consequently, it 'directs the attention of people who want to make the world a better place to the task of transforming these structures' (Collier, 1994: 15–16). (As we noted above, however, this argu-ment would be more impressive if there was any evidence that 'realism' in the social sciences or humanities has done *anything* to 'make the world a better place').

For both intellectual and political reasons, then, 'structural' perspectives have remained dominant in sociology, while the various 'microsociologies' have been both traduced (Maines, 1978: 491; 2001: 249) and criticised for their alleged inability to deal with big real-world issues such as conflict and power. Thus, to take a recent example, Kirchberg suggests that 'the "subjectivity" of existentialism, phenomenology and symbolic interactionism neglects undeniable forces like political power structures' (Kirchberg, 2007: 118; but on this see Dennis and Martin, 2005: 192–194, or Denzin, 1992: 56–63). So it is to the so-called 'microsociologies' that we now turn.

'Micro' sociological perspectives

It is worth pausing to consider three distinctively sociological approaches which have – unjustifiably, in our view – been criticised for their alleged inability to cope with big institutional issues like power, conflict and social inequalities. These are symbolic interactionism, phenomenology and ethnomethodology: all are included, for example, in Collins' discussion of 'The microinteractionist tradition' (1994: 242ff). (We are aware that rational action theory, some versions of exchange theory and similar approaches have also been described as 'micro' sociology, but since these rest on essentially individualistic presuppositions we will not consider them here). Indeed, Collins' use of the term 'microinteractionist' is an illustration of the extent to which the macro–micro binary pervades the sociological discourse. Similarly, we are not persuaded that this opposition is transcended in Maines' (1982) concept of 'mesostructure' – partly because the prefix 'meso' implies an 'above' (macro) and a 'below' (micro), and partly because the notion of 'structure' is retained.

Symbolic interactionism

The figure generally acknowledged as providing the intellectual foundations of symbolic interactionism was G. H. Mead. He, however, was 'primarily a philosopher. He differed from the bulk of philosophers in believing that the cardinal problems of philosophy arose in the realm of human group life and not in a separate realm of an individual thinker and his [sic] universe' (Blumer, 1981: 902). In the present context, it is this emphasis on 'human group life', and Mead's rejection of individualistic assumptions, which is significant. Blumer continues: 'In the case of the "social act", Mead gives us a picture of human group life that exists in the form of conscious ongoing activity ... This process is just not caught by the customary sociological concepts of culture, structure, values, norms, status positions, social roles, or institutions' (ibid.: 903). We can already make three observations about Mead's thought and its influence on Blumer (who coined the term 'symbolic interactionism' in 1937). First, the perspective takes social life to be essentially *collective*, with a focus on 'human group life' in real situations rather than on the unconstrained actions of individuals. Second, both Mead and Blumer respect the empirical reality of social life as *process* rather than structure. Third, and arising from this, 'customary sociological concepts' are found wanting – as abstractions, they cannot provide causal explanations for social actions other than by assuming that the latter are determined by 'forces' external to individuals. So Blumer emphasised that Mead's thought 'points to a different form of analysis' (ibid.: 904) from that which has become conventional in sociology.

Thus Blumer 'viewed symbolic interaction as *the* essential process through which all social phenomena (including structures) are created, maintained, and changed' (Morrione, 2004: *xi*). Perhaps inevitably, his focus on 'both action and the creation of meaning in an *ever-emergent situated present*' (ibid.: *xiii*, emphasis in original), led to accusations of subjectivism and psychological reductionism, positions which Blumer himself found simply untenable (ibid.: *xi*). On the contrary, at the heart of Blumer's thinking is the notion of human action as essentially collective, and he 'represented persistent patterns, enduring organisations, or social "structures" as moving complexes of actions and interactions (ibid.: *xv*). Thus Blumer was at pains to point out that a symbolic interactionist position does not deny 'the existence of structure in human society. Such a position would be ridiculous' (Blumer, 1969: 75). What it does entail, as we suggested above, is a principled rejection of the methodology and theoretical concepts of orthodox 'structural' sociology (Dennis and Martin, 2007: 302) and a commitment to the analysis of 'the natural social world of everyday experience' (Blumer, 1969: 148).

Just as Mead – as a pragmatist – concluded that 'metaphysical problems were unnecessary "riddles" created by dualistic philosophies' (Baldwin, 1986: 24), so Blumer's work aimed to overcome various problematic dualisms in sociology, such as the fruitless opposition between 'structure' and 'agency'. Often neglected in the secondary treatments of Blumer, however, is the fact that he was *also* concerned to show that an exclusive focus on the individual actor could not form the basis of a satisfactory sociological perspective: his rejection of psychological reductionism, subjectivism and solipsism were equally forthright (Morrione, 2004: *xi*). Thus it is quite wrong to suggest that Blumer's symbolic interactionism involves a preoccupation with the individual actor or a subjectivist orientation; rather, his aim was to transcend such dualisms as structure/agency, macro/micro, or objective/subjective by concentrating on 'the social world of everyday experience'.

Phenomenology

Similar points could be made about the tradition of phenomenological thought, which has also been criticised for leading to a subjectivist orientation which runs counter to the very basis of sociological thinking (Ferguson, 2006: 86). According to Ferguson, however, such a view misconceives the real implications of phenomenology for sociology:

> Self-understanding … involves its relation not only with other, already formed, selves, but with an entire shared world; the intersubjective character of reality comes to light as the real foundation of every individual and individually taken acts of consciousness. It is, above all, the intersubjectivity that is concealed in and by the natural attitude. (Ibid.: 60)

Contrary to much received opinion, Husserl himself 'felt that the problem of intersubjectivity was fundamental to the development of phenomenology' (ibid.: 84), while, as we have already suggested, for Schütz the major consequence of phenomenological ideas was not subjectivity but *inter*subjectivity: the subjective world 'is from the outset an intersubjective world of culture' (Schütz, quoted in Ferguson, 2006: 93). In Schütz's terms, for intersubjectivity to be achieved, there must be shared 'typifications', 'stocks of knowledge' held in common, and the assumption of a reciprocity of perspectives among social actors. Thus individual consciousness is a product of the experience of social life, and not vice versa. Moreover, this emphasis on shared meanings shows the extent to which people are constrained by the social environments in which they must think and act: 'whereas European existential thinkers stressed the inner freedom of the subject in the choice of life-project, Schütz turns his attention to the pre-existing contexts of meaning through which such choices emerge' (Ferguson, 2006: 94). So in its attention to intersubjectivity, shared meanings, constraint and the social constitution of individual experience, phenomenology may be seen as consistent with fundamental themes in sociological thought, rather than opposing them.

However, what a phenomenological perspective does not sanction is the reification of concepts which, as we suggested above, is endemic in orthodox sociology. Building on the work of Schütz and the phenomenological tradition, Berger and Luckmann emphasise that:

> institutions, as historical and objective facticities, confront the individual as undeniable facts. The institutions are *there*, external to him [*sic*], persistent in their reality, whether he likes it or not. He cannot wish them away. They resist his attempts to change or evade them. They have coercive power over him, both in themselves, by the sheer force of their facticity, and through the control mechanisms that are usually attached to the most important of them. The objective reality of institutions is not diminished if the individual does not understand their purpose or their mode of operation. (Berger and Luckmann, 1991[1966]: 78)

Not much sign here of a 'subjective' orientation – on the contrary, there is a recognition of the 'coercive power' of institutions which is consistent with much mainstream sociological thinking. But in the present context, our main aim is to emphasise that despite talking of the 'objective reality of institutions', Berger and Luckmann firmly reject any tendency to reify them:

> The institutional world is objectivated human activity, and so is every single institution. In other words, despite the objectivity that marks the social world in human experience, it does not thereby acquire an ontological status apart from the human activity that produced it. (Ibid.)

Berger and Luckmann thus explicitly reject the idea that institutions are real entities with power – in some way – to constrain the activities of individuals.

It should be clear from the foregoing remarks that phenomenological perspectives neither deny the 'facticity' of institutions nor reify them. Nor do such perspectives rest on an unconstrained voluntarism. Indeed, even when speaking of 'society as subjective reality', Berger and Luckmann emphasise the extent to which, through the process of socialisation, individuals 'internalise' the realities which are taken for granted by those around them: we are all 'born into not only an objective social structure but also an objective social world' (ibid.: 151). In emphasising the importance of socialisation and internalisation in the dialectic of social life, then, Berger and Luckmann may be read as echoing fundamental sociological themes developed by earlier theorists, particularly Durkheim and Mead. Their focus is on human social life as a collaborative process, and they consistently refuse to reify the 'objective' structures of the lifeworld.

Ethnomethodology

Phenomenological thought clearly had a major influence on Garfinkel, who is widely held to have initiated the field of ethnomethodology with the publication of *Studies in Ethnomethodology* in 1967. Once again, Garfinkel's primary concern is with what he called 'the routine grounds of everyday activities' (1967: 35) – activities which, he argued, were either presupposed or ignored in conventional sociological studies. Indeed, the explanation of such activities presents both theoretical and methodological problems for orthodox sociology. In Garfinkel's terms:

> For Kant, the moral order 'within' was an awesome mystery; for sociologists, the moral order 'without' is a technical mystery. From the point of view of sociological theory the moral order consists of the rule governed activities of everyday life. A society's members encounter and know the moral order as perceivedly normal courses of action – familiar scenes of everyday affairs, the world of daily life known in common with others and with others taken for granted. (Ibid.)

Like the phenomenologists, Garfinkel's aim is to examine 'the world of daily life known in common with others', and in describing this world as a 'moral order' he is quite explicitly revisiting a theme which runs through Durkheim's work. Indeed it has been argued that ethnomethodology has brought back into sociology themes which were important to 'classic' theorists such as Durkheim and Weber but were subsequently ignored. For Hilbert, Garfinkel's empirical studies relate to 'precisely the theoretical themes Parsons had actively suppressed' in developing his structural-functional model of society (Hilbert, 1995: 163). One of these is the idea of the social order as a moral order: 'Consistent with Durkheim's society/morality equivalence, Garfinkel's studies revealed moral regulation to be a constituent feature of the very order being regulated and produced as factual' (ibid.). Thus the very notion of a 'distinction between factual description and moral prescription' (ibid.: 164) is entirely absent from ethnomethodological analysis.

Similarly, and significantly in the present context,

> in rejecting 'factual order' as an independent existing entity naturally available to science, ethnomethodologists also recovered Weber's doubts about the existence of social organisation independent of the subjective orientations of its members – his warnings about reification. (Ibid.)

Here, too, institutional 'macro' structures are seen as produced and reproduced through the ongoing everyday activities of real people: from an ethnomethodological point of view there is thus no opposition between 'macro' and 'micro' social structures – 'the proper distinction is between structure on the one hand and its artful production on the other, where the latter is the topic of investigation' (Hilbert, 1990: 796). Thus ethnomethodology is concerned primarily with 'concrete empirical practices wherein both macro- and microstructures and their interrelations are produced, reproduced, and managed' (ibid.: 805).

Although ethnomethodology has often been 'misinterpreted as focusing on individual action' and ignoring 'social structures' (Sharrock and Watson, 1988: 62), it is in fact intended as a detailed examination of 'the way in which actions are co-ordinated and concerted', seeing them as 'essentially collaborative phenomena' (ibid.: 63). Thus 'we cannot conceive of an individual action except as an-action-in-a-social-structure, any more than we can conceive of a single word as other than a-word-in-a-language' (ibid.: 64). Moreover, contrary to many accounts of ethnomethodology, this focus on collaborative social action is in no way consistent with the notion of radical voluntarism: the very idea of the 'practical actor ... indicates anything *but* a person under the delusion that they are [*sic*] free to do whatever they like' (ibid.: 74). The opposition between 'individual action' and 'social structure' is thus 'entirely incongruous with ethnomethodology's root conceptions' (ibid.: 64) – the important contrast is, rather, between 'the sociological theorist conceiving "constraints" abstractly, and the practical actor encountering them as real-worldly circumstances' (ibid.: 74).

The social world

Despite various differences between them, our brief discussion of the three perspectives most often described as microsociological – symbolic interactionism, phenomenology and ethnomethodology – does reveal certain important similarities. We wish to emphasise: first, that none of these approaches leads to a 'subjective' analytical orientation; second, that none of them accepts any notion of action as radically voluntaristic; third, that all are opposed in principle to the structure/agency dualism, taking 'social structures' to be generated and maintained through situated collaborative interaction; and fourth, that all are concerned primarily with what Blumer called 'the natural social world of everyday experience' (1969: 148) rather than abstract 'models' of social 'structures'.

Thus each of these approaches develops in its own way the idea that human social life is carried out through processes of interaction among real people in specific situations, and each seeks to avoid the reification of collective concepts – there are no such 'things' as social 'structures', 'classes', or indeed 'societies', yet terms such as these are indispensable, not only for sociologists but for the purposes of everyday communication. As Fine has put it: 'People reify their life worlds, and do not, for the most part, think like interpretivist microsociologists. Macrosociology is a form of folk belief, the way people naturally and commonsensically organise their experiences' (1991: 165). But we take issue with Fine's apparent wish to sustain the macro–micro distinction. Just as problems – some of which have been considered above – arise in adopting the conventional concepts of 'macro' sociology, so too the notion of the 'individual' is equally problematic. (Indeed, from the point of view we are developing, the familiar individual/society binary is another instance of a false dichotomy). Just as 'society' does not exist as an entity, the notion of an isolated, pre-social 'individual' is a theoretical fiction, as the whole tradition of sociological thought has accepted (Sharrock, 1987: 135).

Why is the notion of the individual 'deeply problematic' (King, 2006: 473)? At a 'commonsense' material level, this is obvious: human infants are not viable as 'individuals' at birth or for a long time afterwards, and indeed throughout our lives we are dependent on the activities of others for the goods and services we require. But the basic sociological concept of socialisation goes further, suggesting – as Bourdieu consistently argued – all sorts of ways in which our thoughts, ideas, emotions, feelings and so on are shaped by our cultural environment. We become 'normal' members of society only by accepting established languages and cultural conventions as realities which we must take for granted if we are to act in recognisable and accepted ways (King, 2006: 473ff). So, as Durkheim put it, it is not only in a historical sense that 'society' is prior to the 'individual': languages and cultural conventions exist prior to us, and, as the concept of socialisation implies, are important in constituting us as 'individuals'.

The point that we wish to emphasise has been well made by Anthony King: 'human agency is a collective product, germinated with others and dependent upon the social networks in which we all exist. Human agency is better understood as the collective product of social relations … than as an autonomous individual power' (King, 2006: 475). It is for this reason that we believe the conventional oppositions of individual/society, micro/macro, agency/structure and so on, to be false, scientifically fruitless attempts to capture the realities of social life, which is above all a *process* in which we collaborate with others (or with the products of their actions, such as books, music, video games and so on) in specific situations. All of our experience is derived from such situations. So, as far as human beings are concerned, the familiar opposition between 'culture' and 'nature' is also false – for humans, culture *is* nature, in the sense that the processes of interacting with others depend on the ability to use established cultural phenomena – such as language – in appropriate ways. To repeat, human social life depends absolutely on such processes. Moreover, a focus on the processes of collaborative interaction is to adopt neither a 'macro' nor a 'micro' perspective – rather, it is to focus on the undeniable realities of human social life (rather than on reified abstractions) and to recognise that established patterns of social organisation, which confront every 'individual', are ultimately the outcome of such processes. As one of our contributors, Wes Sharrock, has put it, we are concerned above all 'to examine the ways in which the everyday activities in social life give rise to the stable relationships which we find in society (1987: 152).

Sociological implications

The proper focus of sociological attention, to repeat, is the human world of everyday experience, a world which is neither 'macro' nor 'micro' and cannot be captured analytically by the dualism of 'structure' and 'agency' (or by attempts to 'link' them). There will be some, however, who will remain unconvinced that this focus can comprehend adequately the 'macro' phenomena which have traditionally been the concern of sociologists, and who worry that in directing analytical attention to people-interacting-in-situations we run the risk of ignoring the 'big picture'. To such objections we offer, finally, the following responses.

First, there is nothing in the perspective developed here that would prevent the investigation of social phenomena conventionally described in terms of 'macro' structures. But what we are suggesting is that, for example, the 'class structure' must be conceived as the *outcome* of stratifying processes and practices, many of which – like the grading of students' work or the awarding of educational credentials – may appear to be routine and mundane. Thus interactionist sociologists have investigated the *processes* through which social class differences in educational attainment are produced (Dennis and Martin, 2005: 201–203). Other studies have, for example, investigated the formal procedures through which 'rates' of deviance (e.g. Cicourel, 1967) or 'official statistics' on crime and suicide (e.g. Eglin, 1987) are produced, rather than assuming that such rates and statistics objectively measure characteristics of the social totality. Similarly, patterns of inequality arising from religion, ethnicity, skin colour, gender and so on, must be understood as the result of complex chains of interaction amongst real people.

Second, and following from this, it should now be clear why we argue that it is not legitimate to assume that 'macro' perspectives are somehow 'objective', while 'micro' ones are 'subjective'. As Blumer put it, research conventionally regarded as 'objective' is in fact based on the 'subjective' presuppositions of the researcher (Blumer, 1969: 74), and as far as studies of social class are concerned, this is exactly what we find: 'Marxist' or 'Weberian' assumptions lead to very different approaches, and there are endless disputes about the definition of social classes, or where the 'boundaries' between them should be drawn (Dennis and Martin, 2007: 293–297; Martin, 1987). Perhaps most famously, Blau and Duncan's (1967) representation of the American 'occupational structure' was based on a sample survey of men aged between 20 and 64. Given the exclusion of the young, the old, and all women, it is hard to see how their data are representative of *any* conceivable society (Dennis and Martin, 2007: 296).

The implication of the present argument is that it is not possible to describe societies, social structures or classes (or anything else) in ultimate, exhaustive, 'objective' terms (Kiniven and Piiroinen 2006a and b; 2004). This does not preclude investigations into, for example, population size, income distribution or the extent of immigration, but what must be remembered is first, that the results of such studies are notoriously unreliable (and they are, at every stage, 'political' rather than neutral) and second, that such enquiries are undertaken for particular, practical purposes. The resulting information is not to be regarded as 'objective' but is, rather, knowledge-for-a-purpose, based on specific assumptions and preconceptions and, inevitably, subject to methodological constraints. The present argument, then, does not rule out quantitative studies in the social sciences, but what it does entail is that the results of such studies should not be considered as knowledge of an external, objective, reality.

Third, it might be argued that the perspective outlined here leaves little scope for the 'sociological imagination' – the ability to grasp how the experiences of individuals are shaped by 'the larger historical scene' (Mills, 1959: 5). We would respond to this by turning the issue around, by suggesting that it is precisely the ability to understand how enduring institutional patterns are generated and maintained through situated interactions that is the greatest challenge to the 'sociological imagination', a challenge which conventional sociology has conspicuously failed to meet.

2

The structure problem in the context of structure and agency controversies

Wes Sharrock and Graham Button

Introduction

In denying that the division of sociological theories between 'structure' and 'agency' doctrines effectively captures the divisions amongst them over a century and more, we are certainly not trying to minimise the disagreements that there have been throughout that period. Even though the 'disagreements' are often less disagreements than misunderstandings, we are not saying that better understanding on one or both sides would facilitate bringing together the most prominent of those disputing positions into a coherently unified scheme. The irreducible fact is that an overwhelming part of this sociological controversy involves arguments at cross purposes. In our view, a clearer understanding of the sources of diversity in sociological thought would make the project of theoretical reconciliation by way of a structure–agency synthesis seem much more, rather than significantly less, difficult.

The 'structure-and-agency' discussions in sociology show no sign of reaching a conclusion. Papers by Healy (1998), Perkmann (1998) and Sibeon (1999) have tried to formulate new versions of the 'anti-reductionist' position. Sibeon offers an approach synthesised out of a variety of sources, amongst which Giddens and actor-network theory figure, while Healy proposes that the relationship of individual and society be conceived as one of 'supervenience.' This round of argument was stimulated by reactions from Archer (1982, 1995, 1996a and b), Mouzelis (1991, 1993, 1995) and others (e.g. Holmwood and Stewart, 1991) to Giddens' theory of structuration (1979, 1984), and further fuelled by attempts at the rehabilitation of Lockwood's 1964 paper on social integration and system integration (Mouzelis, 1994; Perkmann, 1998).

The assumption underlying these arguments is that the structure-and-agency problematic is soluble through the synthesis of two sociological traditions, each of which has allegedly misconceived the core issue as being that of structure-versus-agency. Previous theorists are accused of asserting the primacy of either structure or agency, without recognising that structure and agency are complementary features of social reality, and both must be accommodated within any unified theory. However, while many contemporary theorists seem in general agreement on the need for the unification of structure-and-agency, the fact that the dispute continues signifies their inability to agree on how to constitute this unified theory. Thus we are offered 'system' and 'lifeworld' by Habermas (1987a), 'habitus' and 'field' by Bourdieu (1990a) and 'structuration' by Giddens (1984), to take only the most prominent theorists, all of whose syntheses are of only debatable success. (See Chapters 5, 6 and 7 below).

We argue that the structure-and-agency debate cannot reach a conclusion because it is based upon a tendentious interpretation of the history and problematic of sociological theories. In particular, the assumption that prior theories can be simply and crudely divided between either agency or structure is false. In particular, contemporary arguments distort the characteristics of the relevant theories associated with 'agency' – such as methodological individualism, interactionism and phenomenologies – as well as crucial arguments in Marx, Durkheim and Parsons. They exaggerate the differences between the supposed 'traditions' of structure and of agency, consequently *misinterpreting* many of the points of disagreement between contending traditions, and damagingly oversimplifying their theoretical stories, with the result that they misrepresent actual points of difference. We will make our argument in four steps.

First, we show that the problems that are ascribed, mainly to the agency side of the supposed divide, are based upon what are little more than caricatures of the actual sociological positions under consideration. Usually, these are not specifically identified – they are *never* documented in cited detail and are apt to be dubbed in general and anonymous ways (as, for example, 'micro-sociological approaches') – and they are often characterised only in a summary and dismissive way. Second, we seek to amplify this point through an illustration of the way methodological individualism is underestimated by its structuralist critics, leading to the question of how much of genuine substance remains between their positions. Third, we ask: 'what is the notion of "social structure" for'? For example, is it to play the part of a first-order theoretical construct or a second-order collation of first-order constructs? Finally, we turn to the individual-and-society question: it is one thing to say that individuals 'make' society, but there are two very different, and consequential, ways in which this can be taken. Are we talking about individuals and their actions as elemental constituents of society, or are we talking about society as a means-ends product of social actions?

Sociological caricatures of 'agency'

The structure-and-agency 'problem' is too readily accepted as providing a crystallisation of the nodal issues in sociological theory. The articulation of the interrelationship between agency and structure within a unifying scheme is considered by many leading theorists to be the central task of contemporary theory. The founding achievement of recent theorising is, supposedly, to have recognised that 'structure' and 'agency' are jointly constitutive of social reality, thus rejecting the tendency for 'structure' and 'agency' to have been treated as polar conceptions, respectively advocated by rival traditions. However, whilst this diagnosis and prescription may provide the basis for current deliberations, it does not provide a notably perspicuous account of the issues involved.

The reason for this is that contemporary concerns with structure-and-agency are pervaded by an insidious bias that skews the argument towards sociological theories that have advocated conceptions of 'structure', by assuming that the problematic in its present form has resulted from the overassertiveness of the claims of agency. Contemporary theorists are thus more concerned to contain the claims of 'agency', which are conceived as aspiring to appropriate the whole terrain of sociology, than they are with clarifying the relations between and reconciling supposedly complementary camps of sociological theory. However, as we intimate here, a proper clarification would be an essential preliminary to any genuine reconciliation, even though it might only prepare the way for the elimination of the supposed problem. The result is that we are offered arguments championing the *indispensability* of a concept of structure, rather than genuine reflection upon the character of agency. Consequently, the various attempts at unifying theory proceed on the standard premise that 'agency' approaches overreach themselves in their (alleged) attempts to treat social reality as constituted exclusively by agency and so run the risk of occluding real social phenomena from sociological recognition. The championing of a unified theory then becomes little more than a form of structuralist reprise to the (supposed) excesses of agency.

However, the justifications for imposing limitations upon agency are based not upon the actual arguments that have been proposed within the traditions of agency theorising, but upon gross caricatures of the representation of 'agency' within some sociological traditions. In effect, 'agency' is, in these arguments, a straw monument. Here we can only illustrate our argument briefly and therefore choose two of the most important caricatures of 'agency' arguments: first, the idea that individuals are bereft of all constraint, and second, that individuals therefore unilaterally mould social reality.

Taking the first, whose prominence is reflected in Healey's title for his review of manoeuvres around the structure-and-agency arguments ('Conceptualising Constraint'), the introduction of 'constraint' is viewed as providing the bone of contention. Distinct from merely arguing a social determinist line, contemporary structuralist arguments involving the idea of constraint are directed towards limiting what is considered to be the exclusive emphasis upon freedom in agency arguments: see, for example, Mouzelis' comment that the microsociologies conceive people in an institutional vacuum (1995: 175) or Perkmann's insistence that 'voluntarism must be avoided, i.e. it cannot be assumed that any actors have full control over any "system"' (1998: 495). Thus structuralists argue that individuals are not free to do what they want. Archer, for example, argues that there is an unresolved tension between thinking of ourselves as completely free and accepting that we are constrained: 'We are simultaneously free and constrained and we also have some awareness of it' (1995: 1). She refers to this tension as 'an ambivalence' that is reflected in the traditional opposition between structure and agency.

However, the idea of 'ambivalence' here supposes that we have two elements that are antithetical, to the extent that it is possible to conceive of ourselves as being either entirely free or wholly constrained. We confess ourselves baffled as to where in the (so-called) 'agency' literature it is possible to find the view that agency is utterly unconstrained, such that the acknowledgement that we are both constrained and free is appropriately reparative. Within 'agency' arguments the relationship between 'constraint' and 'freedom' is more adroitly dealt with than by merely saying that we are either constrained or free. In those arguments we are only 'simultaneously' free and constrained in the sense that what we will be free to do will be relative to the respects in which we are 'constrained'. For example, we are free to choose, in chess, whether to move a pawn or a knight as our first move, and we are free to choose which of the knights or the pawns to move, but we are not free to move the queen, bishop or castle as our first move – we are 'constrained' from doing so by the rules of chess. Of course, we are free not to play chess, rather than to make any move, but whilst free to decide which of these ten pieces to deploy in the first move, we are not, if we want to play chess, free to move others of our pieces, or to move the opponent's. We are free to throw the board and pieces in the air, but that is not playing chess.

Archer misrepresents the relationship between constraint and freedom as 'an ambivalence' because she has begun with the supposition that 'being free' and 'being constrained' are at odds in some comprehensive sense, as though being in a situation in which we are free in some respects we are not correspondingly constrained in others. Of course, being free to do a certain thing is at odds with being constrained from doing that thing – we are not free to take the next turn on the left if the next turn on the left is closed to traffic, say, but this is hardly a recognition of 'two aspects of a lived reality' (Archer, 1995: 1). It is merely to caricature agency arguments to say that they are attentive only to one such aspect and bereft of the idea of constraint. The issue is not whether we are constrained or not, but what is meant by constraint, and how we are to understand it in the organisation of human conduct.

The second caricature of the agency position at work in the unifying theories is that agency exaggerates the powers of the individual to such an extent that people are conceived as being individually and unilaterally capable of 'moulding' social reality at large. The agency position is parodied as arguing that the individual is entirely self-determining, in unlimited ways. It would follow from this caricature that individuals could simply dictate the nature of social reality and that this would materialise in whatever way they intended it, for, uninhibited by external constraint, they could follow through their intentions and make and remake their world at will.

But has any serious social thinker actually held such a conception? They would have to have done, if many of the rationales for recommending the structural approach as a balancing corrective to agency are to be accepted. In Archer's terms it seems we shall

> delude one another by the pretence that society is simply what we choose to make it and make of it, now or in any generation, for generically 'society' is that which nobody wants in exactly the form they find it and yet it resists both individual and collective efforts at transformation – not necessarily by remaining unchanged but altering to become something else which still conforms to no one's ideal. (Archer, 1995: 2)

But who has pretended that society is 'simply what we choose to make it'? It was Karl Marx, after all, whose general cause structuralists often see themselves as preserving, who tells us that history and society are what active, striving, real individual human beings make it. But does he thereby tell us that society is *simply* or *straightforwardly* what we *choose* to make it? Has anyone supposed that any given, single individual can make society what that individual wants it to be? Or is it that each of many individuals can make society (or social reality) what he or she wants it to be? No one could intelligibly subscribe to either of these views. No one could coherently suppose that the ancient Greek polis, or modern America, were produced by any single individual. And, of course, if each individual could choose how society was to be, then, unless all those individuals concurred in the same choice, either there would be conflict amongst them or each individual would have a distinct, customised reality. When Marx tells us that humans 'make their own history, but they do not make it just as they please; they do not make it under circumstances chosen by themselves, but under circumstances directly encountered, given, and transmitted from the past' (Marx, 1977[1852]: 300), he is surely just telling us that there is no superhuman force, additional to real, striving individuals, that makes or guides history. He is surely also telling us that it is the lives of all those human beings in the largely uncoordinated mass which are the substance of history, not that human beings in any collectively co-ordinated way will the history that results. Who has genuinely supposed differently from Marx on this point? Who has ever imagined that 'we' as some collectively concerted all-inclusive ensemble have directed the production of the society that we have, that we have chosen the society's features, or that the attempts we make to (re)shape ourselves involves 'choosing' how things will be, or that making them the way we want is a 'simple' matter? Certainly no 'agency' arguments entertain these absurd claims.

Nor would it be easy – if at all possible – to find any sociological thinker, or even any person in the street, who *in practice* supposes other than that 'reality ... tends to resist' both individual and collective efforts at transformation' (Perkmann, 1998: 503). It was the methodological individualist Karl Popper who warned that reforms and revolutions do not necessarily deliver their promised results, and even went so far as to identify some candidate laws to this effect:

> You cannot introduce a political reform without causing some repercussions which are undesirable from the point of view of the ends aimed at ... You cannot introduce a political reform without strengthening the opposing forces to a degree roughly in ratio to the scope of the reform ... You cannot make a revolution without causing a reaction ... You cannot give a man power over other men without tempting him to misuse it – a temptation which roughly increases with the amount of power wielded, and which very few are capable of resisting. (Popper, 2002[1957]: 62–63)

What could someone who believed that society did not 'resist' individual and collective efforts at transformation intelligibly believe?

We can only here deal with gross and prominent misrepresentations of agency positions. These caricatures of agency are being used feloniously in the demarcation of distinct sociological traditions. But we question whether any sociological position could possibly possess the characteristics attributed to agency by those making synthesising moves. If our arguments are correct then the rationale for the structure-and-agency synthesis is undermined: if the agency approach does not really lack a concept of constraint, then it does not require a structuralist approach to supply it. Rather, it is the structuralist account that is one-sided, not the agency view that structuralists purport to moderate.

Methodological individualism

We seek to amplify this point through an illustration of the way methodological individualism is persistently underestimated by its structuralist critics, leading to the question of how much of genuine substance divides these two positions. We are not ourselves 'methodological individualists', but we take this example because it would seem that on the face of it there could scarcely be a bigger difference than that between structuralists and methodological individualists. Our aim is to show that the difference between the two positions is not in fact substantial, but only persists because of the misconstrual of the latter's objections to structuralist thinking. Contrary to structuralists' contentions, the methodological individualist position does not eliminate the use of a 'structuralist' vocabulary featuring words or concepts such as social structures, organisations, institutions and other purportedly structural phenomena in the description of social doings. Nor does it inhibit anyone – sociologist or otherwise – from making the kind of empirical statements that the structuralists seem to want to make.

In this respect consider the context of Marx and Engels' notorious claim that the 'history of all hitherto existing society is the history of class struggles'. If we consider this in the context of the sentence which follows: 'Freeman and slave, patrician and plebeian, lord and serf, guild-master and journeyman – in a word, oppressor and oppressed, stood in constant opposition to one another' (Marx and Engels, 1977[1848]: 222), then it is a claim which could as well be made by a methodological individualist as by that supposed doyen of structuralism, Karl Marx. For Marx and Engels then 'cash out' the meaning of the initial assertion in comments about *types* of individuals – which is precisely what the methodological individualist says should be done, or should be doable. A point forcefully argued by Jon Elster (1985: 5–8) was that Marx's concerns to de-reify economic phenomena into people's actions and relations involved a strong, though not perhaps entirely consistent, methodological individualism. There is no reason in principle why the methodological individualist should refrain from asserting that, as a matter of fact, the history of all societies has been one of class struggle. Nor are there principled reasons that prevent methodological individualists from utilising concepts that are allegedly structuralist in kind, such as institutions, organisations, collective movements and so on. Insofar as 'social structure' is deployed as a second-order concept, then those things identified as 'structures' in the structuralists' mouths may be spoken of by methodological individualists without any implication of a supra-individual level of social reality.

The issue, for methodological individualists, is not whether such 'structural' terms are appropriate but, rather, what is being referred to by them. Popper, for example, identifies such 'structural' terminology as part of the vernacular and treats them as functioning there as theoretical, explanatory concepts (Popper, 2002[1957]: 89–95) – devices of indigenous theorising, contrived by members of the society to help them comprehend the observable regularities in their own and other individuals' behaviour. The notions of 'class', 'state' or 'party' are all bona fide parts of the English language, so the issue is not that statements in which they figure should not be made but that such statements should not mislead. As Max Weber (1978[1920]: 13) argued, they must not be understood as referring to anything other – anything more – than the actions of individuals.

Thus a statement about the state's intervention in the economy is a shorthand for a statement about the doings of some number of individuals occupying civil service positions, and the ways in which they are prescribing for, interfering in, and directing the activities of business people and their employees, etc. It would be not merely a mistake, but for some methodological individualists, a dangerous one, to suppose that in talking about the role of 'the state' or 'the class' one is talking about anything other than these individuals. It is thus correct, but not perhaps perspicuous, to say, as Archer does, that individualists are committed to the claim that all social structures are 'attributable to contemporary actors' (Healy, 1998: 517), but the further claim that one can show this is untenable by describing situations where 'the efforts of individuals to change their social structures are constrained by that structure' (ibid.) is not cogent: everyone knows it is very difficult, if not utterly impractical, to try to get large numbers of individuals to do what you want.

The difference between the individualists and a structuralist like Archer is not that the former deny that the efforts of individuals to change 'social structures' are constrained by those 'structures' whilst the latter affirm this. The former can equally well make equivalent assertions, for the states of affairs which these putatively depict are not ones individualism cannot formulate (see the quotation from Popper above). The resistance of the civil service to change is notorious: when politicians attempt to change things, they seldom succeed in getting the changes they seek in quite the form they wanted. They do not succeed because the 'structure' ('tradition' could be used equivalently) of the civil service can prevent them from pursuing their policies and may frustrate, obstruct and eventually nullify their efforts. Anyone can recognise the validity of this argument, methodological individualists included.

Indeed it would be impractical for methodological individualists not to speak in these ostensibly structuralist terms. It might be more strictly consistent with their arguments to formulate assertions about state intervention in the form of a description of the embodied activity that might involved: for instance, 'civil servant A has initiated action under subparagraph 3.19 in the statute for the regulation of the transport of live fish within the UK by dictating to his secretary a letter instructing civil servant B to compose a document to notify the fish transporting organisations in regions of the country with population densities of more than … ', and so on interminably. However, it would be totally impractical to produce this type of description for each and every individual involved in a large-scale organisation such as the civil service. Thus from a methodological individualist position it is good enough for all practical purposes to speak of 'state intervention' and 'the civil service doing X.'

Methodological individualism seeks neither to reduce the vocabulary that we have for speaking about events in society nor to restrict the range of empirical statements about the society's affairs that can be made by way of the vocabulary. It seeks, rather, to strip that vocabulary and those statements of a metaphysical interpretation, preventing them from being misconstrued as involving or requiring reference to social entities other than individual persons – and to delineate the kind of concepts that could appear in 'rock bottom' explanations of the sort that professional theorists might aspire to.

Our arguments may be summarised in three points. First, it is perfectly possible to use 'collective concepts' in *both* structuralist and individualist descriptions of social action. For example, all that structuralists mean by the phrase 'collective concepts' are (to take their own examples) everyday organisations such as 'the Ford Motor Company' or 'the United Nations' (Sibeon, 1999: 9). There is no *a priori* reason that prevents individualist descriptions from utilising these same concepts. Second, the fact that individuals cannot control large-scale social changes is not in itself a criticism of individualism, for individualists also acknowledge 'unintended consequences'. In one sense, this is merely a tendentious re-assertion cast in the disputed terminology. Third, we suggest that there are not necessarily any substantive differences between methodological individualists and structuralists, and that those of the latter who are eager to avoid 'reification' are probably in complete concurrence with methodological individualists, insofar as their anxiety is largely over tendencies to reification.

Illicit moves between first- and second-order concepts of structure

The concept of structure is used in at least two different ways within the structuralist arguments themselves. First, it is used as an intendedly theoretical construct which abstractly specifies observed regularities of social organisation as deductive derivations from its generalities. As such it would be a strictly empirical concept devised according to rules of theoretical formation. Secondly, however, the structure and agency debate operates largely in the *absence* of any substantive theoretical schema of this kind: claims about structure are characteristically made with reference to phenomena which are commonsensically, legally, administratively and even constitutionally defined. These are not distinctive sociological concepts in the sense of having been derived from a sociological theory but are rather vernacular identifications recruited from ordinary social practice to serve as auxiliaries to sociology's theoretical concepts. In this latter use 'structure' actually functions as a 'second-order' construct, one which collects together already-categorised phenomena.

Clearly these two concepts of structure are very different, and the requirements of the first cannot apply to the second. Obviously, the requirement that structure acts upon individuals, although it is not a phenomenon acknowledged by them, can be satisfied by the first concept but not the second, since in the latter case it obviously has to be acknowledged by members of society. Therefore 'the Ford Motor Company', 'the monarchy' or 'the state' cannot be structures in the first sense of structure quite simply because they are recognisably operative within the 'internalist' conception of structure. (We will elaborate on this idea below).

We are not suggesting that these two different understandings of structure are overtly and explicitly counterposed as matters of explicit structuralist doctrine. In practice structuralists do not respect the difference between these distinct kinds of concepts and frequently oscillate between them, with the result that the empirical exemplification of the necessity for a theoretical concept of 'structure' is frequently bogus. This is manifestly displayed in the

fact that instantiations of the doctrines are almost invariably given in illustrations from everyday life. Thus, for instance, illustrations of the determining power of structure will be given by means of examples that are familiar
and known to anyone, such as the insignificance to a bank's management
of a small account holder, or the capacity of car company management to
restructure the 'corporation as a whole' in ways that no individual shop
floor worker could. In this respect structuralists tend to operate with two
understandings of structure, which undermines the initial idea that structure
should be identified with the 'externalist' point of view. Their illustrations
show that they are employing in unstable conjunction notions of structure
from an externalist point of view *and* from an internalist one. This arises, of
course, from the impoverished conception of agency which they have tried
to use as a constructive basis for defining the notion of structure.

Let us try and spell out this problem as it arises in one context in the structure-and-agency debate. One of the central pillars in structuralist thinking is
that structures arise out of the actions of *large* numbers of people. Giddens
emphasises this in his definition of structure as encompassing long periods
of time and large reaches of geographical space (1990: 10–21), combined
with the idea of 'unintended consequences', which holds that people are not
aware of all the consequences of their actions. This sustains the point that
individuals are not aware of the structural level of organisation, since the
latter comprises the unintended consequences of their actions. If these arguments are consistently applied then we have a concept of 'emergent properties', a new autonomous level of organisation distinct from that from which
it arises. This is the rationale for urging the indispensability of a *specifically
sociological* concept of structure to complement that of agency – the latter
cannot, by definition, intentionally produce 'structure' of this kind. Structure is thus an autonomous level of reality in which actors and their actions
merely figure as causal elements interactively contributing with innumerable
other elements in spawning the emergent properties.

However, whilst in the structuralist argument the explicit conception of
structure stands over and above – and outside – societal members' consciousness (and, consequently, their intentional actions), there are concurrently
arguments which treat that structure as standing in a membership relation to
individuals, such that the latter are treated as being able to affiliate or disaffiliate from the structure, or affiliate or disaffiliate from the *status quo*. This
is, though, a contradiction which arises from illegitimate theoretical moves
between first- and second-order concepts of structure through the substitution of vernacular structures for theoretically defined ones. This is the case
quite simply because if structure is a non-intentional emergent by-product
of persons' actions, then it cannot be identified with structures which are
objects of orientation. A state, for example, cannot be both an unintentional
by-product and an oriented-to phenomenon. Thus 'structure' as a casually
generated emergent stratum and structure as the object of membership relations, must be distinct and different orders of phenomena.

Let us pursue this in a more concrete fashion, by considering Giddens' illustration of people 'maintaining the language as a whole' by making a comment in a casual conversation' (Giddens, 1979: 77–78). In Giddens' argument the perpetuation of the language as a whole must be a consequence of a variety of causal, not intentional, connections, and 'the language' therefore must be whatever configuration of causal connections comprise a stable pattern, however that is to be described. The conversational event then merely contributes to the stability of the whole language by whatever extensive and protracted causal connections it has with all the other verbal occurrences generated by speakers. The 'maintenance' of the language is not therefore an intentional phenomenon: actors in conversation are not conversing so as to modify, shape or control the development of a language but are conversing for some specific purpose. (The point presumably applies not to certain specific kinds of conversational contributions by virtue of their particular properties but to conversational contributions in general – or does it?). Their *action* is that of, for example, correcting the previous speaker's mistake, turning the topic to the weather, greeting an old friend or whatever.

Our interpretation here might invite the observation that people *do* take actions to preserve the language, as, for example, teaching their children to speak English and giving them grammar lessons, tools of grammatical analysis, etc. And, of course they do, but to suppose that these kinds of activities *do* (objectively) preserve the grammar is to suppose that the intentions of the actions coincide with their causal properties – but this is just what structuralists insist we must separate. There is thus no reason to suppose that *actions* oriented to preserving the grammar are any more causally effective in preserving the 'system' than those which are not so oriented, or which might even be oriented to subverting 'the language'; the intention might or might not be to preserve one of those properties which is causally efficacious in stabilising the system, but this is not to be assumed. Nor is it to be assumed that 'the language' to which actions are oriented is the same language as that which is being perpetuated at the level of emergent properties generated as causal upshots of action – the 'language' in the former sense is a vernacular construction, not something requiring an 'externalist' point of view for its identification. If 'structures' do indeed require the externalist point of view, then the vernacular object *cannot be the same* as the theoretical one – the means-ends operations of the grammatical utterances instantiate, from the latter point of view, merely more utterances in the causal nexus of utterances. If the argument is the other way around, then of course the *intentional-level characterisation* of the difference between 'just saying hello' and explaining how the verb 'to be' works has been imported into the structuralist discourse. The movement between 'intentional' and 'structuralist' discourse is simply unregulated: are we dealing with two different 'levels' of social reality, a distinction between an autonomous, causal, systemic level, and that of action, or are we dealing with two different kinds of actions which are being distinguished in terms of intentional discourse?

Perkmann (1998), however, attempts to make a virtue out of what we are describing as a vice: the unregulated alternation between structure as a first- and second-order concept. Unlike many other participants in this discussion, Perkmann (following Jessop, 1996) is alert to the fact that the presence or absence of a conception of structure does not differentiate the externalist and internalist points of view. He recognises that 'structural' conceptions are at work in the vernacular and aims to soften the distinction between externalist and internalist. He seeks, however, to perpetuate the distinction by casting the issue in its own terms – actors can reflexively appropriate the externalist point of view, but to adopt this expediency is to have eroded the key assumptions about the relation of 'internal' and 'external' from which this debate began. The concept of structure, it transpires, is available to agency.

Control and definition

One problematic domain of the agency argument for structuralists is what they understand agency proponents to be advancing when they articulate ideas of the 'construction', 'achievement' or 'accomplishment' of social reality. They read these arguments as proposing that individuals unilaterally construct social reality. There are three elements involved here. First, the recurrent contrast between 'institutions' and 'individuals' seems to provide a basis for the alleged difficulty: if 'institutions' are distinct from 'individuals', then those who study 'individuals' must, by definition, fail to access the reality of institutions. This distinction is often formulated as one between 'macro' and 'micro' sociologies, with the latter being condemned for failing to understand that the whole is greater than the parts and for missing the larger picture represented by temporally and spatially extended action. The second alleged deficiency is that *even if you grant* to 'micro' or 'interpretive' sociologists the reasonableness of studying 'individual actions' then they are nonetheless incapable of recognising that individuals are not all equal in their powers, and that some of them can be more influential over the social whole than others. The third problematic for structuralists is that the very ideas of construction, accomplishment or achievement imply a different and inadequate solution to the structuralists' own problems.

We can see all of these misunderstandings in the following remarks by Mouzelis:

> [interpretive sociologists] ignore not only collective actors but also what for convenience one may call 'mega' actors, i.e. individual actors in control of considerable resources, whose decisions stretch widely in space and time;

and

> micro sociologists tend to forget that actors, because of their very unequal access to the economic, political and cultural means of production, contribute just as unequally to the construction of social reality. (1995: 16)

Mouzelis's specific basis for this attribution is that the 'reluctance of interpretative sociologists to deal with macro actors is their populist predilection for
"lay persons", "ordinary members of society", mundane encounters, etc.'
(1995: 16). For Mouzelis (in what must be a world-class example of misunderstanding someone else's position) this means that: 'Attempting ... to
explain the symbolic construction of social whole by exclusive reference to
"lay persons" or "ordinary members" is like trying to account for the construction of a complex edifice by reference only to bricklayers, completely
ignoring the contribution of architects, managers, foremen, accountants,
lawyers, etc' (ibid.).

With regard to the first point, Mouzelis (amongst so many others) is
assuming that there is an analytically relevant difference between studying
individuals and institutions (1995: 175) which is entangled in the macro/
micro opposition. One might characterise much of Erving Goffman's work,
or that of conversation analysis, as 'micro' sociology, since it is specifically focused upon the forms of face-to-face interaction among individuals,
regardless of the establishments within which those activities are set. This
separation will not, however, do for the generality of work carried out by
symbolic interactionists, or ethnomethodologists – try to make the work of
Everett Hughes or Anselm Strauss (or even all of that of Erving Goffman) fit
the category of 'micro' sociology! It does not seem to cross Mouzelis's mind
that the distinction is not between institutions and individuals but between
two ways of studying 'institutions'. In fact it is the individual/institution
contrast that is spurious. The fact that we are studying postal workers does
not necessarily mean that we are not thereby and simultaneously studying
the post office, or vice versa. Individuals are not to be identified independently of their organisational position any more than the organisation is to
be investigated without reference to what these 'individuals' are doing. The
emphasis in ethnomethodology and symbolic interactionism is on studying
institutions-in-action. If anything, Garfinkel's study of suicide investigators
was an attempt to give institutional substance and challenge to Durkheim's
notion of a suicide rate, to treat suicidal death as a legal and administrative matter determined through the practices of the coroner's office staff
(Garfinkel, 1967: 11ff).

With regard to the second point, hard though it is to believe, Mouzelis
has misunderstood the contrast that 'ordinary' is normally used to make
in interpretive sociology. 'Ordinary' is not used, as Mouzelis appears to
imagine, to distinguish 'little people' from 'the great ones'. The contrast is
actually between 'ordinary members' (doing 'lay' sociology) from professional sociological theorists (doing lay and professional sociology). From
this point of view the conventional social importance of different individuals is an irrelevance. This is not to say that there are no differences in power
and influence between heads of nation states and those who clean the streets
of their nation's cities (but this is no professional sociologist's discovery
either – the issue is not whether one is aware of this fact but whether one

makes a meal of it). The interpretive tradition treats the relation between 'lay' and 'professional' sociologies as problematic in a way that structuralists, who do not have a (developed) concept of lay sociology, do not, and it is that problematic that is being worked through in the use of 'ordinary' and 'lay' in relation to members of society.

Given this gross misconception on Mouzelis's part, there will clearly be a problem as to how his other corrective arguments bear upon the targets of his attack. Whilst for Mouzelis it may matter which *kinds* of individuals, in terms of their conventional social importance, you are studying, this does not mean that any particular significance need attach to this in 'interpretative' sociology. If one is interested in – as symbolic interactionists often say they are – generic social processes (e.g. Blumer, 1969) then these are ubiquitous, and one can access them at *any* point in social life. One can study the workings of those processes as they are manifested in the activities of *any* kind of person. Symbolic interactionists were inclined to study 'underdogs' in an attempt to do something corrective in relation to the patronising conceptions that were held, in academic and sociological circles, of these lowly and outcast individuals – beneath the 'ordinary', presumably – but their approach was not therefore restricted to the study of underlings: they also studied 'professionals' in an attempt to diminish the image and influence of some 'overdogs'. To say this is hardly to deny that there are many different kinds of people, or to imagine that they are all equal in respect of their economic, political or cultural capacities, but to recognise this does not require that one *ground* one's sociological scheme in these kinds of distinctions. The distinctions between the more and the less powerful, the superior and the subordinate, the exalted and the lowly are, after all, distinctions that are made *within the society* and in terms of 'generic social processes' rather than ones that originate with or derive from one's sociological scheme.

Hard as it is to believe Mouzelis's mistake concerning 'ordinary affairs', he compounds his misrepresentation of 'interpretive positions' on action by actually imagining that these imply, in their use of terms such as 'construction', achievement' and 'accomplishment', that actors individually mould and shape large scale social reality. The underlying assumption here is that the problematic of sociological analysis is the extent to which 'agents' are in control of their circumstances, the extent to which they have the power to causally determine the nature of situations. The fact that interpretive sociologies employ terms such as construct, define, accomplish, or reproduce tends to be understood as implying an exaggerated view of the powers of agents unilaterally to dictate their circumstances. However, this is to suppose that interpretivists address the same problems as fixate the structuralist, and that the use of those words does – in an interpretivist's mouth – carry that implication. This involves a major misconception about the way in which such words figure in interpretivist discourse. Consider symbolic interactionists' use of the phrase 'definition of the situation'. The term 'define' *can* be used to identify stipulative operations, as when one lays down the definition of a word. The business of 'defining the situation' construed on this usage is presumed to imply that social actors can lay down what the situation really is, that they can individually dictate its nature. Consequently, it seems that actors will be in competition to dictate the nature of situations. 'Define' has, however, another usage, and one which is much more in tune with the use it finds amongst interpretivists – as when it is applied to cases of discernment or clarification, as being involved in ascertaining rather than stipulating. It is surely in this latter sense that interpretivists most commonly speak of the 'definition of the situation' – it refers to the ways in which actors ascertain or determine the nature of the situations in which they find themselves. A definition of the situation is a *premise* of action, not its result: one cannot respond to a situation that is not defined – i.e. is not intelligible. Far from being something over which the individual exercises assertive control, the gist of the idea of the 'definition of the situation' is that definition can be more-or-less problematic. Within the situation-as-defined (and there is no other) the extent to which the actor now has control over it and others in it, depends upon the situation that it is understood to be, and the position that the agent occupies within it. Within a situation in which the actor is defined as, for example, the accused in the dock, that person has little if any control over the outcome of the case, this being down to judge and jury.

Theoretical fiat

Up to this point we have been arguing as if there were such a thing as a structuralist position. However, what is presented as a corrective to the alleged excesses of agency is merely a set of arbitrarily variable definitions of structure. We can conclude by comparing two contributions, those of Sibeon (1999) and Perkmann (1998).

Sibeon's definition of structure begins with a set of ostensibly objective conditions which act in a causal fashion upon agents – otherwise we can only wonder what he means by 'influence' in the following:

> temporally and/or spatially extensive social conditions that to a greater or lesser extent influence actors' forms of thought, decisions and actions, and which, depending on the circumstances, may facilitate or constrain actors' capacities to achieve their objectives'. (Sibeon, 1999: 323)

These are 'the conditions in which actors operate' (ibid.). As such, presumably, structure will be defined in terms of sociological theory, independently of actors' awareness. Sibeon's definition of structure to this point conforms with the received conception of the notion of structure; that is, it is independent of the actor's orientations. However, Sibeon then *decides* to include within his concept of structure the very element that structuralists characteristically rage against – the identification of society from an actor's point of view, through his introduction of 'the objectives of other actors and the variable outcomes of actions taken by other previous as well as

current actions' (1999: 323). Sibeon is attempting to solve the structure/
agency problem by stipulatively recasting the concept of structure and to an
extent that of agency (hoping thereby to achieve a non-reductive concept of
structure).

It seems to us that Sibeon's argument here develops an arbitrary conception of structure depending merely upon how he decides to constitute his
theoretical categories such as 'structure' and 'macro', for he also decides to
recast the macro/micro distinction. With respect to the relation of 'macro'
and 'micro' levels, Sibeon rejects the identification of 'agency' with 'micro'
rather than with 'macro' sociology (1999: 324) as a false conflation. This is
because 'some social actors (for example large organisational actors such as
government departments, the Ford Motor Company, or the United Nations)
are not micro-entities' (Sibeon, 1999: 9). This, however, is only a redefini-
tion of the 'social actor', for assuredly the Ford Motor Company and the
other organisations are not 'social actors' in the sense in which we and
our readers, or even Sibeon, are. The British Government, the Ford Motor
Company, and the United Nations will never be able to read this chapter,
cross the street, get married, meet the neighbours, and so on, though the
British Government, in the person of the Prime Minister, *might* read our
pages.

We are not sure what these arbitrary definitions provide us with, what
turns on redefining a government as a social actor – except, perhaps, providing a means for divesting the concept of structure of its own excesses.
(Certainly this theme is not developed by Sibeon.) This, however, is not the
main point we want to make, which is that the so-called structuralist position merely decomposes into an assortment of heterogeneous stipulations of
definitions of the notion of structure. This may be exemplified by comparing
Sibeon with Perkmann.

Perkmann distinguishes between the 'externalist' point of view – which
is of 'behavioural regularities' constituted 'by institutions' on the basis of
'objective social processes' – and an 'internalist' view of institutions – which
rests on the premise that 'adherence to rules and norms rests with the normative orientations of the actors' (1998: 499). This replicates the basic gist
of the notion of structure, which is to capture a stratum of social reality
other than that of which society's members are aware, and adds to it one
that they *orient to*. It is not, allegedly, possible to comprehend the totality
from within the society, so an alternative theoretical/scientific standpoint is
required – an 'externalist' conception. The properties and relations which
make up the totality are unknown to society's members. Both Sibeon and
Perkmann are attempting to resolve the problem of specifying structure by
redefining the boundaries of the concept, but in doing so make significant
changes to the kind of phenomena that can be included in it, ones which
were specifically intended to be excluded through contrasts with individualism, subjectivity, agency and so on.

Conclusion

Picking up on our observation above concerning structuralists' fears that agency would appropriate the whole field of sociology, it might be thought that our subsequent argument entirely justifies that anxiety. Since we allow no role for 'structure', then presumably we must want to hand everything over to 'agency'. This would be a serious misreading, but, in the history of these arguments, only another one, which is why we take the opportunity to defend ourselves against it. We have tried to show that the notion of 'structure' is in a seriously confused state and that it has no definite sociological role, save as an obstacle to the supposed takeover by 'agency'. Such character as the concept has owes much to its corrective design, which is specifically connected to the supposed deficiencies of 'agency': but if the concept of 'agency' itself is, at best, given only impoverished expression, its actual nature only partially portrayed, then even the corrective effort is misguided (cf. Greiffenhagen and Sharrock, 2008). Most especially, the attempt is made to misrepresent the conflict between structure and agency as primarily over ontology, ostensibly resulting in a disagreement between some who affirm and others who deny what are obvious facts about social reality. It would be much better, we suggest, to see the disagreement as methodological, since there is no genuine disagreement about many of these supposedly crucial social facts, only about the way in which to identify and portray the organisation of these without risk of distortion and reification. 'Agency' just is not what those enamoured of 'structure' imagine, and surrendering the field to it would not involve giving up on recognition of certain domains of phenomena – the consequences of demographic structures, for example – but only a change in the perspective from which these are viewed.

We have argued that the structure/agency debate operates: first, with a thinly characterised and uncharitably interpreted conception of what 'agency' might attain independently of any concept of structure; second, without a clear, settled or even unambiguous conception of structure; and third, without reflection on whether that conception is essential to the purpose it purportedly fulfils.

Rather than attempting to 'link' structure and agency, we contend that it would be more productive to reflectively assess whether the distinctiveness of the notion of 'structure' is largely, if not entirely, a notional one – in this case a matter of saying the same things but in different terms. We have attempted to demonstrate that what the concept of structure can validly say can equally validly be said without it (for demographic structures are surely not a good example – see for instance Poropora, 2007: 197) and to demonstrate that the content which the notion of structure captures is no more than banal, a matter of commonplaces rather than specifically sociological contentions.

3

On the retreat from collective concepts in sociology

Peter J. Martin

Introduction

The aim of this chapter is to consider a general movement in which the collective concepts established by the early pioneers of modern sociological thought have been reconsidered in the light of both theoretical critique and empirical results. The issues raised were already evident in the divergence between the early programmatic formulations of the sociological agenda produced by Durkheim (e.g. 1982[1895]) and Weber (e.g. 1978[1920]), in the subsequent debates about their approaches, and are at the heart of the familiar opposition between the concepts of 'social structure' and 'agency'. In what follows, however, I wish to reject the (somewhat evasive) notion that such terms are simply two sides of the same coin or alternative approaches to the conceptualisation of social order. On the contrary, it will be argued that an examination of the careers of 'collective' concepts demonstrates a progressive realisation of their inadequacies – both theoretical and method-ological – and an increasing acceptance of the idea that social life must be understood as enacted by real people in real situations.

Collective concepts, culture and the sociological discourse

It is widely accepted that the origins of modern sociological thought lay in the emerging critique of the individualism which was fundamental to Enlightenment thought (Hughes, Sharrock and Martin, 2003: 7–10). For Descartes, the thinking individual was the irreducible source of human knowledge; for Thomas Hobbes, the 'social contract' was the result of com-petitive individuals agreeing to political regulation by the sovereign in the interests of all; and – perhaps most famously – economists, in the foot-steps of Adam Smith, developed the concept of 'economic man', a model of human beings which took them to be calculating individuals who, if given the chance, would act rationally in pursuit of their interests. This fundamen-tal idea – that the social order is based on, and can be understood in terms of, the deeds of *individuals* – is also apparent in other influential bodies of nineteenth-century thought, such as utilitarianism and social Darwinism, and in the rise of psychology as a science which sought to understand the mental constitution of individuals.

It was in reaction to this intellectual perspective that certain early modern thinkers developed distinctively sociological ideas as they sought to demonstrate the inadequacies of individualistic premises as the basis for an understanding of human societies. Notable amongst these were the authors of the 'Scottish Enlightenment' whose works in various ways emphasised the fundamental 'sociality' of the human condition: 'Individuals we certainly are and rational we certainly are but an individualistic rationalism is inadequate as a *social* theory' (Berry, 1997: 47–48). In France, too, a tradition was emerging which developed Montesquieu's (1748) insight that the system of laws in a society reflected its basic pattern of organisation. It was Auguste Comte who coined the term 'sociology', arguing for a 'positive' science of society, conceived as an organic whole rather than an aggregate of individuals, and it was against this background that Durkheim famously proposed that society should be conceived as a reality *'sui generis'*, that 'social facts' were 'things' external to individuals and which exerted constraint on them. Indeed, it may be argued that Durkheim's abiding theoretical commitment was the production of a critique of individualistic thought (Lukes, 1975: 13, 22) in the course of which he developed his conception of sociology.

Many other examples – such as the Marxian claim that the real historical actors were social classes rather than individuals – could be given to document the point that many of the roots of modern sociological thought lie in the critique of Enlightenment individualism. As Williams has put it:

> Many of those who have written on the origins of sociology ... have commented that the concepts of society and social structure established during the latter half of the nineteenth century – and thought to be essential for the establishment of this new discipline – were advanced alongside a corresponding neglect of the study of human agency ... classical social theory tended to replace the Cartesian fiction of an originary subject with a new fiction of an abstract social subject. (Williams, 2000: 35)

What is of interest here is the consequence of this intellectual inheritance, this 'fiction of an abstract social subject': the consolidation of an orthodox sociological discourse around a set of concepts denoting various kinds of collectivities – most generally society itself, conceived as an entity with describable properties, but also such familiar terms as social structures and systems, nations and states, communities, institutions, families, classes, formal and informal organisations, groups, professions, tribes, gangs and so on. It is within the parameters of this discourse, moreover, that sociological concepts of culture, and later subculture, acquired their distinctive connotations (Martin, 2004); here it will be sufficient to suggest that such concepts have been shown to be problematic – subcultural theorists have been concerned with the conditions in which people develop divergent views of their social situation, interactionists with ways in which peoples' social locations lead them to develop different 'perspectives', while, as I will suggest below, researchers have been quite unable to relate 'class consciousness' to 'structural' location in any systematic way. These examples raise some awkward issues for the conventional notions of culture and subculture. For if people's ideas and values, perhaps even their sense of identity, are dependent on their experience of different social contexts – class, community, occupation, religion, ethnicity, organisational position and so on – it follows that there will be considerable heterogeneity in the 'culture' of an industrialised, modern (or post-modern) society. If this is the case, then it may not make much analytic sense to speak of a society's 'culture' as more-or-less homogeneous or integrated: even if people speak the same language, for example, they may desire or value quite different things, and possibly even fight each other to achieve them.

Indeed, while Durkheim spoke of the need for members of societies to be sufficiently attached to the *conscience collective*, and other theorists have emphasised 'consensus' as the basis of social order, Weber's general perspective is based on the idea that conflict, competition and the struggle for advantage – as well as co-operation – are ubiquitous, even when overt conflict and physical violence are absent (1978[1920]: 38–40; Bendix, 1966[1959]: 476–477). As Poggi has put it,

> Weber never lets us forget that any social system, no matter how solid and compelling in its apparent facticity, ultimately rests on, indeed consists of, flows of minded activity; and that such flows necessarily originate from individual human beings, engage their energies, express their strategies, convey the meanings they attach to this or that aspect of their existence'. (Poggi, 1983: 34)

What's more, Weber goes to the heart of the sociological matter by focusing his attention on the question of how we are to understand the relationship between 'individual human beings' and the solidity and 'facticity' of the institutions which confront them:

> At bottom, capitalism only exists insofar as a multitude of individuals orient in certain distinctive ways their economic activities ... each actor's economic conduct is largely motivated by the subjectively perceived *necessity* of complying with the system's demands. (Ibid.: 35; emphasis in original)

Thus Bendix wrote of 'Weber's tendency to treat all concepts of collectivities or larger social aggregates as convenient labels for tendencies of action. Wherever possible, he avoided nouns, and hence the "fallacy of misplaced concreteness" (Whitehead)' (Bendix, 1966[1959]: 476). One particularly important instance of this is given by shared beliefs in the 'existence of a legitimate order and in identifiable persons who maintain that order by the exercise of authority'; such an order is likely to endure 'as long as the conception of its legitimacy is shared by those who exercise authority and those who are subject to it' (ibid.: 477).

As I have suggested, this image of societies as pluralistic, and of norms, values and beliefs as contested, also emerges from research in the inter-actionist tradition. For example, in contrast to the Durkheimian idea of laws and social rules as somehow expressing the *conscience collective* of the whole society, Edwin Lemert analysed the process through which, in modern America, laws were enacted as a consequence of the struggle among various interested groups, each pursuing their own point of view. Moreover, such laws will almost invariably bear the imprint of compromises reached in the political process: when incompatible values are involved, 'laws and rules represent no group's values nor values of any portion of a society. Instead they are artifacts of compromise between the values of mutually opposed, but very strongly organised, associations' (Lemert, 1972[1967]: 57). Thus the work of Lemert, and subsequently Becker, on 'deviant' subcultures led them to focus not on the qualities of their members or their activities but on the essentially *political* process (because it involves the exercise of power) through which such subcultures are constituted, identified, stigmatised, mar-ginalised or 'dealt with' by authorities in various ways. (See Becker, 1963: 17–18; Dennis and Martin, 2005). From this point of view the social order is not to be conceived of as a kind of integrated system but rather as the outcome, at any particular time, of a perpetual struggle among individuals and groups as they pursue their interests. Some have many resources, both material and symbolic, others have very few; some get to occupy positions of power and authority, others may challenge or resist them.

But if the concept of a 'culture' at the level of a whole society is inherently problematic, so is the related concept of subculture: the organised patterns of social life are more usefully viewed as a perpetual process of competition, conflict, negotiation and so on, in which people pursue their interests in the light of a whole range of possible values and beliefs (e.g. Strauss, 1978). A further implication should be mentioned at this point, one which suggests itself as soon as we refer to collective concepts such as political parties, churches or heavy metal fans. Quite simply, while it is useful, in fact indis-pensable, to use these terms for the purposes of communication, neither political parties nor churches nor any other such grouping is a homogeneous entity in which all the members share the same ideas and motivations. On the contrary, these sorts of groupings are themselves the sites of conflicts, disputes, negotiations and so on concerning all sorts of practical and ideolo-gical matters. Political parties, for example, are notoriously divided into fac-tions arguing over policies and strategies. Church members and their priests argue over matters of doctrine – disputes about the ordination of women or 'gay' clergy are recent examples. It is doubtful that there is *any* identifiable social group which constitutes the collectivity of 'heavy metal fans'. And so on. Two points of some significance emerge from this: firstly, that for the purposes of sociological analysis the sorts of collective concepts listed above (and all the other possible ones) are useful not as definitions of identifiable groups but rather as *symbolic representations* of fluid, sometimes even amorphous, sets of social relations. Secondly, as interactionists have always insisted, regardless of how orderly, formalised or routine such sets of social relations are – as for example in armies or bureaucracies – they must always be *enacted* by real people in collaboration with others. This may well be a simple, common-sense point – yet its implications have often been forgotten by sociologists who in rightly emphasising the distinctively social aspects of human life, have sometimes wrongly presupposed the ontological reality of collectivities, or ascribed causal powers to them. With these points in mind, it is worth recalling the passages in which Max Weber sought to provide a basic conceptual framework for sociological analysis.

Weber and the 'concepts of collective entities'

It is of some significance for the present argument that, near the end of his life, when Weber set out a systematic outline of the concepts of 'empirical sociology' (1978[1920]: 3), he asserted unequivocally: 'Action in the sense of subjectively understandable orientation of behaviour exists only as the behaviour of one or more *individual* human beings' (ibid.: 13, emphasis in original). This short sentence conveys two of the most fundamental themes of Weber's sociology. The context is his contention that the specific subject matter of sociology is social action; here he repeats, firstly, the idea that action is social 'insofar as its subjective meaning takes account of the behaviour of others and is thereby oriented in its course' (ibid.: 4). Weber is seeking to distinguish social action from analyses of the human individual as, for example, 'a collection of cells' or a series of 'bio-chemical reactions'. Such analyses may be very useful indeed, but they are not sociology, since they are not concerned with 'the subjective meaning-complex of action' (ibid.: 13). It should be clear, too, that – despite the somewhat misleading use of the term 'subjective' – Weber is concerned to describe social action so as to emphasise its collaborative, interactional nature: the ways in which the individual 'takes account of the behaviour of others' by interpreting situations (i.e. giving them meaning), and formulating courses of action in the light of these interpretations.

In these respects Weber's perspective is consistent with that developed at around the same time by G. H. Mead (e.g. 1934), but at present it is the second of Weber's themes which is of particular relevance – the idea that action can only be carried out by 'one or more *individual* human beings'. Again, Weber wishes to separate the sociological from other perspectives, and thus to establish its distinctiveness as a rigorous mode of analysis. It may be useful, for example for legal reasons, to treat collectivities such as 'states, associations, business corporations and foundations' as if they were individual persons. Indeed, for entirely practical reasons we often find it necessary to do so, as when we say things like 'I had a phone call from the hospital' or 'Why don't we go to McDonalds?' Weber's point is that such expressions are to be understood as instances of conceptual shorthand, useful, in fact indispensable, in everyday activities, but quite unsatisfactory for the purposes of sociological analysis: 'for the subjective interpretation of action in sociological work these collectivities must be treated as *solely* the resultants and modes of organisation of the particular acts of individual persons, since these alone can be treated as agents in a course of subjectively understandable action' (1978[1920]: 13, emphasis in original).

Weber makes three further points about the relationship between socio-logical work and 'collective concepts' (ibid.: 13). The first simply amplifies the argument outlined above, that the use of such terms is often necessary 'in order to obtain an intelligible terminology' (ibid.: 14). Once again though, Weber takes the opportunity to re-emphasise his fundamental theme: 'for sociological purposes there is no such thing as a collective personality which "acts". When reference is made in a sociological context to a state, a nation, a corporation, a family or an army corps, or to similar collectivities, what is meant is, on the contrary, *only* a certain kind of development of actual or possible social actions of individual persons' (ibid.).

Secondly, while collectivities in this sense are not 'real' sociological groups, collective concepts are nevertheless used by people *as if* they referred to real entities and, what is more, entities which possess 'normative authority'. Here Weber uses the example of the 'state', which exists sociologically as 'a complex of social interaction of individual persons', but which is treated by citizens as if 'it' had normative authority, so that 'its acts and laws are valid in the legal sense'. Thus an understanding of the meaning and use of collective concepts is essential if the sociologist is to reach an understand-ing of individuals' actions. 'Actors', says Weber, 'in part orient their action to [collective concepts], and in this role such ideas have a powerful, often a decisive, causal influence on the course of action of real individuals' (ibid.). Indeed much of Weber's work was concerned with the ways in which, for example, churches, nations, bureaucracies – or an entire economic order – are perceived as 'legitimate' and so achieve normative authority over those who must submit to 'them': 'by the very logic of its operation ... modern capitalism generates in actors the subjective orientations it thrives on, and to that extent constitutes ... a self-sustaining, going concern (Poggi, 1983: 36). This theme cannot be pursued here, but in many ways resonates with Marx's and Simmel's analyses of alienation; the latter, for example, argued that the

> contents of culture ... are subject to the paradox ... that they are indeed created by human subjects and are meant for human subjects, but follow an imminent developmental logic in the intermediate form of objectivity which they take on at either side of these instances and thereby become alienated from both their origin and their purpose. (Simmel, 1997[1911]: 70)

Thirdly, Weber wishes to emphasise the contrast between his perspective and that of those who attempt to analyse society as an 'organic' whole 'within which the individual acts' (1978[1920]: 14), so that such actions are then interpreted (by the analyst) in terms of the 'functions' which they are said to perform for the whole society. This view of society – as a whole with identifiable component parts – may be useful, says Weber, as a preliminary orientation to an investigation. However, as suggested above, 'if its cognitive value is overestimated and its concepts illegitimately "reified", it can be highly dangerous' (ibid.: 15). Moreover, for Weber, to treat societies as real entities or organic wholes involves not only the logical error of reification: 'functional' explanation *also* inevitably involves the analyst in determining the meaning of activities or patterns of social action, independently of the meanings which the actions may have for the people carrying them out. This external imposition of 'meaning' on actions is clearly incompatible with Weber's insistence that the elucidation of actors' 'subjective' meanings is at the heart of sociological research, since it is only through them that an adequate understanding of social action can be achieved. Although 'functional' analysis in sociology, modelled on the success of biologists in explaining the operation of organisms, and based on an analogy between society and the human body, may appear to be objective and 'scientific', Weber insists that such an approach is both based on a logical fallacy (the reification of society) and incompatible with the actual subject matter of sociology ('subjectively' meaningful social action). Indeed, Weber argues here that since the subject matter of the natural and the social sciences is inherently different, the research methods appropriate to them must also be different. Contrary to those who suggest that the meaningful social world is not amenable to 'scientific' explanation, Weber argues that in fact sociologists are able to carry their analyses *beyond* the point at which natural scientists have to stop: 'In the case of social collectivities, precisely as distinguished from organisms, we are in a position to go beyond merely demonstrating functional relationships and uniformities. We can accomplish something that is never attainable in the natural sciences, namely the subjective understanding of the action of the component individuals' (ibid.: 15). The natural scientist, Weber adds, is restricted to the external observation of events and unable to arrive at this kind of 'subjective understanding', which – however problematic from a methodological point of view – is 'the specific characteristic of sociological knowledge' (ibid.).

It should be emphasised, finally, that Weber's emphasis on the social action of 'component individuals' does not commit him to a radical, and a-sociological, individualism. As Poggi has put it:

> Weber's conception of socio-historical process anchors it in a multiplicity of individual actions, each oriented (also) by what goes on within individual minds. However, he does not ... view that process as a Brownian motion where myriads of unrelated initiatives, attempts, successes and failures collide randomly, signifying nothing. The mental operations them-

selves which inspire and orient the individuals' activities do not spring out of a vacuum. They are de-randomized by the fact that they relate to data, conditions and values, which constitute the historical precipitate of the action of groups held together by, and operating on behalf of, collective interests. (Poggi, 2006: 57)

In short, sociological interest is not in the characteristics of individuals *per se*, let alone their subjective 'states of mind', but in the processes through which they collaborate so as to produce orderly social life.

The deconstruction of collective concepts

It is the argument of this chapter that in the quest for 'sociological know-ledge', the collective concepts which were developed in the early phase of modern sociological thought have been found to be theoretically and empir-ically problematic. In this section I outline a some examples of areas – most of them quite central to the sociological enterprise – in which the reconsid-eration of collective concepts has been evident, as has the reformulation of theories and empirical approaches in ways which are consistent with a focus on processes of *symbolic representation* and the *enactment of social relations*.

Society, the nation-state, and community

Enough has been said already, I hope, to suggest the problems entailed by accepting the concept of 'society' as some sort of homogeneous entity. The related notion of the 'nation-state' has also provided the grounds for much research and theorising, not to mention undergraduate courses on 'com-parative societies' which assume that the 'nation', as constituted politically, is the basic unit of analysis and, often, coterminous with the concept of society (Walby, 2003: 530). Increasingly, however, these assumptions have been questioned, particularly since the appearance in 1983 of Perry Ander-son's *Imagined Communities*. In the present context, Anderson's fundamen-tal argument is highly significant, proposing that the essence of nationhood consists in the ways in which 'the state' is *imagined*:

> It is imagined because the members of even the smallest nation will never know most of their fellow-members, meet them, or even hear of them, yet in the minds of each lives the image of their own communion ... In fact all communities larger than primordial villages of face-to-face contact (and perhaps even these) are imagined. Communities are to be distinguished, not by their falsity/genuineness, but by the style in which they are imagined. (Anderson, 2006[1983]: 15)

There could hardly be a clearer statement of the importance of symbolic representation as the means by which nations are constituted as meaningful entities.

Moreover, in a discussion of recent thinking among archaeologists, very similar ideas are expressed. It is quite wrong, argues James, to accept the traditional view that ancient cultures or peoples were 'sharply bounded' and 'homogeneous internally', or that they were unchanging. Such notions do not emerge from the evidence of artefacts but have been imposed on the data by 'anthropologists and other scholars' (1999: 63). It has come to be realised that their terminology 'reflects a particular set of values and assumptions about the world, and ideas such as "cultures", "nations" or "races", while related to observable human reality, are nevertheless not natural or inevitable categories, but reflect ideology' (ibid.: 64). Thus, James argues, there is no evidence to support the view that the people who came to see themselves as 'Celtic' after around 1700 shared any such sense of identity prior to that time (ibid.: 67). What's more – and of considerable significance in the present context – James continues by rejecting the notions that such group identities are fixed things, or reflect some essence or 'spirit', in favour of an approach which derives from the idea that: 'Ethnicity is lived out, constantly reaffirmed, and ... updated ... Instead of chasing elusive abstractions, this approach seeks the origins and nature of ethnicity in the very nature of our lives, in those patterns of social practices through which a society is constituted' (ibid.: 68).

The discussions by both Anderson and James cast doubt on the analytic value of such collective concepts as nation, people, race or culture, and propose alternative perspectives which are consistent with the kind of sociological reformulation discussed earlier in this chapter. As Walby has argued, 'the typical sociological conception of society, which usually involves the coincidence of economy, polity and culture, is problematic' 2003: 542); there is no empirical support for this assumption, and Walby concludes that 'the nation-state is more mythical than real' (ibid.: 529). Moreover, to this emphasis on symbolic representation in Anderson's and Walby's view of the nation-state may be added, in James's consideration of pre-modern European 'peoples', a focus on understanding those 'social practices' through which the social order is enacted.

Similar conclusions have been reached on the basis of an analysis of the concept of community. For Cohen, the idea of a 'community' should *not* be approached in terms of 'morphology, as a structure of institutions capable of objective definition and description' (1985: 19). Rather, Cohen emphasises the symbolic nature of the concept and the variety of meanings which may be attached to such symbols. The idea of community implies both similarities (i.e. people who have significant things in common) and differences (i.e. that these people are in significant ways different from other groups. Thus the concept of community entails the notion of boundaries, which are 'largely symbolic in character' (ibid.: 13) and which are 'largely constituted by people in interaction' (ibid.). The basic theme here is that using the term 'community' enables us to represent a designated group of people *in a particular way*. To take one of Cohen's (many) examples, people who live in the geopolitical entity called 'Scotland' may be referred to as 'Scottish': however, there may be as much – or more – which divides as unites them in any meaningful way, for instance on the basis of such factors as class and economic interests, occupation, gender, religion, region and so on. Thus the 'symbolic repertoire of a community ... continuously transfers the reality of difference into the appearance of similarity (ibid.: 21).

Cohen's emphasis throughout is on the importance of cultural practices, as opposed to treating patterns of social behaviour as if they were reflections of 'structural' phenomena; indeed he wishes to argue that

> as the structural basis of the boundary becomes undermined or weakened as a consequence of social change, so people resort increasingly to symbolic behaviour to reconstitute the boundary. (Ibid.: 70)

In this, the 'selective construction of the past' (ibid.: 99) is an important part of the 'symbolic repertoire', which can sustain myths of continuity, and here Cohen's argument is consistent with Hobsbawm and Ranger's (1983) focus on the 'invention of tradition' as a means of legitimising distinctly modern institutions and nation-states. In the present context, the implication of the studies considered above is that *for the purposes of sociological analysis* societies, nation-states and communities should be regarded not as describing 'real' collectivities but as ways of representing – and thereby constituting – groups of people in particular ways, for particular purposes.

More recently, Pahl has asked whether *all* communities are what he terms 'communities in the mind', and answered the question affirmatively. The term community is 'as elusive a notion today as it was forty years ago' (Pahl, 2005: 621); and he suggests that the concept does not so much denote a real geosocial entity as reflect the 'conceptual apparatus' (ibid.: 623) employed by sociological analysts at particular periods in time and/or indicate the ways in which people have sought to *represent* places in which they, or others, have lived (ibid.: 633–634). In the present context, the implications of Pahl's discussion may be summarised as follows: efforts to define communities as 'real' collectivities are futile, since such efforts largely reflect the assumptions of the analyst. More positively, communities may be usefully treated as *concepts* which people use to represent important aspects of their situation, so that analytical attention is redirected towards the 'personal communities' which 'provided a bounded holistic social reality in their minds' and which were important in orientating their everyday activities (ibid.: 636).

Social class
The sociological literature on the subject of social class is enormous, much of it inspired by Marx's view of class conflict as the fundamental economic shaping force of history and his claim that modern capitalist societies would inevitably split into two great opposed classes, the bourgeoisie and the proletariat (Marx and Engels, (1977 [1848]: 222). Yet it can be seen immediately that – sociologically – this claim raises some analytic difficulties:

how, for example, are the two classes to be defined? Where can we draw the 'boundary' between them? (e.g. Marshall, 1988: 99ff). And what about the much-discussed 'middle classes' – where do they fit in? In fact, commentators have often pointed out that Marx's own use of the term varies: in contexts where his aim is to raise political consciousness, such as in the *Communist Manifesto* (Marx and Engels, 1977[1848]: 221ff), the development of all societies is explained in terms of the 'antagonism of oppressed and oppressing classes' (ibid.: 230). But when Marx produced a more subtle social analysis of actual events, as in the *Eighteenth Brumaire of Louis Napoleon*, his account of French society in the 1840s takes full account of personalities, political factions, the state bureaucracy, the priests, the army, the press, as well as commercial, industrial and financial interests within the *bourgeoisie* – all leading to an 'unspeakable, deafening chaos of fusion, revision, prorogation, constitution, conspiration, coalition, emigration, usurpation and revolution' (Marx, 1977 [1852]: 309). In short, Marx emphasises the fragmentation of the *bourgeoisie* rather than its class solidarity, and his answer to the question of 'how a nation of thirty six million can be surprised and delivered unresisting into captivity by three swindlers' (ibid.: 304) is that conservative elements of the peasantry rallied to Louis, whom they saw as representing the past glories of the 'Bonaparte dynasty' (ibid.: 318).

It must be said that despite Marx's astute analysis of events in France between 1848 and 1851, and the apparent restoration of the *ancien régime*, he did not lose faith in the eventual victory of the *bourgeoisie*, leading ultimately to a proletarian revolution. However, others have argued that this theoretical 'grand narrative' of historical destiny, based on the dynamic of opposed social classes, neglects both the contingencies affecting actual events and the various factors which, in real societies, tend to inhibit the formation of 'pure' social classes based on a shared awareness of common economic interests (cf. Weber [1920], 1978, 926–940). Inevitably, such problems have generated much debate amongst both Marxist scholars and non-Marxist sociologists; the *concept* of class, however, has usually been retained. Giddens, for example, certainly a non-Marxist sociologist, declared that 'there are only, in any given society, a limited number of classes' (1981[1973]: 106) and that one aim of 'structuration' theory was to identify the factors which generate 'identifiable social groupings' (ibid.: 107).

Despite all their efforts, however, the failure of class analysts to identify actual social classes, or even to agree on how many there are or what their 'boundaries' are, should remind us that the notion of social class does not refer to an observable entity but is, rather, a concept which leads us to think about patterns of social stratification in a particular way. Indeed, such concepts are indispensable if we are to study matters to do with inequality and social stratification. Nevertheless, the essential point here is that they remain *concepts* – constructs through which we can order our perceptions so as to highlight some aspects of the social world at the expense of others. As suggested above, Marx and Engels' usage of the term in *The Communist*

Manifesto may well be a good example of symbolic representation, in which they are concerned to portray social change in terms of economic forces expressed through class conflict, and to encourage their readers to 'see' societies in this particular way. Similarly, sociologists studying the 'class structure' are not simply representing 'reality' in a neutral or objective way: rather, they are engaged in an active process of definition which is based on their own assumptions, beliefs, and theoretical inclinations (Martin, 1987: 68–69).

The ways in which the concept of class has been employed may therefore stand as a useful example of the process of symbolic representation, in both everyday speech and academic discourse. However, it should be added immediately that saying this in no way entails a denial of the existence of social, economic, or any other kind of inequality. What it draws attention to are the ways in which Marx and Engels, sociological researchers, and others have chosen to *represent* the pattern of inequalities theoretically, given that there are all sorts of ways in which this could be done. It should also be added that, contrary to a widespread misconception, an analytic focus on social interaction and modes of representation does not limit the researcher to a concern with 'micro'-level phenomena at the expense of 'macro' issues such as stratification and class. On the contrary, from this perspective the phenomena of 'structured' social inequalities and class relations may be viewed as emerging from, sustained through, and sometimes challenged in, the ongoing interactions of real people in real situations (see Dennis and Martin, 2007). As Schwalbe et al. put it, a sociologically satisfactory explanation (as opposed to description) of patterns of inequalities '… requires attention to the processes that produce and perpetuate it' (Schwalbe et al., 2000: 420).

Once again, a consideration of the concept of class leads to a recognition of the salience of symbolic representations and processes of enactment. It seems clear, too, that in this field as in others, sociological researchers have been moving away from a reliance on traditional collective concepts towards perspectives which focus on inequalities as the outcome of situated actions and interactions. Marshall, for example, questions first, the relevance of Marxian models of class to the 'realities of advanced capitalism in the West' (1988: 121); second, the naïve assumption (of sociologists) that class consciousness, values, or images of society 'can be related directly to highly visible factors in the actor's immediate social milieu' (ibid.: 118); and third, the appropriateness of survey methodology: 'Working-class consciousness cannot … be studied, in the abstract, using highly structured attitude surveys or isolated interviews. It must be investigated as a component or dimension of everyday class practices' (ibid.: 120, 122–123). 'Research strategies that detach consciousness from action are forever fated to generate images of society that are as much an artefact of the research instrument … as they are a genuine attribute of the working-class subject' (ibid.: 120).

For these reasons, and others, Marshall argues that 'the debate about the nature of working-class consciousness [is] grinding to a confused and untimely halt' (ibid.: 105). In order to resuscitate sociological investigation in this field, Marshall suggests, it is necessary to focus on 'the concrete activities of real people or of groups of people' (ibid.: 109), and to restore a genuinely historical or dynamic aspect to analyses by undertaking 'intensive, longitudinal ethnography, in which different aspects of consciousness are located firmly in the context of class practices' (ibid.: 121). Similarly, Savage concludes that 'the British tradition of class analysis ... has failed, both conceptually and empirically' (Savage, 2000: 40). (This must be something of a disappointment to the funding bodies which, since the 1950s, have probably invested more money in this 'tradition' than in any other field of British sociology). To rescue class analysis, Savage argues, it will be necessary 'to see class cultures as contingently embodying forms of individualised identities which operate relationally' (ibid.: 150); he emphasises cultural (as opposed to economic) aspects of class identification (ibid.: 149), the need to abandon the idea that 'class cultures are inherently collective' (ibid.) and the need to understand class in dynamic rather than structural terms (ibid.: 150–151). None of these proposed reorientations, I suggest, are inconsistent with the argument of this chapter; indeed, they raise the question of whether the concept of class retains its analytic validity. At the very least, the concept would have to be used carefully to refer to *processes* of social stratification, yet the notion of 'class processes', while perfectly understandable as conceptual shorthand, is nonetheless an oxymoron.

The relevance of these conclusions to the themes of this chapter should, by now, be evident. Massive inequalities of wealth, income, power and prestige are undeniable features of social life, yet ultimately must be understood as the *outcome* of processes of stratification. In other words, there has been a growing recognition that for all the evident orderliness and obdurate 'facticity' of social institutions (Berger and Luckmann, 1991[1966]: 78), the social order is nonetheless to be understood as the outcome of collaborative interactions among human agents who produce and sustain authoritative meanings 'through the use of methodological devices' (Giddens, 1987: 215). The fact that these words were written by the same author who, in earlier work, declared that there could only be a 'limited number' of social classes in a society (1981 [1973]: 105) and dismissed sociological approaches which were concerned with the 'triviata of everyday life' (ibid.: 15), does indeed suggest that a degree of theoretical reorientation has taken place.

The concept of organisation

The extent of this reorientation may be appreciated through a brief examination of the career of the concept of formal organisation. In the 1950s and 1960s it was common for sociologists studying organisations – strongly influenced by functionalism and systems theory – to regard them as more-or-less integrated 'systems' with 'needs' which had to be met if the organisation was to survive in its 'environment'. It was against this background that

Egon Bittner (1974[1965]) wrote his now-classic paper on 'The Concept of Organisation' pointing out that the notion of the organisation as some kind of entity operating in a particular environment was not a scientifically objective, value-neutral description of it but a particular representation of certain sets of social relationships. As empirical researchers were discovering, neither the 'goals' of the organisation nor the 'rationality' represented by its design were unproblematic. Rather, such a 'rational scheme' expresses the perspective of the 'managerial technician' and is not to be 'treated as having some sort of privileged position for understanding its meaning' (ibid.: 76). That is, the organisation is a *symbolic representation* which expresses the interests of those who seek to control it: the board of directors, for example, as opposed to other interested groups, such as employees (who will typically display their own divergent perspectives), customers, competitors, investors, political authorities, pressure groups and so on. As such, moreover, it may be seen as a 'site of struggle' over whose meanings are to prevail. So from this point of view, 'the organisation' is to be understood sociologically as a symbolic representation of the activities of a wide range of people, a representation which will usually attempt to foster a positive 'image' and a notion of coherence both 'externally' (i.e. in relation to clients, customers and so on) and 'internally' (as when efforts are made to persuade employees to 'identify' with 'the company').

A second theme developed by Bittner is the idea that the organisation as a 'normative idealisation' is a scheme of interpretation which is *used* by individuals and groups as a means of describing actions or events in particular sorts of ways. Thus, for example, managers may argue about whether one or other courses of action are, or are not, consistent with the aims of the organisation. Similarly, activities may be approved, condemned or justified through appeals to the same criterion, as when formal rules may be 'invoked to clarify the *meanings* of actions retrospectively' (ibid.: 77). Indeed, from this point of view, rules are no longer to be seen as prescriptions which simply determine conduct; attention is focused, rather, on the modalities in which rules are established, enforced, selectively applied, challenged and so on (see also Becker, 1963; Lemert, 1972) in contexts where the interests and values of participants may be opposed.

The issue of the establishment of organisational order in the face of the often divergent interests and beliefs of participants was addressed explicitly by Anselm Strauss (e.g. 1964), resulting in his development of the general concept of 'negotiated order'. Originally intended to describe the ways in which various groups of staff and patients – with very different perspectives on purposes and procedures – nevertheless managed to sustain an effective set of working relationships in psychiatric hospitals, the concept of negotiated order has been generalised to provide an interactionally grounded perspective on social order more generally (Strauss, 1978: 11–18). In the present context, what is particularly notable about this is its emphasis, in contrast to certain earlier theoretical approaches, on social order as achieved (rather than emerging spontaneously or being presupposed), as accomplished and *enacted* through the interactions of particular people in specific situations. Once again, then, even a very brief examination of the concept of organisation leads rapidly to a concern with the themes of symbolic representation, and enactment.

Similar points have been made about the concept of profession. In another classic paper, Bucher and Strauss (1961) – like Bittner – rejected the assumptions of 'the prevailing "functionalism"', on the basis of which a profession was viewed 'largely as a relatively homogeneous community whose members share identity, values, definitions of role, and interests' (ibid.: 325). In contrast, using examples largely drawn from their studies of medical work, Bucher and Strauss emphasised the importance of processes of conflict, change and power relations *within* professions, and the extent to which they must be understood as fragmented: 'as loose amalgamations of segments pursuing different objectives in different manners and more or less delicately held together under a common name at a particular period in history' (ibid.: 326). Thus the 'seeming unity' implied by 'such arrangements as codes of ethics, licensure, and the major professional associations ... are not necessarily evidence of internal homogeneity and consensus but rather of the power of certain groups: established associations become battlegrounds as different emerging segments compete for control' (ibid.: 331). Again, the implications of this discussion are clear – the concept of profession is not a neutral or objective description of a particular collectivity but a symbolic representation of a (quite extensive) set of social relations; moreover, sociological interest is directed towards the variety of ways in which 'professionals' enact their working lives (ibid.: 333–334).

The family

In considering the marginalisation of family studies in British sociology during the 1960s and 1970s, David Morgan has noted that in both structural-functionalist theory – widely influential in the early period – and the Marxist perspective which emerged to challenge it, the family appeared mainly as a 'dependent variable' in the context of larger social structures: ' ... a unit or an institution within a wider social system' (Morgan, 1996: 7). In the work of the feminist authors of the 1980s, however, the family was restored to a much more fundamental position as a basic site of the subordination of women and the reproduction of patriarchal relations. Morgan accepts this argument as a much needed corrective, restoring the family to an appropriately central position in our understanding of social order. In addition, however, Morgan pointed out first, that while gender relations are indeed a major aspect of family life, this also involves a wider network of kinship and generation-based relationships, and second, that these are not only about power and oppression, but 'unities and patterns of cooperation' too – not least in the sense of identities that they confer (Morgan, 1996: 9). For Morgan, then, a genuine sociology of the family would have to take account of a far wider network of social relations than those involved in the nuclear family 'unit' of functionalist theory; moreover – and of central relevance here – subsequent studies have significantly extended the scope of matters considered relevant, examining for example ways in which 'family life is implicated in schools and education, systems of transport and urban planning, trends in consumption and shopping and developments in IT and mass media' (Morgan, 2001: 230).

Morgan's conclusion, therefore, was that for the purposes of effective sociological analysis, the family 'is not a thing but a way of looking at, and describing, practices which might also be described in a variety of other ways' (1996: 199). The implication is that in this context the term 'family' should be used as an adjective rather as a noun, qualifying the term 'practices' when these have to do with '*ideas* of parenthood, kinship and marriage and the expectations and obligations which are associated with these' (1996: 11, emphasis added). What is significant for the present discussion is that, once again, a consideration of the concept of the family has led to a recognition of the sociological centrality of the processes of *symbolic representation and enactment*. As Morgan has shown, the 'family' is not a self-evident element of social structure – rather, it has to be constituted as such through representation, both by sociologists who (on the basis of their own theoretical presuppositions) decide how to define 'it', and, more normally, by people in everyday cultural contexts which supply them with a normative sense of the 'expectations and obligations' of family life. It is hardly necessary to emphasise the importance for individuals, in all cultures, of the sense of belonging and identity that family relationships confer, of the countless symbolic ways in which such membership is demonstrated and affirmed. Moreover, it is evident, too, that in recommending that we abandon the idea of the family as a thing or a unit, in favour of an analytical concern with 'family practices', Morgan is drawing attention to the enacted, interactional dimension of social organisation, and to its dynamic, everyday characteristics (1996: 189–190).

Conclusion

What may be seen emerging in the above discussion of some of the 'collective concepts' central to the conventional sociological discourse is a reformulation of these in terms of general processes of symbolic representation and of enactment.

First, the 'collective concepts' discussed above may be understood primarily as symbolic representations of certain sets of social relationships and practices, which emphasise some aspects of these at the expense of others. The term itself has been used by researchers in this way – indeed, as some of the studies referred to above have suggested, such concepts often illuminate the researchers' own assumptions and theoretical preoccupations more than the phenomena allegedly being investigated. Moreover the designation of certain 'groups' – especially if these are portrayed as threatening or harmful – is a frequent and often consequential tactic of the mass media. The designation of such groups may be an important, if diffuse, way in which individuals can experience a sense of inclusion or exclusion, and a corresponding sense of identity. Analytically, the implication of such considerations is to focus attention on *the modalities of the symbolic representation of the social world* rather than on efforts to identify and define actual groups of people, and then to ascribe to them values and practices which are held to be characteristic of collectivities.

Second, processes of representation must be understood as arising in and through the actual practices of individuals and groups in real social settings, in relationships of mutual influence. The experience of a sense of identity or belonging, for example, arises through an active, collaborative process in which individuals participate with others in creating and sustaining a sense of self and others, engaging in certain sorts of activities, which may often have a ritual character (e.g. Collins, 1981) and which confirm and sustain significant meanings held in common. As Finnegan has argued, the active participation of individuals in such social 'worlds' – however transitory, informal and apparently mundane they may seem – is fundamental to participation in social life more generally (1989: 329).

By way of conclusion, it may be added that the argument developed here is in many ways consistent with the work of those who have in recent years detected a significant move away from the theoretical presuppositions and research preoccupations of 'structural' sociology, towards 'interpretive', 'hermeneutic' or 'interactionist' approaches. For Fine, since the 1960s mainstream sociology has been increasingly receptive to various non-positivist perspectives on social life, so that 'increasingly interactionist constructs are integrated into the body of sociological thought' (1993: 67). Indeed, Fine talks in terms of the 'glorious triumph' of symbolic interactionism (ibid.: 61ff), a perspective which, little more than twenty years ago, was widely regarded as having little more than peripheral significance. Maines, too, has drawn attention to the increasing centrality of interactionist premises in general sociology, and explored the paradox in which the sociologists have 'compartmentalised interactionist work and relegated it to the margins of scholarly consideration while simultaneously and unknowingly becoming more interactionist in their work' (Maines, 2001: *xv*; see also Atkinson and Housley, 2003: *x*). For Collins, progress in sociological work depends on the adoption of a programme of theoretical and empirical translation, which 'reveals the empirical realities of social structures as patterns of repetitive micro-interaction'. In the context of this chapter, it is significant that, once again, Collins is drawn to the themes of *enactment and symbolic representation*: the social order, he suggests, may be best understood in terms of 'interaction ritual chains. Such chains of micro-encounters generate the central features of social organisation – authority, property and group membership

– by creating and recreating "mythical" cultural symbols and emotional energies' (Collins, 1981: 985).

In the work of these and other authors there is a recognition that the situated interactions of real people are the fundamental social reality, and that a primary sociological focus on these need *not* entail a neglect of power relations, social structures, and the other apparently 'macro' phenomena of social institutions. On the contrary, it is argued that the latter must be understood not as ontologically independent entities but as arising out of, sustained by, and changed through, collaborative interaction. It is worth recalling at this point Weber's examination of the ways though which, in an economic order such as capitalism, 'economic conduct is largely motivated by the subjectively perceived *necessity* of complying with the system's demands' (Poggi, 1983: 35). So it is important, finally, to emphasise that while individuals may thus be seen to develop 'subjective' attachments to complexes of meanings, to 'make' their identities, and so on, this does not entail that they have the ability to define meanings or construct selves entirely as they please. As Marx put it, 'Men make their own history, but they do not make it just as they please; they do not make it under circumstances chosen by themselves, but under circumstances directly encountered, given, and transmitted from the past' (Marx, 1977[1852]: 300). It is precisely in the collaborative engagement between individual subjectivities and the 'objective facticities' of the social world (Berger and Luckmann, 1991[1966]: 78), that the process of self-formation is carried out. It is this 'human world' (Jenkins, 2002a) which is the proper object of sociological thought.

4

Structure and agency as the products of dynamic social processes: Marx and modern social theory

Alex Dennis

Introduction

Marx, for many sociologists, is a liminal thinker. He is seen to stand between the bogeys of political economy and idealist philosophy on one side and the realm of mature social science on the other. His work is not naïve enough to be that of a mere ancestor, like Hobbes or Comte, but he lacks the sophistication of the other founding figures, Durkheim and Weber. Either he is a (rather too philosophical) critic of, and contributor to, modern economic thought or he is a Hegelian throwback, trying to shore up the 'science' of dialectics in the face of empiricism (although, in this mode, too economistic by half). Somehow, in his critiques and corrections of Smith and Ricardo's foundational works on political economy and Hegel's idealist philosophy, he develops something clearly relevant to the discipline of sociology, but how his work might be integrated into contemporary sociology is problematic.

Such integration often takes the form of reorganising or criticising Marx's ideas on the basis of more contemporary concerns. This has been an ongoing project, which can be traced back at least to Weber's analysis of the varieties of capitalist formations in his *Protestant Ethic and the Spirit of Capitalism* (1905). Marx's tendency to assume that the development of capitalism in Britain was a template for how it would develop elsewhere underemphasised the extent to which the form it takes depends on the social organisation it supplants. Weber's careful comparative analysis of how different religious contexts support or hinder the development of modern, rational capitalism checks this tendency and facilitates a more nuanced, context-sensitive understanding of how capitalist social relations develop in specific cases. More recently, and less convincingly, sociological commentators have argued that Marx neglected all sorts of things – for instance, that class is not the sole basis of social inequality (Gimenez, 2001), that capitalism does not depend for its survival on factory production (Bell, 1974), or that consumption is often more important than production in capitalist societies (McIntyre, 1992). Increasingly, it would seem, the world Marx theorised was a strange and barren place – if these omissions were really his.

Such empirical questions, however, tend to leave Marx's theory relatively unaltered. Marxian thought can be criticised for failing to address particular issues, or 'extended' to bring other social phenomena under its purview. Questions concerning what kind of theory Marx advanced in the first place are more fundamental, however, as they seek to address ways of understanding the social as a whole rather than just particular social phenomena in isolation. The structure–agency 'debate' in contemporary sociological theory has treated Marx's work particularly harshly and will be the topic of investigation here.

It will be argued that the contemporary sociological preoccupation with structure and agency has had disastrous effects on the understanding of Marx's ideas for three reasons. First, neither approach to the social world can be theoretically coherent without systematically distorting Marx's project: Marx was neither a theorist of social structure nor one of human agency (although he did talk about both in different ways). Second, structure and agency necessarily imply one another, and so the work required to make Marx out to be a theorist of one or the other necessitates wasting theoretical time dealing with definitions of 'social structure' or 'the individual', neither of which have to be dealt with in detail to address Marx's theoretical questions. Third, by abandoning the idea that a sociologically useful theory has to fit into the structure–agency framework, Marx's own analyses can be used as effective analytical resources for investigating contemporary social phenomena in a very powerful way.

This argument will be advanced by considering readings of Marx first as a theorist of structure and then as a theorist of agency, demonstrating that neither approach can offer a coherent understanding of the social world or a consistent exposition of Marx's own position. Following this, the concepts of fetishism and alienation will be examined, to show their centrality to Marx's project and their relevance to the structure–agency 'debate'. Next, three key topics from *Capital* – the commodity, work and primitive accumulation – will be examined, to demonstrate that they can be understood more coherently in the original than as the products of either social structure or individual action. Finally, consideration will be given to some ways in which Marx's theoretical framework might be useful as a corrective to contemporary sociological concerns.

Structuralist variants on Marx

Cohen (2000) provides perhaps the most internally consistent case for a structural-determinist understanding of Marx's theory of history. He argues that:

Capitalism arises and persists because it, uniquely, is able to take productive power from the top of level 2 [some surplus production over the immediate needs of consumption] to the bottom of level 4 [massive surplus production over and above the requirements of consumption]. In effecting this progress, it lays up the material requisites of a classless society ... When these requirements are in place, capitalism is no longer justified, and no longer stable. It loses its rationale, and it becomes a 'barrier' to further human development. (Cohen, 2000: 201)

This 'productive power' is the sum total of the productive possibilities available at any one time: the stock of raw materials, factories, machines and so on. The way these possibilities are exploited represents the economic base of the social formation, and this base in turn accounts for the character of many non-economic, superstructural, social phenomena (Cohen, 2000: 216–217). Productive power develops over time as people respond rationally to scarcity by improving their social situations (Cohen, 2000: 152). As productive power increases, however, the economic base must develop to keep pace with such progress. The interests of those advantaged by a particular economic formation – the ruling class – are not served by such a transformation, and so they will tend to resist such change. Thus, revolutionary social upheaval is required for the social formation to realise optimal productive potential: when the relations between classes (constituting the relations of production) are no longer functional they are violently transformed.

Cohen takes Marx and Engels' *Communist Manifesto* (Marx and Engels, 1848) to say that the economic 'base' of a society causes that society's organisation, its class composition, and its institutions, norms, rules, beliefs and so on. A natural progression from one stage of economic development to the next is seen as inevitable, and the vested interests of that society's ruling class as an impediment to such development. The argument is structural to the extent that economic development (through mass production, developing technologies, the efficient deployment of a division of labour and so on) determines all other social phenomena: the social world as we understand it is the result of forces operating 'behind the scenes' and which are largely impervious to attempts to bring them under control.

As Elster (1982) argues, however, Cohen's reading of Marx's theory of history cannot account for human activities in the way it seeks to. This is because it is fundamentally teleological, resting on the assumption that the 'relations of production obtain because and so long as they are optimal for the development of the productive forces' (Elster, 1985: 30). Such an explanation cannot be used to account for the behaviour of real people in a real social context, as it requires one to use the consequences of their behaviour to determine that behaviour's meaning: something which happens to further the development of productive forces is retrospectively determined to be functional, something which has no effect on them is historically unimportant, and something which actively impedes them can only be understood as being dysfunctional. Behaviour is assessed by considering how it affects subsequent economic developments: its 'cause' (what motivated it or what set of circumstances preceded it) being epiphenomenal to this kind of analysis. The sense of human action, its motivation, and the intentions of those who act, Elster (1985) argues, provide a more solid foundation for social and historical analysis as they allow one to describe social phenomena from the point of view of the actor instead of re-describing those phenomena on the basis of a predetermined theoretical schema.

An alternative form of 'structuralist' Marxism, which does not depend on a functionalist analysis of human behaviour, is offered by Louis Althusser. Althusser's contribution to Marxian scholarship centres on his argument that there is a clear break between Marx's early humanism and his later, 'scientific', works:

> In 1845 Marx broke radically with every theory that based history and politics on an essence of man. This unique rupture contained three indissociable elements:
>
> (1) The formation of a theory of history and politics based on radically new concepts: the concepts of social formation, productive forces, relations of production, superstructure, ideologies, determination in the last instance by the economy, specific determination of the other levels, etc.
> (2) A radical critique of the *theoretical* pretensions of every philosophical humanism.
> (3) The definition of humanism as an *ideology*.
>
> This rupture with every philosophical anthropology or humanism is no secondary detail; it is Marx's scientific discovery. It means that Marx rejected the problematic of the earlier philosophy and adopted a new problematic in one and the same act. The earlier idealist ('bourgeois') philosophy depended in all its domains and arguments (its 'theory of knowledge', its conception of history, its political economy, its ethics, its aesthetics, etc.) on a problematic of human nature (or the essence of man). For centuries, this problematic had been transparency itself, and no one had thought of questioning it even in its internal modifications. (Althusser, 1969[1965]: 227, emphases in original)

Althusser's argument appears to avoid the flaws of Cohen's insofar as it does not rest on functionalist premises. According to Althusser, the central theme in (the mature) Marx's work is the denial of the individual – as a mere product of ideology – as an historical agent. Economic development does not, however, drive social organisation in a simple manner (as Cohen might argue), but is mediated through a number of superstructural, ideological, phenomena. Thus, for example, if the church is ideologically dominant in a particular society it might for some time successfully prevent developments in the economic base from manifesting themselves in changing productive relationships. Although the economy is the determinant of social organisation 'in the last instance' that does not mean that it will necessarily determine that organisation in particular cases. By extending Cohen's argument beyond class interests and into the realm of the 'social formation' more broadly, Althusser is able to avoid the functionalist explanations of social organisation that Cohen is forced into.

Althusser's argument, however, reveals something interesting about structuralist explanations more broadly. He is able to demonstrate the centrality of structural features of the social formation (the economy, the ideological apparatus of the state, and so on) only if one is prepared to accept his apparently introductory comments about the non-existence of the individual. Although this might appear to be a way of eliminating 'humanist' errors to reveal what Marx was 'really' arguing (in his 'scientific' later works), in fact Althusser is advancing an alternative theoretical view of agency: by denying the existence of 'human nature' Althusser is able to redefine the individual actor as a bearer of ideology. This allows a more thoroughgoing structuralism than that offered by Cohen – in Althusser's version the individual's actions are merely the practical workings-out of 'real' structural imperatives, as opposed to things that can only retrospectively be assigned an historical sense – but it also provides the analyst with the privileged position of being able to determine what an action or event 'really' is. An act of rebellion, for instance – from petty vandalism to the foundation of a revolutionary party – cannot be described from the point of view of its instigator or others in the field, but must be subsumed under a pre-existing theoretical understanding of the social setting as a whole to determine its sense. Description becomes entirely subservient to explanation, and explanation is something always undertaken on the basis of an *a priori* understanding of the nature of the 'social formation'. In short, the nature of the social is worked out in advance, and then its theoretical constitution applied on each occasion to the subjects of its 'analysis'. The human agent is not denied, but his or her avowed motivations and meanings are – to be replaced by the analysts' 'scientific' understanding of what is 'really' going on. Althusser's theory, then, only allows one to construe the world as based on the workings of autonomous (and semi-autonomous) structural phenomena to the extent that the 'problem' of agency can be resolved by replacing what people think with what must really be making them do whatever it is they do: agency remains but is ironicised, and agents are only amenable to analysis as long as they can be treated as 'judgemental dopes' (Garfinkel, 1967).

Individualist variants on Marx

If 'structural' explanations require either a teleological orientation to the function of social activities (Cohen) or the substitution of the 'actor' for a theoretical model of the actor (Althusser), then, it is tempting to think that starting from an 'agency' perspective on Marx might be more fruitful. This, however, is not the case. The two most influential Marxian theorists of agency, Norman Geras and Jon Elster, provide interesting and fruitful criticisms of their structuralist counterparts, but their own attempts to refound

Marx's ideas are less convincing.

Geras (1983) offers a strident critique of Althusser's position by challenging the idea that one could understand Marx as someone who denies the existence of 'human nature'. Geras concentrates on the sixth of Marx's 'Theses on Feuerbach', the text Althusser takes as demonstrating Marx's 'radical break' with humanist thought. This aphorism is as follows:

> Feuerbach resolves the religious essence into the human essence. But the human essence is no abstraction inherent in each single individual. In its reality it is the ensemble of the social relations.
>
> Feuerbach, who does not enter upon a criticism of this real essence, is consequently compelled:

> (1) To abstract from the historical process and to fix the religious sentiment as something by itself and to presuppose an abstract – isolated – human individual.
> (2) Essence, therefore, can be comprehended only as 'genus', as an internal, dumb generality which naturally unites the many individuals.

> (Marx, 1977[1845]: 423)

Althusser takes this somewhat opaque fragment to imply that 'the ensemble of human relations' determines human nature, where this 'ensemble' is structural. Geras takes issue with this claim by questioning whether one must understand this comment in such a way, and whether such an understanding is congruent with the rest of Marx's thought. Geras offers three possible understandings of this fragment:

> (1) In its reality the nature of man is conditioned by the ensemble of social relations.
> (2) In its reality human nature, or the nature of man, is manifested in the ensemble of social relations.
> (3) In its reality the nature of man is determined by, or human nature is dissolved in, the ensemble of social relations.

> (Geras, 1983: 46)

Geras points out that the third interpretation – that made by Althusser – is no more convincing than either of the first two, neither of which requires that one denies the existence of 'human nature' or the individual. Furthermore, he argues, the first two interpretations are perfectly consistent with many things Marx argued both before and after this 'radical break with humanism' – whereas the third interpretation is not. The idea that Marx denied the existence of human nature, then, can only be accepted if one is prepared to treat as central 'a freak remark, of an idea which is a departure from the mainstream of his [Marx's] thought and therefore has no bearing on its interpretation' (Geras, 1983: 58).

This is all well and good, and it provides a scholarly basis for questioning Althusser's interpretation of the later Marx. Certainly, by removing the idea that Marx broke with the idea of 'the individual' it prevents Althusser from substituting ideology for meaningful action. What Geras does not do, however, is offer a positive definition of what sort of 'human nature' Marx might have believed in. Demonstrating that Marx did not deny a human essence is very different from demonstrating what kind of thing 'human essence' might be in Marx's work as a whole. Some clues do exist, though. In the 'The economic and philosophical manuscripts', for example, Marx argues that it is:

> in his fashioning of the objective that man really proves himself to be a species-being. Such production is his active species-life. Through it nature appears as his work and his reality. The object of labour is therefore the objectification of the species-life of man: for man reproduces himself not only intellectually, in his consciousness, but actively and actually, and he can therefore contemplate himself in a world he himself has created. (Marx, 1992[1844]: 329)

Later, in *Capital*, he further argues:

> We presuppose labour in a form in which it is an exclusively human characteristic. A spider constructs operations which resemble those of the weaver, and a bee would put many a human architect to shame by the construction of its honeycomb cells. But what distinguishes the worst architect from the best of bees is that the architect builds the cell in his mind before he constructs it in wax. At the end of every labour process, a result emerges which had already been conceived by the worker at the beginning, hence already existed ideally. (Marx, 1990[1867]: 283–284)

Both these extracts indicate the centrality of labour to the human essence – what distinguishes humans from other animals is their capacity to act on the basis of plans and to shape the world (to objectify it) through their actions. Nevertheless, this does not help us to develop an agency-based understanding of the social world. A means of understanding how people combine and operate collectively is required, and if we are not to revert to the structuralism of Cohen and Althusser it is unclear how this can be developed without adding more components to an agency-based theory.

Elster (1982) seems to offer such an addition. To avoid functionalist teleology, he argues, one must start with what motivates individuals to act in the ways they do – their motivations lead them to act in particular ways, and the manner in which they change and affect their environments are determined by how they understand the world and their place in it. Furthermore, Elster argues, people will tend to select courses of action that seem most likely to bring them beneficial results: they act rationally. Such courses of action are never conducted in isolation, however, and so the rationality or utility of any one actor's plans requires that he or she must also take others' courses of action into account. Thus, for instance, it is in the interests of any particular worker to maximise the sum they can command for their labour power. To do this by blacklegging in a strike, however, would have a wide range of known and unknown negative consequences: trying to predict what these might be forms part of the process of deciding what to do in such a strike situation. The short-term gain of maintaining an income could have longer-term negative consequences, such as attacks by striking colleagues or the risk of unemployment or reduced wages if the strike fails. Individuals, then, although they might compete with one another in particular ways, have some shared interests, and it is on the basis of those that 'classes' are constructed.

Elster's methodological individualism seems to offer us a way of understanding 'structural' phenomena without either resorting to functionalist teleology (as with Cohen) or privileging theoretical understandings over individuals' actual motivation (as with Althusser). His argument, however, requires us to ignore an enormous part of Marx's thought. Most importantly in this, his use of the concept of 'rationality' assumes that an individual's motivations are those of 'economic man', a creature seeking to maximise its returns. By reducing the human actor to this model, Elster presupposes that the logic of capitalist societies, rational self-interest, is the basis of human endeavour, something which begs more questions than it answers. By making this assumption Elster substitutes an historically specific way of engaging with the world for something eternal and essential to the human actor. While this makes sense in capitalist societies – where rational self-interest can be understood to be the same thing as rationality more generally – it is difficult to see how it could be applied to the ties of obligation that characterised feudal social formations, or indeed the ideal of the free human being under communism. By modelling the actor the way he does, Elster seems to deny the possibility of different motivations being 'rational' in different social settings. In short, he forecloses the possibility of revolutionary social change by making rational self-interest a universal human phenomenon rather than one shaped by capitalist social relations. Furthermore, he neglects the role of ideology in contemporary consciousness: the rationality he takes for granted maps closely onto the ideologies of free-market entrepreneurialism and neo-liberalism. In his attempt to refocus Marxian theory on the individual he seems at times to revert to the models of man advanced by the very political economists whom Marx sought to criticise.

Fetishising the social world

Neither structuralist nor individualist readings of Marx make sense. Elster correctly criticises Cohen for his teleological functionalism, but his own theory is open to the criticisms of the concept of the individual which Althusser advances. Althusser's position, as Geras argues, does not square with the 'mainstream' of Marx's writings; however Geras' careful analysis of this mainstream does not provide us with a workable basis for social theory. It is at this point that the 'structure-agency' debate might find purchase.

If neither position can provide a coherent understanding of Marx's position, it might appear that a perspective that unites the two would be more productive. To think this, however, would be a mistake. Neither position is coherent in its own terms, and so an attempt to synthesise the two is likely to add to the confusion.

Both the structuralist and the individualist positions outlined above are instances of fetishism. The concept of fetishism in *Capital* (Marx, 1990[1867], chapter 1) refers to the tendency of political economists to see the socially particular features of commodities (their 'value' as expressed through the market) as essential and their concrete features (what they actually are) as peripheral. A particular way of looking at things is privileged as 'real' and 'eternal', despite the fact that it is an historically specific accident of the way production and consumption happen to be organised. That is not to say that it is a mistake – to be sure, commodities are produced to be sold, and must be bought prior to being consumed – but it is nevertheless the basis of confused thinking. By starting with goods and services as saleable, capitalist, commodities, political economists presuppose just those aspects of the social world they are supposed to be explaining: that is, how production, distribution and consumption are socially organised. It is impossible to question the bases of capitalist social relations if those bases are foundational to one's theory – hence *Capital*'s subtitle, *A Critique of Political Economy*.

To step away from the positions advanced so far, then, does not mean picking and choosing the least incoherent parts of them and attempting to put them together in a new combination. Instead, it requires us to rethink the assumptions they make. The concept of a 'factual social world', something that resists our individual (or collective) efforts to change it, and which provides a context in which we act, does not require that we reify that world into a 'social structure'. To do so fetishises the 'obdurate character' (Blumer, 1969: 22) of social reality as a 'thing', something which has autonomy and intentions of its own. Equally, to characterise the 'individual' as the basic building block of society requires us to fill his or her head with particular contents – either the products of ideology (Althusser) or the 'rationality' of capitalist self-interest (Elster) – which are theoretically rather than empirically derived. Instead of examining human behaviour to try to work out what meanings people might attach to the objects of their attention, we are required to fetishise people as 'instances' of something else, and evaluate their behaviour against what our theories would predict.

One of Marx's most fruitful contributions to social thought, then (to return to the theme with which this chapter commenced), might be to make us suspicious of giving sociological categories life of their own, treating them as 'things' capable of driving activity rather than relatively stable features of the social world which are reproduced through activity. The social world does shape what is or is not possible, and human beings do act on that world in particular ways, but it is not necessary for us to treat either 'social structure' or 'the individual' as *a priori* 'real' phenomena. To illustrate this point further, three concepts from Marx's own work will be described to demonstrate that construing them in relation to 'structural' or 'individualist' understandings weakens their theoretical utility. These are the commodity, work and primitive accumulation.

The commodity

Capitalist social relations – how people combine and organise their joint actions in capitalist societies – depend on the commodification of life: making things which were previously shared or held in common capable of being bought and sold. In the first chapter of *Capital*, Marx (1990[1867]) demonstrates how the difference between things 'in themselves' (things capable of being used, use-values) and those same things as bearers of value (things capable of being exchanged, exchange-values) is central to this commodification. Commodities are not static 'things', however. As use-values they embody 'concrete labour', the particular skills required to produce the object at hand. A suit embodies the concrete labour of a tailor, and a laptop computer embodies the concrete labour of designers, component manufacturers, assembly teams, researchers and so on. As exchange-values they embody 'abstract labour', the amount of time it takes to produce the commodity in question – which forms the basis of the commodity's value, the basis of what it can be exchanged for. Something which takes a worker or workers a week to produce must have an exchange-value sufficiently high to allow its producers to reproduce themselves for that period of time – it must be exchanged for at least its 'value'.

In these two ways, then, commodities embody joint activities. They do so firstly by crystallising human activity into an objectified form, by making concrete the particular skills and abilities of particular people, working in particular circumstances, and secondly by embodying social relations, by having so much time devoted to their creation, where time is the measure of value. Commodities are, therefore, capable of both qualitative and quantitative examination, depending on whether one seeks to consume them or to exchange them for other commodities. From the point of view of (political) economics, though, the commodity is not something which requires explanation but is the starting point for analysis.

The existence of commodities as 'things', for Marx, does not indicate that they can be taken as the starting points for theory building. Indeed, *Capital*'s theoretical thrust is based on the analysis of the commodity into the different ways it can be valued. Central to this analysis is an understanding of the commodity as an embodiment of both human activity and the relations of production. The way things are treated is determined by both what concrete labour they embody (determining what they can be used for) and how much abstract labour was required to produce then (what their value is, which in turn determines the lower limit of what they can be exchanged for). Marx defines capitalism as social relations between people mediated by the commodity, and a central part of his argument is that these relationships come to dominate more and more of our lives over time. There is a tendency for our relationships with other people to become organised around these 'things', which in turn makes the commodity-form appear more natural and normal – something which cannot be questioned. The products of our activities come to confront us as the things around which we have to organise our relationships with other people (Marx, 1990[1867]).

Thus, for Marx, capitalism represents a particular way in which our collective activities are embodied in the products of labour, and a particular way in which those products come to confront us. Other ways in which people can relate to one another – through communal action, through ties of mutual responsibility, through gifts, and so on – are replaced by the commodity relationship, which comes to seem 'natural' and unquestionable, as demonstrated by the political economists' commodity fetishism. In the sphere of labour we come to be defined as 'workers' or 'employers', while in the sphere of consumption we are 'sellers' or 'consumers': the social categories of commodity exchange determine our identities, and – through the expansion of the commodity-form – more and more parts of our lives are devoted to labour or consumption. Although Marx's work is largely about the ways in which the commodity-form comes to dominate the kinds of relationships human beings can have with one another, this is not the consequence of any 'structural' features of the world. Our activities produce commodities, which come to dominate the relationships we have with one another. From start to finish human interaction is central to Marx's analysis, producing both the constraints that operate upon us and the identities we take within those constraints.

Work

Commodity exchange is nothing new or unique to capitalist social organisation. In feudal societies things were exchanged and, more importantly, things were produced for exchange. The simplest division of labour requires this, as those who specialise in one task must exchange the thing they produce (or the service they provide) for the other necessities of life. What is unique about capitalism is that, as a mode of social organisation, it allows some people to get something for nothing – to exchange what they have for something more valuable. This ability, being able to get something for nothing, provides the impetus for capitalist expansion and the colonisation of more and more areas of life by the commodity-form.

Again, however, this is not something 'structural', predetermined by economic development, or 'individualistic', the result of particular (bad) people choosing to behave in particular (bad) ways. The capacity to sell something for more than its value – to generate surplus value – is a function of the special features of labour-power as a commodity. Capitalist societies are based on particular class relationships: one class of people are only able to support themselves by selling their labour-power, their capacity to work, to an employer, who will pay them a wage or a salary for the amount of time they work. Another class of people own the means of production – the land, equipment, buildings etc. – which are required for complex labour to be undertaken. The purchase of labour-power is the basis of the production of surplus value.

Labour-power as a commodity is purchased for its value – what it costs to reproduce the worker and his or her family. A wage must minimally provide workers with the income required to shelter and feed themselves and their families, to ensure that they are able to maintain the value of their labour-power and reproduce it (through raising the next generation of workers). Some workers require higher wages than others as, for example, it costs more to reproduce the labour-power of a surgeon than to reproduce that of an unskilled labourer. As with any commodity, the price that labour-power can command at market (its exchange-value) will tend towards how much it costs to (re)produce it (its value). By increasing the length of the working day, requiring higher productivity (levels of production) or by cutting wages, the purchasers of labour-power can use their employees to produce more goods or perform more services for the same outlay. The logic of capitalist accumulation leads to 'less profitable' employers being unable to compete against 'more efficient' ones and so going out of business. Thus, there is a tendency for the production to be continually reorganised to allow more value to be extracted from a workforce for less cost: wages are driven downwards and productivity increases.

In any particular case, these relationships are determined by the relative strengths of workers and employers. Some groups of workers are indispensable, and so are able to command greater bargaining power, higher wages and better terms and conditions. Newspaper print workers and coal miners were two such groups in the United Kingdom prior to the 1980s. Without the former's goodwill newspapers could not be produced at all (even if the content was produced and the distribution channels waiting): because of this, print workers were able to command far higher salaries than others with similar skill levels and in comparable industries, and were able to have a decisive effect on the organisation of the companies they worked for. Equally, the overall dependency of the energy market on coal gave miners the capacity to bargain with their employer, the National Coal Board, in the knowledge that withdrawing their labour would disrupt the workings of the British economy as a whole. Workers behave rationally given the constraints they operate under, and if those constraints are weak they will seek to hold back the tendency for wages to fall and productivity to rise.

As owners of the means of production, however, employers also behave rationally. Although they might be perfectly pleasant people, they are obliged to ensure the profitability of their productive processes, which means not just selling goods and services for a profit but also ensuring that they are as cheap as those of their competitors. Thus, in the event that particular elements of the workforce are able to reduce their rate of exploitation (like the print workers and miners) there will be a tendency for consumers to buy alternative commodities – coal imported from countries with a weaker mining workforce for example. Capitalists will thus either face bankruptcy or have to reorganise their enterprises, either by producing abroad or by changing their working practices. In the case of the British coal industry, capital investment fled abroad in the face of worker militancy: the vast majority of the coal consumed in Britain is now imported, and alternative sources of energy (some heavily state-subsidised) are used instead. In the case of the newspaper industry, printing is now largely automated, with print workers replaced by technicians who simply serve to ensure the smooth operation of the machines they are responsible for. In both cases capitalist restructuring outmanoeuvres the workforce's strong bargaining position.

The commodity of labour-power, then, while subject to the specific strengths of purchasers and sellers in any one case, does not just drive capitalist profit-making but also forms the basis of the dynamic for capitalist expansion and development more generally. Capitalist production is not a 'structure' with an autonomous existence but is the product of conflicts between workers and capitalists. As worker strength and militancy develops in an industry, that industry's capacity to increase exploitation is checked. But, as a consequence of this, investment will move to those sections of the industry ('poles of capital') with weaker workforces or production practices that are able to sidestep their workers' power. What appear to be 'structures' of production and consumption are generated and maintained by the ongoing struggles over work – and, as this process develops over time, the 'freedom' of both workers and owners becomes more and more constrained by the circumstances in which they find themselves. Neither 'the individual' nor 'social structure' make sense unless understood as part of this dynamic.

Primitive accumulation

Marx does not see this state of affairs as being 'normal' or 'natural', however. It developed out of a specific set of circumstances, and, again, these are neither 'structural' nor 'individualistic'. The movement from pre-capitalist to capitalist social relations was an immense social change. First of all, it should be (re)stated that capital is not a thing but rather a relationship between people mediated by the commodity. This means that people come into relations with one another as buyers or sellers rather than as colleagues, friends, lovers, enemies, relatives and so on. Clearly, not all of our relationships, then, are 'capitalist': we relate to one another in different circumstances in all kinds of different ways, and many, perhaps even most, of those relationships have nothing directly to do with the commodity form. But it appears that more and more relationships have become organised through the commodity nexus: people relate to one another through things rather than directly. The relationships of obligation, honour and affiliation that characterised feudal society, for instance, have been replaced by the contractual relationships of worker and employer, landowner and tenant, lender and borrower, and so on. Capital dissolves many 'traditional' ties and replaces them with pure commodity-mediated contractual arrangements.

This changes the nature of social relations *tout court*: one particular kind of relationship comes to replace many others, and the nature of social life and social structures changes as a consequence. Most obviously, the roles of seller or buyer come to supplant other roles, and one set of stable role-based relationships is replaced by another. The tie between a worker and an employer comes to be organised around working hours, productivity and wages, and other potential frames of reference (expertise, guild membership, family tradition and so on) lose their legitimacy in this contract. Indeed, this is formalised in public liability. Firms have an obligation to maximise share-holder returns, and a failure to do so has negative economic repercussions and can even be deemed a breach of company law. According to Marx, the commodity relationship between worker and employer (organised around wages) is central to capital's expansion and development, as it is the sole form of exchange that allows 'value' to be created: the difference between the rate at which labour-power is purchased and the value it produces is the only means (in the first instance) whereby capital can valorise itself.

To treat these changes as structurally determined or historically inevitable, however, requires us to believe just the kinds of notions that the political economists sought to advance – and which Marx sought to criticise. Early political economists argued that such a social change was the result of particular people being more 'frugal' or 'investing more wisely' than others – a myth that 'plays approximately the same role in political economy as original sin does in theology' (Marx, 1990[1867]: 873). What is interesting about 'structuralist' accounts of all kinds is that they reproduce the same form of this myth: the idea is that something 'structural' changes, which shapes and determines what human actions are possible – something happened in the past which changed the nature of society, making it what it is today. But, as discussed above, the world is not a particular kind of (stable) place as a consequence of now-completed historical changes but rather a constantly shifting dynamic set of activities, characterised by conflicts between different groups of people which drive economic and social restructuring on an ongoing basis.

Atemporal and homeostatic readings neglect two important issues. Firstly, the 'change' from one 'social system' to another was the result of the actions of real people. The Duchess of Sutherland, for instance, removed 15,000 inhabitants from her estates between 1814 and 1820, replacing their habitations with sheep-walks and later forests for deer hunting (Marx, 1990[1867]: 891–892). This massive restructuring was not inevitable but was the result of her need to increase her household income, the relative weakness of her tenants, and changes in social expectations (codified in law and the changing nature of the state) that allowed her to get away with such an action. It is not the case that enclosure inevitably proceeds by its own logic: it is the outcome of real people's actions, and has itself a number of real human consequences. In this case, these consequences crucially include the production of a landless mass of people, ready for capitalist employment – with only their labour-power to sell. Secondly, 'primitive accumulation' – the enclosure of common land and its use for commercial purposes – is the model of subsequent capitalist development. Although in the first instance, such accumulation depends on the enclosure of common land, subsequent enclosures are based on the capacity of 'entrepreneurs' to locate an unexploited resource and find a way to commercialise it. The privatisation of public spaces and commercialisation of leisure activities would be just two examples of how this same logic proceeds. Capitalist societies, and the subsequent development of capital, then, are the products of real human activities (and not abstract social forces), and furthermore are dynamic rather than static entities: the extent to which capital is capable of developing and enclosing 'things' depends on the relative strength of those who seek to impose it and those who seek to resist it. The Duchess of Sutherland was not able to 'persuade' the clans to leave their land – without the British soldiers capable of enforcing the imposition of sheep-walks, or with a stronger and better armed population, such an imposition would have been impossible.

Conclusion

Sociological readings of Marx that rest on 'structural' or 'individualist' assumptions, then, are internally incoherent and neglect those central aspects of Marx's theory that emphasise the dynamic aspects of social development. Struggles between groups – particularly over work – determine how people live and, crucially, what kind of world they live in, and such struggles cannot be reduced to either structural imperatives or to the particular motivations of particular participants. Both the nature of the individual and the shape of the world they live in are produced by human activities, and these activities are always analytically primary in Marx's work.

In this sense, then, Marx's arguments are relevant to sociology in at least three ways. Firstly, they demonstrate that appending a structure–agency dualism to an existing body of work only reveals the incoherence of that dualism: regardless of which 'side' one takes, one cannot build a theory on such distorted bases. Furthermore, such a dualism does not clarify but obscures the sense of the work being examined: in no case can a theorist of either 'structure' or 'agency' deal with the totality of Marx's thought – in each case they have to assert that only part of what Marx wrote about is relevant, useful or accurate. Secondly, Marx's arguments show that it is perfectly possible to describe and explain many aspects of contemporary social life on the basis of dynamic patterns of joint human activity: one does not have to define or specify 'structure' or 'the actor' in order to produce comprehensible accounts of social situations. This is not an accident. Marx was well aware of what he was doing theoretically. Thirdly, and finally, Marx's arguments show that the 'stable' features of both individuals and the social world can be shown to be the products of social relationships, underpinned by dynamic social relations that are the 'real' foundations of social reality. To imagine that these 'stable' concepts are 'real' is not to re-interpret Marx's theory but to reduce it to a fetishised state.

PART TWO

Recent social theorists

5

The two Habermases

Anthony King

Introduction

Jürgen Habermas is one of the most prominent figures in contemporary social theory. This status is deserved: he has produced an impressive opus which has addressed critical contemporary social and political issues. Habermas has also been a consistently brilliant exegete, lucidly describing a wide range of philosophical and sociological literature. In the specific field of social theory and, in particular, in the debates about ontology, Habermas has also made a decisive contribution, demonstrating the undeniable importance of meaning to human social life. All social practice presumes a lifeworld of shared understandings which co-ordinate interaction. In this Habermas is like many of his contemporary social theorists: Giddens and Bhaskar, for instance, have also always insisted that there is a meaningful dimension to human social life. However, like some other social theorists, Habermas has also insisted that society cannot be comprehended only in terms of shared understandings and the social practices which are conducted on the basis of them. Modern society is not just a lifeworld but a system in which the economy and state bureaucracies exist independently of the collective understandings of those who work within them. In this way, Habermas' work replicates the contours of contemporary social theory more generally: he advocates a dualistic social theory of structure and agency.

In his discussions of Weber, Pierre Bourdieu suggested that we must think with Weber against him (1990a: 49). That is, in reading Weber, Weberian insights must be turned against those parts of his opus which are flawed and inadequate. A similar strategy might be used against Habermas: an attempt will be made here to turn Habermas' lifeworld against his concept of the system. In particular, it will be argued that the idea of lifeworld invalidates his concept of system. The codes and systems which Habermas invokes are in every instance reducible to the lifeworlds which he advocates in other parts of this work. By thinking with Habermas against Habermas, the contradictions within his writing come into full view – but their resolution is also eminently possible. In place of ontological dualism, Habermas promotes an interactional account of human social life. Of course, since Habermas is such a prominent social theorist, the resolution of the conflicts within his work has much wider resonance. The lifeworld which is – sometimes unwittingly – at the foundation of his sociology, and the contradictory advocacy of dualism, feature very widely in contemporary social theory. Thus the recovery of the lifeworld in Habermas' work and the rejection of dualism can rectify the shortcomings of contemporary social theory more generally.

The lifeworld

In *The Philosophical Discourse of Modernity* (1987a), Habermas argues that from Hegel on, modern philosophy has fatally limited itself to individual consciousness, rejecting theological appeals to God or any other metaphysical entity on which human knowledge can be grounded. Knowledge can be established only through the rational self-examination of individual consciousness: reason must ultimately provide its own foundations. *The Philosophical Discourse of Modernity* describes how some of the key figures in Western thought – Hegel, Marx, Nietzsche, Adorno and Horkheimer, Heidegger, Derrida, Bataille and Foucault – have all in turn failed to provide an adequate basis for the philosophy of consciousness. In each case, these philosophers failed to provide a firm grounding for knowledge because they limited themselves to a subjective philosophy of consciousness. Each remained wedded to an individualistic ontology, which provided no route out of epistemological nihilism and ethical individualism. Alone, individuals have no external reference to the world beyond their own experience. They know the world only through their own senses and can never be certain that their knowledge is accurately grounded. Individuals can never reach a grounded position on the basis of their own knowledge alone, because that knowledge has no external referent against which to confirm itself; any knowledge they have is the product of the very senses that are suspect in the first place. On this basis, individuals can never know whether their own knowledge is accurate or not. Of course, Descartes' meditations constitute the most important and clearest statement of this problem, where the Cartesian ego, potentially deceived by 'some malicious demon', was forced into a position of radical doubt:

> I shall think that the sky, the air, the earth, colours, shapes, sounds, and all external things are merely delusions of dreams which he [the demon] has devised to ensnare my judgement. I shall consider myself as not having hands or eyes, or flesh or blood, or senses, but as falsely believing that I have all these things. (Descartes, 1994: 79)

Similarly, by reference only to themselves as individuals, it is impossible for humans to establish a stable ethical position for themselves. Once theological legitimations are removed, individuals must establish their ethics on the basis of personal belief and experience. The problem here is that while modern philosophers have sought to ground individual ethics in a rationality which is universal, they have been constantly troubled by the fact that even a rational ethics, like the categorical imperative, ultimately draws on individual judgement for its application. Modern philosophy strives for a universal ethics on the basis of subjective experience, but any universalism is constantly compromised by its reference to and origin in the individual. Based on the concept of the individual, modern ethics is constantly troubled by solipsism, and the philosophy of consciousness is fatally compromised by the subject–object dualism at its heart, which it cannot overcome. The individual can only know the object through the mediation of the senses and, therefore, the object remains an unknowable thing-in-itself.

Habermas has brilliantly illuminated a route out of the self-defeating subject–object dualism of modern philosophy. For him, modern European philosophy has failed to recognise that humans are social animals who learn within communities. This is a decisive fact which transforms the nature of philosophical inquiry. The communities in which humans live provide verification for knowledge which is impossible for the individual alone: 'The concept of communicative reason that transcends subject-centred reason, which I have provisionally introduced, is intended to lead away from the paradoxes and levelings of a self-referential critique of reason' (Habermas, 1987a: 341). While individuals cannot confirm their own knowledge, social groups provide the possibility of such verification – humans can mutually verify their own experience of the world with other members of their social group. That is, other members can affirm or reject the individual's experience as valid. Other people provide the external reference which is lacking for the lone individual: 'The transcendental-empirical doubling of relation to the self is only unavoidable so long as there is no alternative to this observer-perspective ... As soon as linguistically generated intersubjectivity gains primacy, this alternative no longer applies' (Habermas, 1987a: 297). Group members mutually provide each other with an account of the world which is independent of the other's senses.

Yet, the social basis of knowledge is more significant than this, as Habermas suggests in his other writing. One of the central concepts in Habermas' work from the *Theory of Communicative Action* onwards is the notion of the 'lifeworld'. This term was originally invented by Edmund Husserl, who was himself influenced by Wilhelm Dilthey's hermeneutic concept of 'life'. For Habermas, the lifeworld consists of the 'more or less diffuse, always unproblematic, background convictions' in which 'the interpretive work of preceding generations' is stored (Habermas, 1991: 70). The lifeworld therefore refers to those 'taken-for-granted' understandings, the importance of which were exposed in Schütz's phenomenology. These background convictions are essential for human interaction: members of any society are always already part of a particular lifeworld, in which they have to operate: 'Communicative actors are always moving *within* the horizon of their lifeworld; they cannot step outside it' (Habermas, 1987b: 126). The implications of Habermas' notion of the lifeworld are profound and extend beyond ethical or epistemological considerations. Groups do not merely verify individual senses or ethics with others: Habermas is, above all, concerned to develop a theory of communicative action. For him, intersubjective communication in the lifeworld is a means not merely of attaining knowledge but of acting in the world together. In order to collaborate, participants need to be able to co-ordinate their actions. Consequently, they must communicate with each other in order to reach shared intersubjective understandings. As they develop shared understanding, actors orient themselves to joint goals and to the collective practices by which these are attained. Without shared understandings directing actors to collective goals, humans could never co-ordinate their actions and would engage in instrumental, individual acts. Intersubjective communication is, therefore, the most important aspect of human social life, facilitating co-operation in pursuit of distinctively collective goals. Despite Habermas' rigorously theoretical approach, the concept of the lifeworld is utterly concrete: it describes how people are able to do things together. Habermas insists that any serious social theory has to recognise that humans necessarily live within lifeworlds: they are always part of one lifeworld or another, interacting with others on the basis of shared understandings.

Social theorists are indebted to Habermas. He has demonstrated the fallacies of subject–object dualism, which arise from individualist philosophies of consciousness, in favour of the lifeworld in which shared understanding is central to all human practice. Habermas recognises that humans live in social groups and that this primary fact of their existence must be recognised when studying any specific human practice. Habermas de-centres the individualism of modern philosophy and sociology. In place of the subject confronting an object, he prioritises the community – social groups – oriented to collective goals. Community members, bound in dense webs of interaction and oriented to common goals, develop knowledge and morality which are compatible with what they – not the isolated individual – are collectively trying to achieve. Social reality is not reduced to any individual's interpretation of it but depends upon how the participants in a lifeworld collectively understand what they are trying to achieve together. Consequently, Habermas' concept of the lifeworld drives theorists to consider the most concrete forms of social practice. Humans live in a myriad of lifeworlds, each oriented around a specific form of practice co-ordinated by shared understandings. That is a critical insight.

The system

Despite the force of his argument, Habermas fails to recognise the theoretical implications of the concept of the lifeworld. Even as he lays out a genuinely interactive social theory, focusing on collective practices co-ordinated by understanding – or communication – he reneges upon it. This retreat from an interactive theory back to precisely the subject–object dualism which he comprehensively refuted is particularly evident in his exchange with Hans-Georg Gadamer in the early 1970s. Decisively, in this exchange, Habermas re-interprets hermeneutics until it becomes a facile and obtuse form of idealism. Against the universality of the lifeworld, he claims:

> There is good reason to conceive language as a kind of metainstitution on which all social institutions depend. For social action is constituted only in ordinary-language communication. But clearly this metainstitution of language as tradition is dependent in turn on social processes that cannot be reduced to normative relations. (Habermas, 1988: 172)

For Habermas, there are also objective forces which take precedence over understanding: 'The nonnormative forces that enter into language as a metainstitution derive not only from systems of domination but also from social labour' (Habermas, 1988: 173). Of course, Gadamer never denies the reality of labour, technology and the economy in modern society; he promotes, rather, an account of social reality consistent with Habermas' concept of the lifeworld. Thus, Gadamer stresses that 'the cultural heritage of a people is preeminently the heritage of forms and techniques of working, of forms and techniques of domination, of ideals of liberty, of objectives of order and the like' (Gadamer, 1975: 495). However, Gadamer proposes that these phenomena cannot be analysed independently of the understandings of those groups in which they are established. For instance, governance cannot be comprehended independently of the political ideas which co-ordinate state institutions around common policies and processes. Like Habermas' original concept of the lifeworld, Gadamer's hermeneutic focuses concretely on human practice; it recognises only that collective activity is never independent of how those engaged in it understand their practices. Given Habermas' own eloquent discussion of the lifeworld, it is extremely strange that Habermas should revert to such a crude misreading of hermeneutics, casting it as mere subjectivism. It is true that, if conceived as referring to individual interpretation, hermeneutics can no longer provide an adequate account of social reality since it is clear that social reality is not reducible to an individual's understanding of it. That reality is unchanged, however a particular individual might interpret it. Thus, the capitalist economy or state bureaucracy will persist even if any particular individual is unaware of its workings. Consequently, confusing hermeneutics for idealism, Habermas is necessarily forced to develop a new social theory. Although he demonstrates that intersubjective communication is the ground on which humans exist and that the lifeworld is universal, he finally reneges on this interactive position. Having held it out as ultimately a solution to subject–object dualism, Habermas rejects the notion that the lifeworld constitutes an adequate account of social reality in itself.

Consequently, as Habermas stresses with increasing conviction from *The Theory of Communicative Action* on, there is 'system'. Thus, he proposes 'that we conceive of societies *simultaneously* as systems and lifeworlds'

(Habermas, 1987b: 118). In contrast to the lifeworld of interacting participants co-operating in collective practices, the institutions of the system
function causally. The system refers to the operations of the state and the
economy which supersede shared understanding and collective action. In
modern European society, the system, as opposed to the lifeworld, becomes
prior: 'Whereas primitive societies are integrated via a *basic normative consensus*, the integration of developed societies comes about via the *systemic
interconnection of functionally specified domains of action*' (Habermas,
1987b: 115). Habermas' conviction that there is a distinction between the
lifeworld and system constitutes a fundamental tenet of his later work.
Although sociologists have to recognise that individuals can interact with
each other on the basis of meanings, modern society itself does not function
solely on the basis of shared understanding. A critical social theory has to
recognise this material dimension to social life.

> It has to opt for a theoretical strategy that neither identifies the lifeworld
> with society as a whole, nor reduces it to a systemic nexus. My guiding
> idea is that, on the one hand, the dynamics of development are steered
> by imperatives issuing from problems of self-maintenance, that is, prob-
> lems of materially reproducing the lifeworld, but that, on the other hand,
> this societal development draws upon structural *possibilities* and is subject
> to structural *limitations* that, with the rationalisation of the lifeworld,
> undergo systematic change in dependence upon corresponding learning
> processes ... A *verstehende* sociology that allows society to be wholly
> absorbed into the lifeworld ties itself to the perspective of self-interpreta-
> tion of the culture under investigation; this internal perspective screens out
> everything that inconspicuously affects a sociocultural lifeworld from the
> outside. (Habermas, 1987b: 148).

Here, Habermas repeats his misinterpretation of hermeneutics, confusing
interpretive sociology for subjectivism, where the social theorist takes
'the self-interpretation' of individuals in the society as reality. Habermas'
'guiding idea', by contrast, is that society consists of both lifeworld and
system. In the lifeworld, individuals interact with each other on the basis
of common understanding, engaging in collective practices. The system,
by contrast, operates on the basis of causal function and has an objective,
structural status. Consequently, individual action in the system is organised
in a distinctive fashion:

> The transfer of action coordinated from language over to the steering media
> means uncoupling of interaction from lifeworld contexts. Media such as
> money and power attach to empirical ties; they encode a purposive-rational
> attitude toward calculable amounts of value and make it possible to exert
> generalized, strategic influence on the decisions of other participants while
> *by-passing* processes of consensus-oriented communication. The lifeworld
> is no longer needed for the co-ordination of action. (Habermas, 1987b:
> 183)

Actors in the system no longer co-ordinate their practices and interactions by reference to shared understandings. The lifeworld has become rationalised. Habermas concurs with Weber that *'formally organised domains of action* emerge that ... are no longer integrated through the mechanisms of mutual understanding' (Habermas, 1987a: 307). Rather, on this account, individuals enact rationalised codes in order to pursue their own private interests, and so may ignore intersubjective consensus in favour of these. Nevertheless, purposive-rational codes, it must be inferred, become sufficiently established and generalised that, although they are essentially private, members of modern societies are able to co-ordinate their purposive interactions to reproduce the social institutions in which they are operating. The system is coherent because the majority of individuals follow the same rationalised codes. In contrast to the lifeworld, the system, as a functionally interacting structure, is reproduced by individuals enacting rationalised codes. Thus, 'in capitalist societies the market is the most important example of a norm-free regulation of co-operative context' (Habermas, 1987b: 150). Individuals do not collaborate through intersubjective communication but independently follow codes for private gain. All of these individual purposive-rational acts taken together produce an objective social system which operates functionally. The rationalised codes serve an important purpose – to provide a bridge between the objective social system and independent individuals, ensuring the reproduction of the system through individual conformity. Intersubjective interaction is broken up as isolated individuals reproduce the system through the private enactment of codes. The interaction order of the lifeworld is replaced by a dualism of system and individual or, in the language of many social theorists, structure and agency.

According to Habermas, the lifeworld persists in modern society but only in an etiolated form. In contrast with primitive society, it becomes almost superfluous (Habermas, 1987b: 186, 201). The lifeworld no longer provides the background for every interaction but itself becomes dependent upon the economy and state bureaucracy, and it diminishes until it survives only in the private sphere of the family, where individuals create their own personal forms of social interaction: 'Familial lifeworlds see the imperatives of the economic and administrative systems coming at them from outside, instead of being mediatized by them from behind' (Habermas, 1987a: 387). As the system predominates, the lifeworld becomes fragmented. It no longer underpins the social order through powerful ritualistic affirmations but becomes dispersed across a fragile archipelago of private spheres. Each home provides a temporary haven from a heartless world while the system, which provides the material basis for each island of meaning, functions on the basis of purposive-rational codes. Here Habermas echoes Parsons' middle-period work on systems theory. Distinctively, however, Habermas endows lifeworld and system with separate ontological status. In the lifeworld, participants do not merely do different things and engage in different relations. They act and interact with each other in a fundamentally different way from their activities in the system.

The critique of purposive codes

Habermas retreats from his concept of the lifeworld in most of his writing. Nevertheless, although he fails to see the implications of the lifeworld, this concept can be used against Habermas' notion of the system. It is possible to think with his lifeworld against his system; with his interactionism and against his dualism. According to Habermas, the system is the product of the enactment of abstract rationalized codes by individuals. The correct application of these codes in practice does not require shared understanding or negotiation; their application is self-evident. There are two possible interpretations of his concept of purposive-rational codes: a strong one and a weak one.

A strong version account of purposive-rational codes is evident in some parts of *The Theory of Communicative Action* and Habermas' other work. Thus, in *Knowledge and Human Interests*, he draws on psychoanalysis as a model for his critical theory. Psychoanalysis attempts to cure patients by helping them recognise the psychological repressions which bring them into contradiction with themselves. 'Analysis has immediate therapeutic results because the critical overcoming of blocks to consciousness and the penetration of false objectivations initiates the appropriation of a lost portion of life history; it thus reverses a process of splitting-off' (Habermas, 1971: 233). Through psychoanalysis, the false code leading to irrational practice is made explicit and replaced by a coherent one. Habermas' critical theory follows an analogous course. In the system, individuals can follow the codes unknowingly to engage in purposive forms of action; these sublimated codes have to be uncovered. Individuals are effectively cultural dopes.

Similarly, Habermas' ideal speech situation emphasises that the members of modern society are not aware of the codes which prescribe their actions. In order to overcome distorted communication it is insufficient to consider shared understandings; these may be false. Rather, it is necessary to imagine what individuals would agree to in conditions of equality: 'A social theory critical of ideology can, therefore, identify the normative power built into the institutional system of a society only if it starts from the *model of the suppression of generalizable interests* and compares norms formed, *ceteris paribus*, discursively' (Habermas, 1976: 113). In this way, the ideal speech situation illuminates the hidden injuries of purposive-rational codes. In his more recent discourse ethics, Habermas draws heavily on Kohlberg because, once again, he must go beyond how the members of modern society understand themselves: it is necessary to 'transcend this specific conversational context, pointing to something beyond the spatio-temporal ambit of the occasion' (Habermas, 1990: 19). In this way, tacit codes leading to irrational and exploitative action can be replaced by conscious, consensual ones: the system can once again be brought under control of the communicative action of the lifeworld. Whatever the validity of Habermas' critical method from the ideal speech situation to discourse ethics, it implies a strong version of the purposive-rational code. Codes, which drive individual action, exceed individual understanding.

There are serious theoretical problems with this strong account of codes, which represents a typical example of sociological determinism. People are not seen as conscious actors but as agents of structural imperatives, of which they are not fully aware. This account explains the coherence of the system. Since, conveniently, all individuals are similarly programmed, it is possible for them to co-ordinate their actions and to produce the bureaucratic monoliths which characterise modern society. Yet, in arguing thus, Habermas also disparages the role of human consciousness and understanding, and simply renounces a central claim of his own social theory. He claims that human understanding is always central to social life, but, with the strong concept of codes, he then denies this view of agency. Moreover, with the strong concept of code, the fact of social change becomes problematic. If individuals are directed by pre-conscious codes into regular patterns of behaviour, it is difficult to see how they could change their practices. Their actions are already pre-structured by codes which they do not recognise and, like the psychologically ill, they merely repeat pathological behaviour. On this account of codes, individuals are not able to reconsider their practices; they are not fully aware of the codes that inform action and so cannot change them. Yet, Habermas' critical theory relies precisely on this ability to reconsider and collectively identify new goals. For him, it is a principle that humans are able to criticise purposive codes and to create a new consensus on the basis of which they may interact. Thus according to Habermas' own theory, codes cannot really be unknown and pre-conscious – they must be able to be understood by actors. Although Habermas' critical theory implies that codes are hidden, at the same time they must actually be known to the individuals that follow them.

Consequently, there is another possible interpretation of purposive-rational codes. Codes are known by individuals, but instead of being directed by codes independently of their consciousness, individuals follow codes knowingly but independently. Codes are not part of a public consensus, established by collective debate and agreement, but they are understood by each individual, so that codes act as rules for individual action. Each individual follows codes in pursuit of their private interests and to the ultimate detriment to others, but all follow the codes knowingly. On this account of the code, individual agency and consciousness are preserved. Individuals have to know what the codes imply. It is also eminently possible to expose and change the codes. However, on this interpretation, the existence of the system becomes a mystery. If individuals merely followed abstract codes for their own ends without confirming their common goals with their fellow group members, humans would not engage in regular and predictable activity. If individuals followed the codes independently without consensus about ends, then there is nothing to suggest that they should follow them in the same way. Individuals could just as easily apply the same code in a different way in order to pursue different ends. The codes would not co-ordinate human action, giving rise to the system, but would lead merely to a diversity of practices as individuals followed their own private interests. Of course, the problem was famously exposed by Wittgenstein in his so-called 'sceptical paradox' (Kripke, 1982) in which he noted that on such a rule-individualist account, 'every course of action can be made out to accord with the rule' but also 'to conflict with it' (Wittgenstein, 1967[1953]: 81). Although it appears obvious how to follow a rule in any particular situation, it is theoretically possible to interpret a rule in a multiplicity of ways. If individuals followed rationalised codes independently of one another, with no communal agreement on what these rules actually implied, each individual could follow the code in a different way, producing random forms of action. The system would not exist; there would be only incoherence.

In arguing for internal codes which determine individual action, or which individuals follow, Habermas impales himself on the horns of a dilemma which is typical of contemporary social theory, oscillating between randomness and determinism, depending on the ontological status of the purposive codes. Either codes determine action independently of consciousness – in which case social change and human agency are denied – or individuals follow rules independently, in which case there would be no reason for them to converge on similar purposive forms of practice. On Habermas' account of codes, modern society with its institutional system could not exist, unless human understanding were denied and individuals not fully aware of what they were doing. His account of the system is thus fundamentally flawed and must be rejected.

The lifeworld of the system

Purposive codes, followed by or inscribed on individuals, cannot explain the existence of the modern social system. Consequently, it is necessary to reconsider the nature of modern institutions such as capitalist corporations and state bureaucracies. There must be other processes which Habermas ignores and which explain their manifest persistence. Significantly, despite Habermas' Weberian pessimism about the 'iron cage' of bureaucracy, the empirical study of organisations demonstrates that these do indeed operate on a quite different basis than Habermas' concepts of system and codes envisage. Organisations may aspire to the kind of purposive-rational decision-making which Habermas describes; in reality, however, organisations operate quite differently.

In his work on organisations, Bittner recognises the importance of rules in co-ordinating institutions; purposive-rational codes are central. However, no matter how formally rational these rules, they cannot in themselves explain organisational coherence. In contingent situations, members of the organisation might negotiate an agreement between themselves nominally on the basis of the rules which, in fact, undermine the unity of the organisation as a whole (Bittner, 1974: 78). What, according to Bittner, finally unifies the organisation as a coherent social entity is not the rules themselves but the collective belief shared by employees that they are members of an organisation. The contingent interactions in an organisation are orchestrated into a coherent organic whole by the shared belief that participants are members of an organisation – they recognise that they are members of an institution, and this fact in itself mediates relations among them. Shared understanding is a self-referential act of unification; 'The dominant consideration underlying this construction would not be found in the field of means-end relations but in an all-pervading sense of piety' (ibid.: 78–79). Surprisingly, the collective belief of employees that they constitute a unified entity gives their interactions a special, even sacred, quality – no matter how mundane their work seems to be. It is this belief – not the rules or codes themselves – that are critical to the existence of organisations and precede any code or rules which they may try to follow.

March and Olsen's well-known work further undermines the notion that organisations can be understood merely in terms of purposive-rational codes (March and Olsen, 1976). They have famously proposed a 'garbage can' theory of decision-making in which the internal social dynamics of the company and various extraneous contingencies drive strategy. These factors fall together randomly like rubbish to produce a decision. March and Olsen's point is not merely to demystify company strategy but also to emphasise that, even in the best companies, the ideal rational decision-making process is unrealisable. In order to make a decision, the subgroups within the organisation come together to reach a collective agreement on strategy. Each has its own understandings and interests which frame planning. As individuals and these subgroups interact, the planning process itself takes on an autonomous dynamic where the social interactions between particular parties, the joint understandings they reach for often quite local political reasons, reverberate out through the organisation. March and Olsen do not deny the expertise of some large organisations but, even in the most efficient, decisions cannot be understood in terms of a rational choice model. The activities of modern organisations cannot be understood merely in terms of the application of purposive codes, either by the corporate body as a whole or by individual executives. At each point, employees, themselves organised into a hierarchy of subgroups, co-ordinate themselves through a common understanding of their collective goals. The organisation's collective goals and the means of achieving them are a product of these dense and complex interactions among subgroups within the organisation. An organisation is ultimately no different from a lifeworld. It involves participants interacting with each other on the basis of shared understandings and mutually committing themselves to collective goals. Even if the company decides to exploit third-world workers, sack people or destroy the rainforest at the end of the decision-cycle, executives will engage in a social process which is in essential respects similar to the interactions of family members planning Christmas. These decisions are complex collective products. However apparently clinical, they are not the simple product of some purposive-rational code which designates an obvious utilitarian course of action. Humans knowingly arrive at these decisions together, even if the decisions themselves, driven by social and institutional dynamics, are seen to be completely irrational or exploitative.

Similarly, against the concept of a purposive-rational code determining the use of money, John Searle has described how the evolution of money as an institution is dependent on collective public understanding: 'I think we can better understand what is going on in the evolution of money if we explore the relation of constitutive rules to the creation of institutional facts' (Searle, 1995: 42). Thus, 'when we say that such and such bits of paper count as money, we genuinely have a constitutive rule' (ibid.). When money is given a new function 'there has to be collective agreement ... both in the imposition of that status on the stuff referred to by the X term and about the function that goes with that status' (ibid.). Economic actors are only able to use money insofar as they collectively understand what money stands for in the particular situation they are using it. The usefulness of money is ultimately dependent on that collective decision. Certainly Searle fully recognises that once that collective understanding has been reached – and becomes routinised as a co-ordinating signal – individuals can trade without apparently thinking about the shared understanding. They simply act; and they seem simply to follow a rationalised code. They can barter, trying to dominate and exploit each other. Nevertheless, despite the routinisation of interaction, the most apparently code-driven and unconscious individual act presumes collective understandings about money: (X) counts as something specific (Y) in a particular situation (C) (ibid.).

Habermas may be right to dislike modern bureaucracies – and he may find a capitalist money economy personally alienating – but these institutions exist only insofar as participants in them are oriented to collective understandings which they repeatedly affirm and re-negotiate in an eternal myriad of social interactions. Executives in organisations may interact differently with their professional colleagues from how they interact with family and friends, but the social process is not ontologically different. In both cases, the corporation, like the family, is sustained through a series of interactions and exchanges based on certain common understandings and expectations. The shared understandings and the unifying practices are different in a bureaucracy or in a money economy, but the participants in these spheres, as in the family, nonetheless collaborate with each other on the basis of shared understandings about ends and appropriate means. The systems of power and money – which Habermas presumes are created by individuals as they apply rationalised codes – are in fact lifeworlds of collective practice, constituted by shared understandings.

Of course, Habermas in fact always recognises this point. There are various passages which re-describe the system in ways which are compatible with his concept of the lifeworld, the most obvious of which is the ideal speech situation. Although it is often uncertain whether the ideal situation is an actual historical moment, which once occurred in modern society (1996), the continuing process of political discussion in modern societies (1995a: 86) or a transcendental condition which underlies all public debate in any society (1979; 1995a: 57), at certain moments Habermas suggests that the ideal speech situation is an actual political reality whereby the legitimacy of any particular regime is established. For instance, he suggests that a real equivalent of the ideal speech situation has grown empirically out of the transformation of the public sphere (Habermas, 1996) while in *Legitimation Crisis*, he postulated the ideal speech situation in the context of the crisis of the post-war settlement. In the face of economic crisis which jeopardised the state's ability to deliver prosperity and security to its citizens, the legitimacy of the state has been threatened since the 1970s. The post-war social demo-cratic lifeworld which unified the system has collapsed. Habermas remains at a level of abstraction above historical and political detail, and never explic-itly states whether the ideal speech situation is the means of resolving this particular crisis, or whether it is a universal principle which underpins or should underpin the public sphere in modern society. Nevertheless, whether a specific resolution to the 1970s crisis or a more general proposition, Hab-ermas seeks to solve the state's steering problems by re-establishing its legiti-macy to manage the economy and society. With the ideal speech situation, Habermas attempts to re-establish a collective normative basis for the state and its bureaucracies, the system. He intends to re-create a public lifeworld which re-connects all the archipelagos of private lifeworlds to produce a normative grounding for the entire system. Individuals are no longer alien-ated from a system which is not theirs but in Hegelian fashion they are an intrinsic part of it. They subject themselves only to the normative require-ments that they have created. 'We do not adhere to recognised norms from a sense of duty because they are imposed upon us by the threat of sanctions but because we give them to ourselves' (Habermas, 1995a: 42).

Again echoing Parsons, Habermas recognises the obligatory nature of common norms; once accepted, they bind humans to each other in mutually recognised social relations. The ideal speech situation provides a normative basis for the system. Therefore, and by means of it, Habermas is able to re-couple social integration with system integration. Individuals are no longer oppressed by an alien system nor do they follow abstract codes, the implica-tions of which they do not recognise. Through the ideal speech situation, individuals establish certain norms to which they willingly and publicly consent. They recognise themselves as a social group which interacts on the basis of these common understandings, and indeed, as members of this social group, they are obliged to act in accordance with these norms. The system is guaranteed not because individuals independently follow abstract codes but because members of the society have collectively established common goals and ways of attaining them. In this way, collective action is enjoined on the part of every member of the society, and the steering problems which threatened the legitimacy of the society are overcome.

Although Habermas avowedly assumes a dualistic ontology, the ideal speech situation reveals that the system relies at each point on continuous communal agreement, even if the agreement is circumscribed within dominant organisations. The entire edifice of the theory of communicative action (and his subsequent discourse ethics) is based on the assumption that shared understandings are constitutive of all forms of social life including institutional ones. Participants in each sphere of human activity have to recognise their collective goals and the shared means for achieving them. Without collective understandings orienting them to common goals, they cannot co-ordinate their actions. There would be no co-operation and no collective practice. To repeat Habermas' claim, this time against him: 'Communicative actors are always moving *within* the horizon of their lifeworld; they cannot step outside it' (Habermas, 1987b: 126). Even the most rigid and apparently objective institutions are, in fact, sustained by the shared understandings affirmed and re-affirmed in recurrent interactions between participants who work in these institutional contexts. (Faceless institutions are, in fact, completely human, even though they may well be inhumane.) The dependence of even the most rigorous institutions on shared communication does not deny their manifest reality or power. However, the shared understanding of any organisation, disseminated through complex chains of communication which orient its members to a multiplicity of actions, will determine what any institutional reality is.

Habermas rejects any reduction of society to a lifeworld, yet his social theory ultimately rests upon it. For him, modern society is always the product of prior social agreements which orient the members of that society to collective ends. Despite Habermas' claims to the contrary, the system ultimately presupposes a myriad of lifeworlds where local groups of bankers, lawyers, doctors, academics, soldiers, politicians and so on interact and commit themselves to their respective collective goals. These interactions and collective practices constitute the complex social order which Habermas calls 'the system'. At each point, his social theory ultimately appeals neither to objective structures nor to the isolated individual but to the lifeworld; to participants engaged in social practices on the basis of shared understandings. His critical theory should be understood, then, not as an attempt to replace the system with a lifeworld but, rather, to rein in the domineering lifeworlds of states and corporations under a universal, public and democratic lifeworld. That is a worthy project. The problem is that by operating with a dualistic ontology of systems and individuals directed by codes, he cannot hope to achieve it.

Conclusion

Habermas is one of the most prominent social theorists writing today and his work illustrates central characteristics of contemporary social theory more widely. The majority of his work revolves around questions of structure and agency. On this ontology, the individual reproduces the social system through following a set of codes. Yet as *The Philosophical Discourse of Modernity* demonstrated, this account of social action is totally inadequate. I have argued that regular social interaction and collective practice is inexplicable on the basis of it. Habermas' work also involves an alternative ontology. Especially in *The Philosophical Discourse of Modernity* – but also in other texts in sometimes subordinate ways – the ontology of structure and agency, of object and subject, is replaced by the idea of the lifeworld. Here, individuals do not enact codes to produce institutional structures. Humans live in lifeworlds: they form social groups and on the basis of shared understandings they do things together. They co-operate and collaborate in pursuit of collective goals. These lifeworlds consist not merely of the warm and intimate relations of family and friends but of large and consequential networks comprising a myriad of potentially antagonistic and competitive interactions. Soldiers, bankers and even lawyers live in lifeworlds too; even the most brutal institution is a lifeworld, the members of which interact with each other and define themselves on the basis of shared meanings. The idea of lifeworld, in fact, envisages society in a genuinely sociological way. On this account, society consists of people engaged in collective social activity conducted on the basis of shared understandings. To some, this may seem a frail basis for the grand institutions of modernity – but there is no other reality out of which these institutions can be built. The fact that complex and powerful institutions exist should not lead sociologists to appeal to a different, dualistic ontology. It should have a quite different effect: to inspire sociologists to examine the precise way in which groups and networks of participants interact with each other to sustain their relations over days, weeks and years. Habermas' social ontology of the lifeworld should demand a genuinely sociological approach in contemporary social theory – where humans, their actions and interactions are the focus of attention. It should offset the unfortunate tendency in contemporary social theory towards ontological dualism and theoretical abstraction.

6

Pierre Bourdieu: from the model of reality to the reality of the model

Richard Jenkins

The sociological and anthropological work of Pierre Bourdieu, from the 1960s through to his death in 2002, is among the most impressive examples of sustained, consistent social science that the field has produced during the century and a half or so that it has existed as an institutionalised academic endeavour. Despite the criticisms to which it is vulnerable, Bourdieu's *oeuvre* is a distinguished and challenging combination of extreme theoretical ambition and systematic empirical investigation across a range of substantive topics, from the matrimonial strategies of the Kabyle of Algeria to the reproduction strategies of the French ruling elite. It is, in fact, all the more distinguished and challenging precisely because of that, regrettably all too unusual, combination.

Among the programmatic meta-objectives that Bourdieu identified as distinguishing features of his work, perhaps the most striking – certainly the most resonant with the themes and concerns of this volume – was the epistemological and theoretical transcendence of what he considered to be the 'ritual either/or choice between objectivism and subjectivism' (Bourdieu, 1977: 4), or, put another way, 'the scientifically quite absurd opposition between individual and society' (Bourdieu, 1990a: 31). Given that these oppositions are so deeply dyed in the post-Enlightenment Western intellectual wool as to be nearly invisible much of the time – they are, after all, 'the conceptual dualisms upon which nearly all post-Cartesian philosophies are based' (Bourdieu and Wacquant, 1992: 122) – why did Bourdieu find them so problematic, and how did he attempt to transcend them?

In seeking to answer these very specific questions I will concentrate, in the main, on *Outline of a Theory of Practice* (1977), and *The Logic of Practice* (1990b). These books can, in all respects, be considered to be different versions of the same text: in addition to covering precisely the same intellectual agenda and advancing exactly the same arguments, whole passages of *Outline* are repeated nearly verbatim in *Logic*. Although I will refer to other texts as appropriate, *Outline* and *Logic* are the definitive theoretical summaries of Bourdieu's systematic general social theory, and, his early research aside, that theory informed his work throughout his career. The reader looking for more general surveys of Bourdieu's work is recommended to Calhoun (2003c) or Jenkins (2002b), for discussions that are, respectively, more and less sympathetic.

Absurd oppositions

In the pursuit of what he saw as a genuinely dialectical social science, Bourdieu spent a considerable amount of energy attacking intellectual dualisms wherever he found them: theory and practice, *langue et parole*, the primitive and the civilised, materialism and idealism, it would be possible to draw up a long list. The contrasting concepts with which I am concerned here form a cluster, addressing what are obviously related issues:

objectivism : subjectivism
structuralism : existentialism
social physics : social phenomenology
determinism : voluntarism
external : internal
structure : action
society : individual

I could add other items to this list (Bourdieu, 1977: 72–78; Bourdieu and Wacquant, 1992: 5, 7–11), but the point is already made. At the risk of being accused of lapsing into structuralism, these oppositional pairs appear to be transformations of a common root dualism, variations on a basic dichotomous theme:

> Of all the oppositions that artificially divide social science, the most fundamental, and the most ruinous, is the one set up between subjectivism and objectivism. The very fact that this division constantly reappears in virtually the same form would suffice to indicate that the modes of knowledge which it distinguishes are equally indispensable to a science of the social world that cannot be reduced either to a social phenomenology or a social physics. (Bourdieu, 1990b: 25)

When he talked in this way about objectivism and subjectivism, what did Bourdieu mean? The first thing to note is that they are epistemological positions: alternative, and mutually exclusive, ways of seeing the world. He did not – at least not in the first place – offer them as models of *what* or *how* the world *is*. Thus, by objectivism, Bourdieu was referring to the business of knowing the social world by means of establishing 'objective regularities (structures, laws, systems of relationships etc.) independent of individual consciousnesses and wills' (ibid.: 26), an enterprise which privileges analytical models over actors' folk models and theoretical knowledge over practical knowledge. Subjectivism, on the other hand, is a matter of attending to the unreflexive individual experience of self, others and the environment, the 'apprehension of the world as self-evident, "taken for granted"' (ibid.: 25). Practical knowledge is not ignored by subjectivism; it is, rather, the *object* of the analytical exercise. Neither option, in Bourdieu's view, is adequate:

> rejection of mechanistic theories in no way implies that ... we should reduce the objective intentions and constituted significations of actions and works to the conscious and deliberate intentions of their authors. (Bourdieu, 1977: 73)

To begin with objectivism, Bourdieu argued that it does not reflect on the consequences of the research process and the researcher's fundamentally objectifying stance towards social reality. Furthermore:

> because it ignores the relationship between the experiential meaning which social phenomenology makes explicit and the objective meaning that is constructed by social physics or objectivist semiology, it is unable to analyse the conditions of the production and functioning of the feel for the social game that makes it possible to take for granted the meaning objectified in institutions. (Ibid.: 26–27)

In other words, objectivism, failing to take account of the epistemological distance which it necessarily demands – failing to objectify the act of objec-tification – cannot, therefore, begin to grasp how people live their lives and, even more to the point, how they *produce* their lives as structured patterns of practices. This is not all, however. By virtue of this epistemological blind spot:

> objectivism is condemned either to ignore the whole question of the prin-ciple underlying the production of the regularities which it then contents itself with recording; or to reify abstractions, by the fallacy of treating the objects constructed by science, whether 'culture', 'structures', or 'modes of production', as realities endowed with a social efficacy, capable of acting as agents responsible for historical actions or as a power capable of constrain-ing practices; or to save appearances by means of concepts as ambiguous as the notions of the rule or the unconscious, which make it possible to avoid choosing between incompatible theories of practice. (Ibid.)

So, objectivism has three options: first, to be merely descriptive of regularities and patterns; second, to be doomed, in an attempt to explain these objective realities, to resort to attributing causal powers to abstract reifications; or third, to be forced to deploy ambiguous, shifty concepts, to 'explain away' rather than explain. Particularly in the case of the last two options, this is a move from 'the model of reality to the reality of the model' (Bourdieu, 1977: 29; 1990b: 39).

   Given the remarks quoted above about social phenomenology, one might, perhaps, expect Bourdieu to have treated subjectivism a little more kindly (if nothing else, it necessarily recognises the epistemological rupture between social science and its subjects). Not a bit of it: the same problem, the impossibility of apprehending how social reality is made – and in deference to his own use of language, I baulk at imposing on him any allusion to 'social construction' – presents itself immediately. Subjectivism, he argues, cannot do better than describe lived experience:

> This is because it excludes the question of the conditions of possibility of this experience, namely the coincidence of the objective structures and the internalized structures which provide the illusion of immediate understanding, characteristic of practical experience of the familiar universe, and which at the same time excludes from that experience any inquiry as to its own conditions of possibility. (Bourdieu, 1990b: 25–26)

So, subjectivism is, first, merely descriptive of individual experience and, second, incapable of 'getting' the illusion that constitutes and defines that experience and, in addition, renders it incapable of understanding itself.

What is this illusion about which Bourdieu was so concerned? Basically, it is anything that smacks of free will, particularly decision-making and choice:

> The conditions of rational calculation are practically never given in practice: time is limited, information is restricted, etc. And yet agents *do* do, much more often than if they were behaving randomly, 'the only thing to do'. This because, following the intuitions of a 'logic of practice', which is the product of a lasting exposure to conditions similar to those in which they are placed, they anticipate the necessity immanent in the way of the world. (Bourdieu, 1990a: 11)

In this vein, it is worth noting that Bourdieu always preferred to talk about 'agents' rather than 'actors' and that he was at his most ferociously scathing – something for which he had an undoubted talent (Jenkins, 2002b: 167–168) – when discussing existentialism or rational action theories: neither was offered any quarter (Bourdieu, 1990a: 12; 1990b: 46–51; Bourdieu and Wacquant, 1992: 124–127). Since this is such an important aspect of Bourdieu's theory, here is another quotation to flesh out his argument:

> The paradoxes encountered by the endeavour to conceive belief in terms of the logic of decision show the real acquisition of belief is defined by the fact that it resolves these antinomies in practice ... The logic of the acquisition of belief, that of the continuous, unconscious conditioning that is exerted through conditions of existence as much as through explicit encouragements or warnings, implies the forgetting of acquisition, the illusion of innateness. (Bourdieu, 1990b: 50)

Thus the 'logic of decision' is not merely implausible or infrequent owing to the everyday constraints on time and information; it is, Bourdieu insists, simply *wrong*, it is an incorrect account of 'the way of the world'. At which point it might well be suggested that he himself was slipping from a model of reality to the reality of his own model, in dismissing subjectivism not because – or not *only* because – it cannot grasp the world adequately but because it will always be checkmated by how things really are.

But how are things, *really*? As I have already suggested, Bourdieu espoused a radical denial of individual agency. As far as he was concerned, although individuals might routinely believe that they make decisions and can to some degree influence the course of their own lives, in this they are fooling themselves. Or, rather, they are being fooled. But fooled by what? Bourdieu's answer was, by their habitus. The linked illusions – a word that occurs again and again throughout his discussions of these matters – of agency and knowledgeability are fundamental to how the habitus works to generate practices:

> Individualistic finalism, which conceives action as determined by conscious aiming at explicitly posed goals, is indeed a well-founded illusion: the sense of the game which implies an anticipated adjustment to the necessities and probabilities inscribed in the field does present itself under the appearance of a successful 'aiming' at the future. Likewise the structural affinity of habituses belonging to the same class is capable of generating practices that are convergent and objectively orchestrated outside of any collective 'intention' or consciousness. (Bourdieu and Wacquant, 1992: 125)

With the introduction of the notion of 'habitus', it is time to move on to the next section and the question of how Bourdieu claimed to have transcended the 'ruinous opposition' between objectivism and subjectivism.

Before doing so, however, one last observation is in order. I have already suggested that Bourdieu brought objectivism and subjectivism to book on different charges: while he convicted each of epistemological incapacity, of only being able to arrive at limited and partial – albeit different – apprehensions of the social world, subjectivism was also found guilty of qualitatively misunderstanding the nature of the human beings who live in, and whose practices generate, that world. In fostering the wrong-headed notion of meaningful individual decision-making, subjectivism can at best offer no more than a sociologised version of the illusions that individuals hold about their own knowledge, rationality and capacities for social action. So, while neither objectivism nor subjectivism is, in itself, adequate as an epistemological position, subjectivism, in addition, is ontologically wrong.

The inescapable conclusion is that before Bourdieu's bench subjectivism was a much more heinous sociological offence than objectivism. This impression can only be reinforced by his argument, when introducing the 'theory of practice' as an alternative to the 'ruinous' 'ritual' choice between the two alternatives, that 'this sort of third-order knowledge does not cancel out the gains from objectivist knowledge but conserves and transcends them' (Bourdieu, 1977: 4). Although he talked about the need to preserve the virtues of both epistemological positions (1990b: 25), it is the significance of 'objective' phenomena, the need to document pattern and regularity – even though it brought its own pitfalls with it – and the vital necessity of objectification in the research process that are consistently and regularly emphasised (Jenkins, 2002b: 45–65). He comes down very definitely on the objectivist side of the fence.

It is not, in fact, clear that Bourdieu saw any virtues in subjectivism. As already mentioned, he certainly appeared to see none in the two main versions of subjectivism that he regularly attacked, existentialism and rational action theory. Using his own definition of subjectivism, quoted earlier, its only persistent residue in Bourdieu's work is the emphasis on the unreflexive, taken-for-granted nature of human experience and practice. Since this is, to put it mildly, an extremely idiosyncratic account of subjectivism anyway (lack of reflexivity does not figure in many people's understanding of the subjectivist options in social science) we may perhaps be forgiven if we interpret this as indicating a further inclination to objectivism.

The transcendent alternative

Despite the fact that Bourdieu was, to say the least, a closet objectivist, he knew, as suggested above, that there are problems inherent in objectivism. In fact, it may even be true to say that, precisely because of his leanings in that direction, objectivism provided his alternative theory-making with a more creative foil – or proved to be a more worthy opponent, to use his own favourite metaphor of 'the game' – than subjectivism. This is certainly one plausible reading of the following:

> In order to escape *the realism of the structure*, which hypostatizes systems of objective relations by converting them into totalities already constituted outside of individual history and group history, it is necessary to pass ... from statistical regularity or algebraic structure to the principle of the production of this observed order, and to construct the theory of practice, or, more precisely, the theory of the mode of generation of practices, which is the precondition for establishing an experimental science of the dialectic of the internalization of externality and the externalization of internality, or, more simply, of incorporation and objectification. (Bourdieu, 1977: 72, emphasis in original)

The passage from regularity and structure to the principles of their production can be said to be the primary concern of Bourdieu's general social theory, if we strip it down to its barest essentials. The key fundamentals, for my limited purposes in this discussion, are 'practice' – not, it is important to note, 'social action': Bourdieu, despite his more or less approving name-checks of Weber, was ploughing a very different furrow – and habitus.

With respect to practice, the important thing to grasp is that, although people routinely do things in relative harmony or accord with whatever those around them are doing, things that are apparently intelligible to those others and to themselves, we should not make the error of thinking that they *know* what they are doing in any profound, or even self-conscious, sense.

Quite the reverse:

> Each agent, wittingly or unwittingly, willy nilly, is a producer and repro-
> ducer of objective meaning ... It is because subjects do not, strictly speak-
> ing, know what they are doing that what they do has more meaning than
> they know. (Ibid.: 79)

While Bourdieu would never have denied that human beings can, if asked,
generally explain what they are doing and why they are doing it, we should
not forget that in his scheme of things those explanations, those quotidian
projects and reasons, are illusory. The only meaning that appears to count is
'objective meaning', which, lacking 'subjective intention', is to be found in
the eye of the analytical beholder (Bourdieu, 1990b: 62).

A good example of this is the notion of the 'rule'. While everyday life
and sociological accounts of everyday life are full of rules, which apparently
explain this or that pattern of behaviour, for Bourdieu rules of this kind
were, at best, 'official representations'. They do not cause practices – not
even practices that are apparently observant of an explicit rule:

> the rule is never ... more than a second-best intended to make good the
> occasional misfirings of the collective enterprise of inculcation tending to
> produce habitus that are capable of generating practices regulated without
> express regulation or any institutionalized call to order' (Bourdieu, 1977:
> 17).

It is the 'collective enterprise of inculcation' – socialisation by any other
name, although he forbad his translator to use the word (Richard Nice, personal communication) – that produces in individual agents dispositions to
produce generally conforming practices. Rules are *ex post facto*, relevant in
the breach not the observance (and rules as formulated by sociologists are a
model of reality that have no bearing on the reality itself).

The product of collective inculcation is habitus, a concept originally
derived by Bourdieu from Panofsky, with an earlier history in the work
of Hegel, Husserl, Weber, Durkheim and Mauss (Bourdieu, 1990a: 12).
Originally referring to the habitual condition and appearance of the
body – 'how people hold themselves' would be one way to summarise it
– in Bourdieu's usage habitus came to be defined as 'an acquired system of
generative schemes objectively adjusted to the particular conditions in which
it is constituted' (Bourdieu, 1977: 95). The circumstances are important:

> The structures constitutive of a particular type of environment (e.g. the
> material conditions of existence characteristic of a class condition) produce
> *habitus*, systems of durable, transposable dispositions, structured struc-
> tures predisposed to function as structuring structures, that is, as principles
> of the generation and structuring of practices and representations which
> can be objectively 'regulated' and 'regular' without in any way being the
> product of obedience to rules, objectively adapted to their goals without
> presupposing a conscious aiming at ends or an express mastery of the

operations necessary to attain them and, being all this, collectively orchestrated without being the product of the orchestrating action of a conductor.
(Ibid.: 72)

It is perhaps no wonder that Bourdieu, despite his protests to the contrary
(Bourdieu and Wacquant, 1992: 135–137), found himself described as a
determinist (and often a materialist determinist, at that).

Leaving aside until later the issue of determinism, in the concept of the
habitus Bourdieu was trying to find one word in which to bundle together
adequately the complexities of the embodied 'practical sense' or 'logic of
practice' that enables people to do competent things without having all the
time to think about what they are doing. At its most extreme, and in explicit
opposition to an 'objectivist model of the mechanical interlocking of pre-
regulated actions', this is 'the "art" of the necessary improvisation which
defines excellence' (Bourdieu, 1977: 8). As he said in a number of places, it
is the 'feel for the game', neither conscious nor unconscious and impossible
to rationalise. It is what people just *do*.

Although it is unclear how much he was inspired by earlier work – such
as Goffman's subtle accounts of interaction, or Schütz's explorations of
habituation – in the notion of the habitus Bourdieu was definitely grasping for something genuinely significant. There is no doubt that the 'ways
of the world' operate as much off the radar screen as on it, and there is
equally no doubt that, as a consequence, we often find behaviour difficult
to understand and predict. Even our own behaviour may sometimes be difficult to 'put into words'. However, if we look a little closer at how Bourdieu
believed the habitus works, serious problems begin to multiply. Not the
least of these are his bald refusals, already discussed, to acknowledge first,
that decision making and rational calculation play *some* part in shaping
how and why people do things; second, that people are, as Giddens, for
example, recognises, authentically knowledgeable about what they do; and
third, that knowledge is explicit as well as tacit.

These refusals often look like doctrinal prohibitions, orthodoxy in the
strict theological sense of the word; it is certainly difficult to imagine what
their origins might be, other than a fervent allergic reaction to existentialism. They lead him into ever more labyrinthine elaboration, and ever further
away from the observable realities of 'the way of the world'. His is a case of
'part right being all wrong'. Since there is no space here for a more detailed
forensic dissection (see Jenkins, 2002b: 74–84), I will focus on two key
matters: first, the collective adjustment to each other of different individual
habituses (the question of conformity) and second, the individual adjustment to restricted life-chances (again the question of conformity).

The first version of the question of conformity may be stated thus: if
each individual is genuinely an individual, with his or her own individual
habitus, and if each habitus – i.e. each embodied set of dispositions and
principles, which *generate* practices rather than *cause* them – works in ways
that are not conscious or witting and therefore cannot be the subject or

object of explicit negotiation and transaction, how is an orderly human world possible? The answer has already been implied in some of the quotations above: 'The homogeneity of the mode of production of habitus (i.e. of the material conditions of life, and of pedagogic action) produces a homogenization of dispositions and interests' (Bourdieu,, 1977: 63–64). In other words, shared/similar experiences of life and socialisation produced shared/similar dispositions and generative principles (habitus), which generate shared/similar practices. The 'interests' that are referred to here are worth pausing to consider: are these interests in the subjective or the objective sense of the word? 'I am interested in …', or 'It is in your interests to …'? This looks like a typical example of the deliberate conceptual fuzziness – 'a certain vagueness' – that Bourdieu claimed to cultivate, because 'this openness of concepts … gives them their "suggestive" character, and thus their capacity to produce scientific effects' (Bourdieu, 1990a: 40–41).

This perspective is, according to Bourdieu, the only way that one can account for social order without having recourse to structuralism or functionalism:

> if it is not seen that the relationship between the various sub-systems is established only through the mediation of class membership, i.e. through the actions of agents disposed to actualize the same basic types of habitus in the most diverse practices (fertility, marriage, economic, political or educational conduct), one is in danger of reifying abstract structures by reducing the relationship between these sub-systems to the logical formula enabling any one of them to be derived from any other; or, worse, one is danger of reconstituting the appearances of the real functioning of the 'social system', as Parsons does, only by giving the sub-systems the anthropomorphic shape of agents linked to one another by exchange of services and so contributing to the smooth functioning of the system which is nothing other than the product of their abstract compounding. (Bourdieu and Passeron, 1977: 204)

Here, then, we have one of the reasons why agents do not, apparently, know what they are doing, or why. It's because *they* do not, in fact, appear to be *doing* anything. Or, rather, what they are doing looks suspiciously like the social equivalent of Brownian motion: little more than a result of the combination of energy, environment and the properties of matter (in this case, humans). If this is practice it appears to be mindless. Taking this formulation at face value, it is true that neither are agents the bearers of abstract structure's imperatives (Althusser) nor are they beavering away in order to keep those structures going (Parsons). Bourdieu's alternative is, however, no better; the reproductive reality of his model smacks of the beehive or the anthill:

> Since the history of an individual is never anything other than a certain specification of the collective history of his group or class, *each individual system of dispositions* may be seen as a *structural variant* of all the other group or class habitus. (Bourdieu, 1977: 86, emphasis in original)

This impression of a relatively closed circle of reproduction is reinforced when we look at the second version of the question of conformity, which may be stated thus: how do social arrangements that are typically, one might almost say *always*, characterised by hierarchy and unequal access to resources (in Bourdieu's terms, economic, social, cultural and symbolic capitals), retain considerable stability over time, persisting and only very rarely changing significantly? Bourdieu's answer can be found in the notion of the 'subjective expectation of objective probabilities', which also appeared in his work as dialectics of 'the internalization of externality and the externalization of internality', 'incorporation and objectification', 'objective structures and incorporated structures' and 'objective chances and agents' aspirations'.

What these expressions indicate is that, without realising that they are doing it or intending to, individuals, having grown up within, and been socialised into, a specific social order and material circumstances, take them for granted as 'the way of the world' and produce practices– generated by their habitus, which is, of course, conditioned and formed by circumstances and socialisation – that are harmoniously adjusted to those circumstances and that social order. The concept of the 'subjective expectation of objective probabilities' provides the analytical clockwork for Bourdieu's model of formal education, in France and elsewhere:

> The subjective expectation which leads an individual to drop out depends directly on the conditions determining the objective chances of success proper to his category, so that it must be counted among the mechanisms which contribute to the actualization of objective probabilities. The concept of subjective expectation, conceived as the product of the internalization of objective conditions through a process governed by the whole system of relations within which it takes place, has the theoretical function of designating the intersection of the different systems of relations – those linking the educational system to the class structure and also those set up between the system of these objective relations and the system of dispositions (ethos) which characterizes each social agent (individual or group), inasmuch as when agents make up their minds, they always, albeit unwittingly, make reference to the system of the objective relations which make up their situation. (Bourdieu and Passeron, 1977: 156)

People are thus predisposed not to rock the boat; not because they are satisfied with their lot in life, not because they are forced to acquiesce, and not even because they have decided that resistance is useless, but because they literally do not – cannot – recognise any other option. The end result cannot be other than reproduction, the perpetuation of the existing arbitrary *status quo*:

> Every established order tends to produce (to very different degrees and with very different means) the naturalization of its own arbitrariness. Of all the mechanisms tending to produce this effect, the most important and the best concealed is undoubtedly the dialectic of the objective chances and

> the agents' aspirations, out of which arises the sense of limits, commonly
> called the sense of reality, i.e. the correspondence between the objective
> classes and the internalized classes, social structures and mental structures,
> which is the basis of the most ineradicable adherence to the established
> order. (Bourdieu, 1977: 194)

However, in a modern nation-state, for the system to tick over, everything
has to appear as if meritocracy is at work or individual choice has been exercised. The legitimation of 'the circular reproduction of social hierarchies
and educational hierarchies' is at stake (Bourdieu and Passeron, 1977: 208).
The role of the institutions and practices of formal socialisation in achieving
this is crucial:

> For social destiny to be changed into free vocation or personal merit ... it
> is necessary and sufficient that the School, 'the hierophant of Necessity',
> should succeed in convincing individuals that they have themselves chosen
> or won the destinies which social destiny has assigned them in advance.
> (Ibid.)

Bourdieu was, one imagines, aware that this can be read, without stretching
anyone's credulity, as another version of Althusserian 'determination in the
last instance'. Hence the need to acknowledge that agents play at least some
part in the legitimation of the system, that it doesn't 'just happen'. This
need is satisfied for Bourdieu by his notion of 'misrecognition' (*méconnais-
sance*), which is 'the process whereby power relations are perceived not for
what they are but in a form which renders them legitimate in the eyes of the
beholder' (ibid.: *xiii*).

Misrecognition looks suspiciously like 'false knowledge' and, once again,
underlines Bourdieu's emphasis on objective rather than subjective knowledge. In addition, it introduces a contradictory element into the model: on
the one hand agents can appreciate – albeit less than consciously, through
the generative workings of the habitus – the objective probabilities of their
situation and produce appropriate practices, while on the other they mis-
recognise the realities of that situation. The 'sense of reality' and systematic
misperception converge on the same point, the reproduction of hierarchy
and the existing social order, in what looks like belt-and-braces overdeter-
mination. Either way, agency is denied and the objective knowledge of the
sociologist is paramount.

In closing this section, two comments are due. The first is that there is
more than an air of ontological uncertainty about the habitus: what actually
is it? Bourdieu consistently resisted the easy reduction of habitus to 'culture'
and wrote about habitus as a property of both individuals and collectivities,
such as classes. While there is nothing to prevent theoretical concepts applying to both individuals and collectivities – in fact social theory arguably
needs more concepts of this kind – greater clarity in this respect, or even just
a recognition of the ontological problems posed by his formulation, would
have been most helpful. His bald assertions of the individuality and collec-

tivity of habitus are certainly less than helpful.

Second, given the almost overwhelming fatalistic determinism of Bourdieu's model – 'social destiny' is, indeed, a telling phrase – we are entitled to ask: whence comes change, how do social transformations occur? 'Change' is, unsurprisingly, an entry for which one searches in vain in most of the works by Bourdieu that I have drawn upon in this chapter. Nevertheless, Bourdieu did not completely ignore the problem, or the charge of determinism that accompanied it. To summarise his response in his own words, transformation is the product of 'a social trajectory leading to conditions of living different from initial ones' and can be '*controlled* through the awakening of consciousness' (Bourdieu, 1990a: 116, emphasis in the original). I take this to mean that changed circumstances – largely material circumstances, given what he has to say elsewhere – are the motor of change, and, once change is in train, politics matters in that it decides what is to be done in response. How changed circumstances arise, other than from external pressures, is not clear, and where consciousness might come from, given everything else he had to say about that, is a moot and problematic point.

Objective structures

There are many things about Bourdieu's theoretical enterprise that are not merely intellectually and politically attractive but actually necessary if we are to continue to aspire to a rigorous yet non-reductionist social science. In particular, his appreciation of two important observable realities in the human world – that not everything humans do is consciously executed or can easily be brought to consciousness, and that not all collective phenomena are explicitly organised – is timely, and both points are well-taken. The wonderful image of the 'conductorless orchestra' is just one of the many that he conjures up to put imaginative flesh on dry theoretical bones.

These comments are not offered as the ritual faint praise that often serves as a conscience-saving prelude to an exercise in damnation. If social theory matters – and I take it that it does, otherwise the contributors to this volume would have found something better to do – then consciousness and collectivity are important matters and Bourdieu's contribution to how we can think about them is significant. It is, therefore, all the more frustrating that, in refusing to recognise that decision-making and calculation are routine, non-remarkable parts of the human repertoire, which have considerable influence on what people do, and that people do know a good deal about what they're doing and can talk about it, Bourdieu squandered not only the good will of many readers but also, more importantly, many if not all of the theoretical gains that he promised us.

These very specific refusals, which were arguably crippling in terms of the theoretical programme that he outlined for himself, were underpinned by other, more general, themes in Bourdieu's intellectual make-up and formation. Perhaps the first of these, and the most damaging, is that, despite setting out to transcend the fallacies of objectivism and subjectivism, his attachment to objectivism proved much too strong for him to abandon it. In all of the respects that I have already discussed, Bourdieu remained, fundamentally, an objectivist; and not a faint-hearted objectivist either. So much so, in fact, that whenever he uses expressions such 'objective relations', 'objective regulation', 'objective adaptation' or 'objective structures' – and there are many other variations on the theme to choose from – the notion of objectivity looks very like a gloss for reality, and hence 'truth'.

In the first place, he, of course, takes 'objective' simply to refer to pattern in the data that is independent of the perceptions and knowledge of the people whose practices are documented in those data. Thus objectivity apparently refers to the eye of the beholding sociologist. In the second place, however, over and over again he refers to those 'objective' patterns or processes as causal factors in the social situation that is under examination, and in the lives of those people. This is merely one example:

> The objective homogenizing of group or class habitus which results from the homogeneity of the conditions of existence is what enables practices to be objectively harmonized without any intentional calculation or conscious reference to a norm and mutually adjusted *in the absence of any direct interaction* or, *a fortiori*, explicit co-ordination. (Bourdieu, 1977: 80, emphasis in original)

This is not epistemological objectivism; it is, rather, steely ontological objectivism. While he is loudly warning everyone else about the danger of doing so, Bourdieu quietly slips, over and over again, from a model of reality to the reality of his model.

This consistent and unacknowledged slippage probably explains the next problem. Despite the combative vigour with which he consistently denied the charge of determinism (Bourdieu, 1990a: 14–17; Bourdieu and Wacquant, 1992: 135–137), it is difficult not to conclude that Bourdieu's is a model of social reality in which phenomena that are located outside individuals determine what those individuals do. Even while explicitly refuting accusations of determinism, Bourdieu could not break out of the deterministic circle, in which objective structures produce habitus, which generate practices, which reproduce structures, and so on:

> Social agents are the *product of history*, of the history of the whole social field and of the accumulated experience of a path within the specific subfield ... social agents will *actively* determine, on the basis of these socially and historically constituted categories of perception and appreciation, the situation that determines them. One can even say that *social agents are determined only to the extent that they determine themselves*. But the categories of perception and appreciation which provide the principle of the (self-)determination are themselves largely determined by the social and economic conditions of their constitution. (Bourdieu and Wacquant, 1992: 136, emphasis in original)

Despite the authors' protests, it is hard to imagine how else this might be read, other than as determinism.

The final background current in Bourdieu's theory is structuralism. If I am correct about objectivism and determinism this is not too surprising, in that it could be argued that they came as a package in post-war France. It is a current that can be found throughout his academic writings – it is telling that he reprinted 1970's 'blissful' structuralist analysis of the Berber house as late as 1990, in *The Logic of Practice* (1990b: 271–283) – and it can be seen in a number of the quotations above. While Bourdieu may have intended to pass from structures to the principles that produced them, what he in fact did was to find, in habitus, 'structured structures predisposed to function as structuring structures'.

I have already suggested that objectivism, determinism and structuralism may be mutually entailed in each other, particularly in the French context. Looking at Bourdieu's intellectual biography (Jenkins, 2002b: 13–20, 24–44) it may be defensible to suggest that, in his case, structuralism was the cornerstone. His entire enterprise suggests that it may not be possible to use the notion of 'structure' at all, even in the loosest of senses, without simultaneously importing objectivism and determinism (something that I discuss further in Chapter 9). What is certain is that the more than residual long-term influence of structuralism on his work, coupled with the ferocity with which he rejected the French existential tradition, doomed his transcendent theoretical ambitions to failure. The true dimensions of that failure can best be appreciated in his robust rejection of individual agency as a contributor to the production and reproduction of human social life and its patterns, and in the concepts of 'habitus' and the 'subjective expectation of objective probability', in both of which oversocialised humans are apparently doomed to reproduce the existing objective structures within which they found themselves.

To close, there is one last irony, for a writer whose work abounds in them. Bourdieu, as we have seen, argued that objectivism had no option but to attribute causal powers to abstract reifications, or to use vague or nebulous concepts to explain away social reality rather than explain it. He was probably right. Both criticisms can certainly be applied to his own work.

7

The production and reproduction of social order: is structuration a solution?

Wes Sharrock

Through a critical evaluation of 'structuration theory' as a purported synthesis of 'structure and agency' (or, alternatively, structuralism and hermeneutics), I will argue that the whole idea of a structure-and-agency 'problem' mythologises the fracture lines that *do* run through relatively recent sociological thought.

The structure-and-agency 'problem' is contrived by a powerful structure 'lobby' in sociology that takes its own baseline suppositions as self-evident. It, as in the case of structuration theory, considers the 'problem' in a conciliatory manner: structure must not be absolutely asserted over agency – only extreme structuralists are relentlessly anti-humanist. It is, rather, conceived as the 'problem' of striking an appropriately blended balance of 'structural' and 'agency' elements. In that context, it becomes relevant to ask whether, for example, Bourdieu gives too little emphasis to agency and overdoes the determinism of structures (cf. Jenkins, Chapter 6), or whether Giddens goes too far in the other direction.

As Baldamus (1976: 6–7) pointed out, sociology is enraptured with dualisms, so that structure-and-agency discussions are usually organised in terms of putative oppositions – such as agency and structure, individual and collective, subjective and objective, voluntarist and determinist, and so on, so that the two 'sides' may be lined up on one or other end of these familiar axes. The gross structure-and-agency strategy is to convert such dichotomies to continua and to regard society as (conceptually at least) Janus-faced, leaving the tricky question (on which there is an array of possible combinations, as is testified by the numerous and diverse 'solutions' to the problem) of how far, and in what ways, society is 'objective' or 'subjective'.

The demand for such a synthesis usually arises from those who see the notion of 'structure' as under threat; there is little sense of dialogue with those presumed to be the advocates of 'agency' in these synthesising constructions, for they are commonly presented as correcting utterly naïve misunderstandings about social life on the part of the 'agentists'. For example, it sometimes seems as though 'agency', unless conjoined with 'structuralism', must entail the most thoughtless egalitarianism, imagining that each individual has just as much influence on the run of social affairs as every other one (e.g. Mouzelis, 1995), naïvely overlooking the plain fact that some individuals may make more decisive contributions to practical outcomes than others (Dennis and Martin, 2005: 208–209).

Theoretical syntheses are convenient for the structure 'lobby' insofar as they leave its fundamental suppositions intact, thus disregarding the extent to which disagreement may not be about the balance of 'structure' and 'agency' but a matter of questioning fundamental assumptions about sociological theory in an attempt to disengage from the dualisms which are supposedly constitutive of the structure/agency contrast. For example, presenting the contest as between 'objective' and 'subjective' simply ignores the extent to which this pairing can be displaced by the notion of the 'intersubjective'.

No action in action theory

The structure-and-agency conception does not appreciate that a shift in problematics is involved. There is room here for only the briefest delineation of a fundamental point. It can be legitimately observed of the contemporary 'social action' tradition – which is supposed (e.g. Campbell, 1996) to include such would-be synthesists as Giddens and Habermas – that it shows little interest in the examination of actual social action. This also used to be observed of Talcott Parsons' social action theory, though the accusation is probably more fairly made of recent theorists. Indeed, it is reasonable to complain that prominent contemporary 'action' theorists show little interest in the organisation of action and interaction: there is little that either symbolic interactionists or ethnomethodologists would find recognisable as empirical studies in most 'synthesising' literature. So Blumer's (1966: 538) complaint about theorists' treatment of action, especially action-in-interaction, as a 'neutral medium' remains valid for attempts at structure-and-agency syntheses, for in the latter it is generally assumed that the overall organisation of 'action systems' can be understood *without* understanding how action itself is organised.

The aim here, however, is not to pursue a general disparagement of the spurious structure-and-agency nexus as a vehicle for understanding social thought in the recent past and present but to evaluate the way in which the synthesising project plays out in one case, that of structuration theory. There will, however, be continuity, for the fundamental point is that Giddens' attempted synthesis, too, is one-sided, and that the sociological preoccupations which are adapted to his master scheme are to be understood only in relation to his own problematic. I will try to show that symbolic interactionists and ethnomethodologists may legitimately resist the idea that 'structuration' in any way improves on their conceptions. The issues of the organisation of action, the distinctiveness of Giddens' concept of structure, the role of unintended consequences, and of 'knowledgeability' will be reviewed.

Agency in structuralist terms

The 'duality of structure' notion (Giddens, 1984: 25; see also Giddens, 1976 and 1979) advises us that action is produced in structures, and that structures are end products of action. Thus the concepts of 'action' and 'structure' are both seen as indispensable, and two different kinds of relationships are held to be involved – those in which structures give rise to action, and those in which actions bring about structures. The putatively synthetic achievement of the 'duality of structure' is to acknowledge (to borrow Layder's summary) that the 'actor is a centre of meaning, a free agent who creates the social reality around him or her', but also to moderate a view of human actors as 'solely a product of the constraining influences of social structure … ciphers of structural demands … condemned to repeat and reinforce the very conditions that restrict their freedom in the first place' (Layder, 1994: 133). The 'production' of social life has to be understood as a matter of 'the way in which social life is produced (or created) by people as they engage in the social practices which are the substance of their lives and social experience', whereas the 'reproduction' side asks about the fact that social life 'becomes patterned and routinised' (ibid: 132); in other words, how are institutions, organisations and cultural patterns reproduced over time?

   This proposed solution is a response to the presumption of a freedom/determinism duality. If individuals have freedom, what stops them constantly exercising it to make life unpredictably variable? If individuals can do whatever they want, why do they act much as others do? The overall conception is neither original nor striking – individuals have freedom, but to a limited degree. This is evidenced in a kind of personal customisation of standard practice: individuals act in accord with standardised social forms, but in a manner which reflects some of the distinctive – unique, even – things that make us the particular individuals we are. Layder again: 'We act "creatively" in this sense by bringing to bear our unique characteristics upon socially shared knowledge' (1994: 134), a view which reflects the frequent conceptualisation of compliance in socially standardised forms as creatively null, mere mechanical conformity, with 'creativity' to be found only in (marginal, minimal) embroidering upon the standard forms.

   The story seems a wholly familiar one, of 'agency' conceived as spontaneity and freedom, and 'structure' as the mechanical acting out of that which is predetermined. (cf. Rawls, 1987: 138). If it were so, one could see why an approach which emphasised agency only would involve drastic voluntarism, since it would have to conceive of life as a succession of spontaneous and unreproducible instants. Agency is thus seen as the antithesis of structure, but it would be faulty 'structuralist' logic to eliminate agency altogether. Rather, what is required is a cyclical relationship between spontaneity and routinisation, between moments of individual creativity and their 'objectivation' (in Berger and Luckman's terminology; see 1991: 49ff) in impersonal social arrangements.

That a notion of 'structure' curbs the voluntarism of endless existential moments is perhaps logical, but there are good reasons to ask whether it has any significant application to the history of social thought. In Chapters 1 and 2 it was argued that there was no settled concept of 'structure' of the kind needed if a thorough unification of sociological thought were in prospect. I suggest that attention now be turned to 'action', to enquire whether the work that this concept does in, for example, symbolic interactionism (SI) and ethnomethodology (EM) is underestimated in efforts to line them up as contributors to 'structuration' (e.g. Giddens, 1984: 6–7). It is seldom noticed that SI and EM are quite sociologically traditional in one major respect: both concur in the widespread view that in sociology the relationship between theory and research is at sea. Theorising, the widespread complaint goes, typically has little empirical content, and no ways of linking with research that does (e.g. Blumer, 1969: 45). Attempts were made to bring sociological theory and research together through middle-range theorising, but this did not prevent a resurgence of 'grand theory', which continues to be empirically free-wheeling, without significant concern for how its generalities may be validated. The recent wave of 'grand theory' is not conceptually innovative but consists in recycling and rearranging existing ideas.

Dissatisfaction with theorising's remoteness from the world of action is hardly unique to symbolic interactionists and ethnomethodologists, but it is shared by them. Garfinkel's (1967) insistence on prioritising researchable phenomena encouraged attention to social life as action, finding social order through the examination of cases where people are observably engaged in carrying out society's everyday affairs. One can, as synthesisers do, suppose that focusing upon action ultimately provides only an impoverished understanding of social life, but this is because they commonly have an impoverished idea of what 'action' is. (The important differences between SI and EM are not of primary concern here, so they will subsequently be treated together).

Structure/agency synthesis thus conceives of two different kinds of, or two different aspects of, action: that which belongs to 'society', and that which is personal or belongs to the 'individual'. For proponents of that synthesis, the failing of structuralism is not an inadequate conception of action as a mechanical process playing out the demands of society, but in overgeneralising that conception, thus leaving no room for spontaneity. Reciprocally, it is allowed that 'hermeneutics' is right to conceive action as spontaneity, but guilty of overgeneralising this conception, as though autonomous conduct represents all action (cf. Giddens, 1984: 2). Adjust for exaggerations, and we see that society involves both action required by society and that which is free of its dictation.

How to think about action

Neither SI nor EM conceive action thus. The shortest way to explain this is to say that both see action as problematic, recognising that courses of action – even routinised ones – involve their 'working out'. The examination of 'the actor's point of view' and the study of 'action' are interwoven, since the meaning of any action is constituted by the understandings its perpetrators have. The attempt to investigate action as an observable phenomenon directs attention to the necessity of conceiving the actor's point of view in 'real-time': 'What is someone doing?' can only be answered in relation to where the person is in the course of the action sequence. This is not very different from Weber's initial treatment of action (1978: 4) as a matter of its meaning to the actor – but the concern in both SI and EM is to use this to convert sociology's theoretical themes into empirically observable topics. SI and EM are less involved in manoeuvring within the objective/subjective polarity than in empirically 'objectifying' social reality, ensuring that actual social activities are represented in the research reports that sociology assembles. Constructing large warehouses of abstract theoretical concepts is not useful in identifying the forms of action organisation which constitute the observable occurrences that are the ongoing life of society. Whereas middle-range theories sought to ground their venture through 'objective' methods, SI and EM demoted (and in the latter's case eliminated) the concern with theorising, adopting naturalistic observation as a means of objectifying sociological discourse. The exhibition of closely observed or recorded observations of activities embedded in social scenes was meant to ensure that one could at least understand what it was that abstract sociological schemes might aspire to represent. This is a quite alternative response to the deficiencies of the middle-range programme to that of those who 'return' to 'grand theory' (Skinner, 1985): not one that stipulatively abolishes complex organisational forms, but one that requires instead that they be subjected to an empiricising demand – that their presence and properties be found in action and be recoverable from witnessable, reportable, recordable occasions in social life.

SI gives prominent treatment to the 'definition of situation' as a real-time process, assuming that courses of action are 'emergent' assemblies, that action is 'interaction' involving the joint construction of lines of action, and that communication is the facilitator of the mutual and ongoing 'adjustments' that are achieved through the 'negotiations' that shape the further form of the action's course. On the ethnomethodological side, there is an equal concern with serial organisation of action-in-interaction (the turn-taking of conversation being the most vivid application), and with the extent to which serial organisation is an 'artful' matter, involving practical skills, and pervasively subject to the exigencies of specific circumstances, thus acknowledging that there is an 'impromptu' aspect to even the most routine affairs. The outcomes of action are to be viewed as 'achievements', and the assembly of a course of action is understood, if I can put it this way, as an extensively 'technical' matter. (If SI is disposed towards attempts to identify generic relations of action and interaction, abstracting those forms from what, in Simmelian terms, is their content, then EM instead insists on attending to the organisation of action as an enactment of its content). A course of action is then analysed as an assembly of 'parts', and the organisation of action is understood as a product of the actor's grasp of the nature of such 'parts' and the practicalities of their effective organisation. The artful work of getting a natural science investigation to work out, for example, is a matter not of employing generic methods but of possessing discipline-specific ones (Lynch, 1985).

SI and EM are often singled out as – radical, even – species of subjectivism or voluntarism, and there is every likelihood that they would count as instances of subjectivism by Stones' criteria: 'subjectivism reduces the whole of social life to the actions of individual agents or groups, their actions, interactions, their goals, desires, interpretations and practices. Subjectivism uproots agents from their socio-structural context, treating them as deracinated, free-floating, individuals' (Stones, 2005: 14). Such a characterisation is almost entirely useless as a guide to identifying any actual 'subjectivists' in the history of sociology. It is also quite surprising in what it includes within its catalogue of symptoms – what is 'subjective' about 'groups' or 'practices'? And what remainder is excluded by the alleged reductionism: 'institutions', perhaps? But what are institutions other than standardised practices which have become established across a wide range of territory, groupings and individuals? It is as though reflective attention to 'the actor's point of view' as a principal focus involves endowing it with a unilateral status, as though the 'definition of the situation' conceives the actor as literally laying down – spontaneously dictating – how situations are defined and who may define them, however he or she pleases. It is also as though the power to define the situation was to be understood as self-fulfilling, as if actors may effectively define situations according to whatever preferences they have (for example, deciding to define myself as invulnerable I therefore become invulnerable). This is patent nonsense, of course, but not nonsense advocated by SI or EM. The 'definition of the situation' affiliates, rather, to the problematic nature of action, to the way in which action involves figuring out emerging situations, managing to make determinate sense of the circumstances of action, working out what is actually happening. Equally, the notion of action-as-practical in EM's Schützian legacy is also disregarded: the whole notion entails 'constraints' through heterogeneous conditions that are taken into account in any action project, from watching an evening's television undisturbed to building a major dam.

Thus, 'the society' is the environment of action, and the actor's point of view is more usefully conceived not as a mere perception of an immediate situation confined within the forty square feet of office space and to three people, but as an understanding of (some of) the ways of the society, which are involved in any understanding of what the three people in this room are doing. Projects of action can be large and complex, collaborative (not necessarily or pervasively co-operative) and the fact that 'situated' is sometimes appended to 'action' is only a pleonasm of the sort that Baldamus

(1976) tells us also proliferate in sociology. 'Situated action' cannot identify a distinct kind of action, but can at best serve to emphasise the patent – if neglected – fact that action takes place in situations (its very identity being connected to its circumstances). That actions take place in situations does not, however, entail the reduction of social reality to a series of discontinuous and self-sufficient moments of interaction – any adequate understanding of 'the situation' involves apprehension of its relation to spatiotemporally extended collaborative affairs. It does not need a sociological analyst to externally establish connections between one situation and others, for the understanding of a situation as 'placed' within collective affairs belongs to the situation itself, indeed is integral to grasping the sense of what 'the situation' is.

These cursory remarks on the practically problematic character of action should suffice to show that the idea of action as an acting-out of structural necessities is inadequate, not because it is insufficiently voluntaristic, but because it fails to grasp the mechanics of real-time organisation of action, or to appreciate the 'practically problematic' character of even institutionalised practices. So a refusal of the structuralist conception does not deny that there are institutionalised practices, and hence does not risk lapsing into extreme voluntarism. Nor is the supposed error of such voluntarism – the exemption of action from all constraint – any risk, for action-as-practice *necessarily* involves determination of what 'constraints' those doing the actions must manage. These 'constraints' are multiple and heterogeneous, and they may include some which have, for the participants, the sense of being 'structural'. Again, there is no denial of the commonsense recognisability of 'structural constraints', but real-time analysis of action in real-world situations does not require singling out such constraints as a specialist topic merely because they are the preoccupation of many interpreters of classic theory. Structuralists seem often to identify 'constraint' with 'structural constraint' alone, and thus to conceive it much too narrowly to be relevant to studies of action (cf. Rawls, 1987: 138).

Giddens' notion of 'structure'

It is admitted by Giddens' sympathetic interpreters that the notion of structure as a 'virtual order' (Giddens, 1984: 17) of rules (and resources) causes chronic troubles of interpretation, but this arises only because of the degree to which the notion is barely distinguishable from what have elsewhere been called shared understandings. In Giddens' words, 'structure exists ... only in its instantiations in [social] practices and as memory traces orienting the conduct of knowledgeable human agents' (ibid). By undertaking to set out an ontology Giddens puts himself into a corner, and the adoption of the 'virtual' strategy is the result. Such difficulties are also evident in an ambiguity that permeates Durkheim's thought: Durkheim desired to identify society as a real entity with independent existence but knew, equally well, that the fact that society is more than the product of any one individual does not make it anything other than the product of many individuals. In fact, Durkheim's concept of society turns out to consist in shared understandings (otherwise 'collective representations'; cf. Bloor, 2000). If there is 'more' to society than shared understandings, it is not much, and it is hard to make out just what it is.

Giddens struggles with the same issue, one which is inherited from Durkheim, if not directly, then through the lineage of Saussurean linguistics. The 'language system' sounds like an ontologically independent entity, encouraging Lévi-Strauss, for example, to think of it as something that operates in and through the individual's unconscious (e.g. Lévi-Strauss, 1968). However, whilst one may describe the 'language system' in terms of a structure of differentiation, one is only describing organisational features of shared understandings – the generality of the 'language system' comes from the commonality of the understandings, not vice versa. Giddens affiliates only to the most stripped-down of post-Saussurean structuralisms:

> [The] accomplishment of the task of integrating semiotic studies more closely with other areas of social theory, demands abandoning most, if not all, of the oppositions that have been taken over from Saussure ... In their place, we may expect to develop a theory of codes, and of code production grounded in a broader theory of social practice, and reconnected to hermeneutics. (Giddens, 1979: 48)

That 'expect' is unrealistic, and 'a theory of codes' – an entirely programmatic construct – is another unredeemable theoretical promissory note, but one, like so many of the IOUs churned out by sociology's optimistic printing house, that the issuer hopes someone else will redeem. Giddens' assignment of virtuality to structure seems, then, like a half-hearted attempt to maintain the ontological autonomy of 'structure' in face of the recognition that *de facto* one is talking about nothing other than shared understandings. It is difficult to find a spatiotemporal location for such a 'structure', for it is no more than an abstract representation of the understandings of individuals. It is easy enough to find spatiotemporal locations for actual languages, of course, for one can indicate the locations of the populations that speak them over time and across space. But the 'language system' can't be located in twentieth-century Spain, in Barcelona, or wherever, and must therefore be extricated from 'space and time', and consigned to a virtual realm. However, from this virtual realm it cannot exercise determinate causal influences on events, and so has to be reinstated in space-time to play its putative part in the production and reproduction of social organisation. The 'virtual' structure is realised in the brains of individuals who then, in the case of language, operate according to understandings common to other speakers of the same language: 'language use is primarily methodological and ... rules of language are methodically applied procedures implicated in the practical activities of day-to-day life' (Giddens, 1984: 21). Little is gained by such manoeuvres, and 'virtual' status seems to involve residual reification into an abstract systematic representation of the (complex and uneven) organisation of a set of shared understandings.

If this is unsatisfactory in the language case, then it is not likely be effective more generally when taken, as Giddens takes it, to exemplify the moment–totality relationship between an individual action and the 'overall society':

> When I utter a sentence I draw upon various syntactical rules (sedimented in my practical consciousness of the language) in order to do so. These structural features of the language are the medium whereby I generate the utterance. But in producing a syntactically correct utterance I simultaneously contribute to the reproduction of the language as a whole. The importance of this relation between moment and totality for social theory can hardly be exaggerated, involving as it does a dialectic of presence and absence which ties the most minor of trivial forms of social action to structural properties of the overall society, and to the coalescence of institutions over long stretches of historical time. (Giddens, 1979: 114)

The idea that a language is 'a whole', in the sense in which a nation state is one, is surely spurious. What is presented as a part–whole relationship is, in respect of language, close to, if not actually, a tautology. It is certainly not the case that in producing a 'syntactically correct utterance' I do anything *additional* to 'reproduce the language as a whole'. In other words, it seems as if it is enough to 'reproduce the language as a whole' that one continues to speak it (the language, presumably, since one does not speak 'the language as a whole'). I speak English, and I speak English on the basis of my understanding, which is sufficiently well developed to be described as an 'understanding of English'. My participation in the English language is pretty much the same as that of any other mature speaker: that is, we have pretty much the same understandings about basic syntactic organisation, vocabulary, and so on. My speaking is not participation in part of English, nor does my use of English act out my part in the English language. What else can be concluded, save that I reproduce the language 'as a whole' by continuing to speak according to my understanding of the language, and that the same goes for all those others who share my understandings of it. In my own case the notion that I 'reproduce' the language is presumably semantically identical to the fact that my understandings are continuing ones, which are shared with many others, and can be picked up by those who do not yet have them (they are public properties). If I pass on my understandings to others (through speaking with them on the basis of those understandings) then the language will continue to be spoken even after I cease to speak it, though, of course, the understandings I employ may cease to be shared by other speakers. My 'part' in the English language is surely nothing like my part in modern British society. To give the simplest example, the connection between my action of posting a letter, and someone else's action of delivering it does not consist in shared understandings (though it involves some, obviously) but presupposes a complex organisational inter-mediary, the arrangements of the postal services. Does my posting a letter contribute to the reproduction of the post office? Not if the government has decided that a rearrangement of the whole thing is called for. And so on.

Unable to find robust supra-individual entities occupying identifiable space-time locales, structural theorists seek to give substitute effect to the idea of the supra-individual, by appeal to the 'common' or 'shared'. At this point, however, it becomes difficult to understand how such structuralists are to be differentiated from those they accuse of falling into 'subjectivism' for daring to suggest that social phenomena are constituted in significant part, and in many ways, in terms of the understandings (not necessarily shared) of those who participate in those phenomena. 'Structure' has become so vague that it seems no more than a restatement of the truism that individuals possess understandings which they have acquired from others – in other words, that they are 'socialised'.

What work does action do?

The idea of a 'duality of structure' (Giddens, 1984: 25) – which could just as well be a duality of action – does nothing to correct any voluntaristic risk associated with SI or EM. It is notable that the instances Giddens provides of extreme voluntarism are at the outermost periphery of sociological dis-cussion; G. L. S. Shackle and Jean-Paul Sartre are nominated (1979: 34). Structuration as propaedeutic to excessive voluntarism is insurance against a largely absent risk. Could focusing on action alone possibly yield more than a partial account of social reality, and only a partial understanding of the mechanisms by which action contributes to the formation of social reality? Structuration affirms that action produces structure, but – the duality – structure produces action. This implies two kinds of role that action plays: that of giving rise to new structures and that of reproducing existing structures (which parallels the contrast between action which is spontaneously creative and action cast in forms that have become institutionalised). 'Reproducing existing structures' is treated as much the same as reproducing the existing order of institutions, and it is assumed that attention to action alone cannot comprehend how the existing social order is maintained and transformed. The relation between 'action' and 'structure' is conceived as a part–whole relationship, and exclusive focus on the parts is held to occlude their con-nection to 'the whole'. At this juncture, the notion of 'unintended conse-quences' comes into play, as a means of bridging the gap between specific actions and their totalised outcomes (Giddens, 1984: 9–14).

It is not clear whether a solecism is involved. Here's the fallacious form: actions are explained by their intentions (save for the – gratuitous – addition of a notion of 'the unconscious'). But actions do not only produce the results they intend – they produce consequences which are unintended, especially when considered collectively. Therefore actions do not explain their (collective) outcomes. The proper form, by contrast, reflects what everyone who does things knows: a person's intentions can be appealed to in explanation of what they do. That a person is acting in a certain way is explained by his or her intention to do something. However, persons' intentions do not – alone – explain the outcomes of their actions. Actions do not necessarily follow their intended courses, nor do they necessarily achieve their intended outcomes. It is the actions that were taken, not the action-in-intention, that explain outcomes, and actions that are taken have both intended and unintended consequences. A favoured sociological example of unintended consequences is the 'self-fulfilling prophecy', in which people's own actions frustrate their purposes – as when there is a banking panic, and individuals, intending to save their money by closing their accounts, overwhelm the bank, bring about its collapse, and lose their money (Merton, 1968). It ought to be clear that the individuals' intentions explain their actions: their intention to save their money explains why they act to withdraw it. It is their actions, their collective attempt to save their money which has the effect of forcing the bank out of business.

The fallacious form seems to be presupposed in structuration's attempt to make unintended consequences provide the mechanism of structural stabilisation (e.g. Giddens, 1984: 14), but the treatment of this as a puta- tively synthesising measure again involves uncritical adherence to a prob- lematic that others, such as SI and EM, have abandoned. The claimed necessity of 'structure' arises from the idea that a rounded sociological approach is one that provides a solution to the problem of the stabilisation of social order and that a focus on action alone cannot give such a solu- tion, since the stabilisation of the social order is not an intended outcome. In addition to actions there is a need to postulate a systematic treatment of the relations amongst, and the stabilising feedback effects of, the unin- tended consequences of action. A notion of 'structure' is then indispensable to provide an identity for that-which-is-to-be-stabilised, and which is to be stabilised by actors playing out institutionalised patterns of action that have consequences that unwittingly feed back into the maintenance of those insti- tutionalised pattern.

Could SI and EM benefit by distinguishing the production from the reproduction of social order? Is the 'production of social order' not to be understood as the maintenance of the existing one? If so, then the issue is one of stabilisation – what keeps a regime in place? – which is classically understood as a motivational matter. For example, Weber and Parsons treat social order as a matter of motivated compliance, asking what keeps the members of a society acting in ways that perpetuate that form of society, and under what conditions they could possibly break with the institutional forms that identify that society. It is this problematic to which Giddens' has affiliated himself. A contrast between this political 'problem of social order', inherited from Thomas Hobbes, and the problem of the practical constitution of orders of ordinary action can emphasise the presence of two very different problematics, and at least indicate that they are not going to be accommodated within a unified theoretical scheme, especially if their difference is obscured.

What does action organise?

The political 'problem of order' is not the concern of SI and EM. In these approaches 'social order' refers to the ordering properties of social affairs and, from their point of view, the work that action does is that of ordering itself, of putting its course together in ways which will enable the interrelation of activities. The 'orderliness' of action is the orderliness that participants in activities depend upon to assemble designed and practically effective projects of joint action. Take, for example, 'organising a course of action to do something unprecedented', such as the astronomical task of optically locating a pulsar in the first place, and 'organising the optical location of a pulsar as something that can subsequently be done repeatedly'; in either case, the analysis that EM undertakes attends to the 'technical structure' of the course of action – i.e. what specific actions are needed to achieve the outcome, to produce, in the first case, an assured finding and, in the second, a reproducible procedure. The focus is on how 'stable' courses of action are developed and implemented. In sum, the work that action does is organising.

It is clear that action is self-organising, and – a guideline idea – predominantly does this in and through interaction. Action therefore organises interaction, and one can – as Erving Goffman and conversation analysis (CA) notably did – focus analytical attention on the ways in which action organises interactional moments, identifying the forms of orderly interaction and the ways in which the these are produced. Indeed, the work of Goffman and CA has been so notable that it is not unusual for it to be assumed that these represent the entire domains of SI and EM respectively, and for these then to be described as 'microsociology'. However, it is equally plain that action organises the affairs of everyday life through situations of action and interaction, and that situations may be understood as sites for the formation and execution of joint projects, which range from personal projects to those organised on a societal scale. It is clear, too, that situations are sites for diverse forms of participation in organising a large project, with the sense of whatever is being done in any situation having a concerted relation to the extended collaboration (from, for example, the situation of those carrying out the local chores of a national election campaign, such as folding leaflets or putting them in envelopes and 'central' meetings of those who are 'masterminding the campaign'). These differences are not between ontological domains, only between intra-organisational locales. In any such case, then, the action's form is that of participation in the project, whatever that may be. Identifying a coherent form for any collaborative project is done in and through its occasions and their modes of participation in the collective, in and through the actions which organise it.

I have tried to show that SI and EM inquiries do not address 'the problem of order' as specifically a matter of regime stability: their problem is not to identify the causal conditions for an inter-institutionally stable pattern of arrangements across some social totality. This concern is displaced, so that the idea of the 'production of social order' identifies the way in which order is enacted, brought about by action, focusing, as indicated above, on how action does the work of ordering itself into situations and projects. It is not a matter of 'how does action first produce order?' and 'how does action then reproduce order?' but only 'how does action generate orderly organisation (on whatever scale) in a social setting that is already organised?' This question is to be answered by seeing how orderly organisation is enacted – what, in terms of the working up and working out of action sequences, is done to realise what might be, jargonistically, a feature of the social structure. The fact that some pattern of action recurs does not, of itself, ensure a further occurrence; for the pattern must be actualised, the next occurrence of 'the same' action made to happen, delivered in action.

Consider, for example, what Giddens latterly regards as deeply entrenched rules of action, those of conversational turn-taking. Note that whilst CA provides a portrayal of conversation in terms of a set of rules of turn-taking, it does not treat those rules as providing the organisation of conversation, for, of course, the organising of the conversation is to be done amongst the conversationalists themselves. CA's formal model of turn-taking is identified as 'participant managed'. The participants in conversation have to find ways of organising their talk through the turn-taking arrangements; they have to design the forms of expression that occupy a turn and that accomplish, for example, a transition of speakers, doing so under the condition of 'recipient design' – the requirement that the designed expressions are attuned to the characteristics of co-conversationalists. The turn-taking system has to be actualised in the detailed specifics of each individual conversation through 'artful' practices. Is 'order' not, then, reduced to the order-that-action-intends, standing in direct contravention to the plain fact that 'the social order' is not necessarily what anyone intended, just like those occasions where the successful candidate is everyone's second choice? Mustn't there, therefore, be something in addition to action that determines the outcomes of action with respect to the social order?

Unintended consequences again

'Unintended consequences' are important to Giddens, being pivotal to structuration processes – that people reproduce the totality by merely going about their business would seem, as far as the theoretical problem is concerned, the happiest of coincidences. In a putatively systematic story, it cannot, however, be that, and so it is not the intended outputs of action but their further consequences, especially those which ramify across the actions of very many individuals, which can develop into stable feedback patterns relative to the initial 'structural' conditions under which the actions were produced. Giddens thus congratulates (an otherwise reviled) functionalism for having given prominence to unintended consequences, which, he complains, '[s]ome philosophers' have failed to do (Giddens, 1984: 8). As with so many of Giddens' capsule reviews of the intellectual situation, it is hard to tell quite what has correctly or mistakenly been done to earn or lose his approbation – who, in this case, falls within action philosophy? It is possible that a failure to give unintended consequences their due is a failure to mark them out as a single identified topic, and perhaps the assumption is that paying attention to these would inevitably lead to the recognition that they play a decisive role in the production of social order.

It may seem fair to say that 'unintended consequences' have not been given their due, for one can look in vain throughout the literature of SI and EM for a discussion of 'unintended consequences' that is labelled as such. However, the contention that in both approaches action is seen as problematic gives explicit recognition to unintended consequences – organising action patently involves managing its consequences, for actions may fail to deliver their intended consequences or may deliver consequences additional to those intended, even inimical to those desired. Drivers surely don't intend to produce the traffic jams that they nonetheless encounter each day after they leave the office, yet they know perfectly well that they, along with the other drivers, are creating them. As indicated above, it is not even the case that the 'intended consequences' of a course of action are necessarily all that determinate (cf. Garfinkel's 'certifying an event one did not bid for'; Garfinkel and Sacks, 1970: 363). However, Giddens' theoretical discourse of 'structuration' proceeds untroubled by the fact that for even a single action, sociologists might have trouble totalising the action's consequences, let alone being confident of distinguishing those that were and were not intended. Giddens proceeds in terms of what we could theoretically do if we could track the consequences of large numbers of actions, their interactions, and the interactions amongst their consequences as far as spatially, temporally and organisationally remote states which are to be understood as 'outcomes' of those interlocking actions and their intended and unintended consequences.

From the point of view of action, there are, of course, connections between instant actions and spatiotemporally or organisationally remote, large or complex outcomes; but, whilst these connections are recognised, they must, from action's point of view, take care of themselves, be relied upon to yield the desired outcome, or be regretted as being intractable to local control when not desired. Sociological schemes which invoke the independence of outcomes from intentions do not involve an understanding different from commonsense ones, nor are sociologists in any position different from or better than practically engaged participants to understand how, in any case, the articulation of unintended consequences works out.

Knowledgeable agents

The attribution of 'knowledgeability' might seem a conciliatory gesture toward, for example, ethnomethodology. Giddens again:

> It is an essential emphasis of the ideas developed here that institutions do not just work 'behind the backs' of the social actors who produce and reproduce them. Every competent member of every society knows a great deal about the institutions of that society; such knowledge is not incidental to the society but is necessarily involved in it. (Giddens, 1979: 71)

First, what does the attribution of 'a great deal' of knowledge about 'the institutions' of the society actually involve? In Giddensian terms there is both 'discursive' (or reflective) consciousness of these and, more importantly, practical consciousness, but what does this classification achieve? Giddens' argument is obviously addressed to the 'ideological dupe' problem rather than the 'dope' problem that ethnomethodology raises. The 'ideological dupe' notion is concerned with general orientations, conceiving of actors' general orientations as being ones that are characteristically given to them by society: people believe certain things because it is in the interest of society that they should do so. The beliefs mislead, serving to pull the wool over people's eyes and making them more docile and unquestioning than they would be if they had a better grasp of realities. Again, the theoreticist understanding of the concerns of classic social theory is manifested: these concerns are focused on the conditions under which orders of domination are stabilised or destabilised. It is in this context that 'agency' comes to be conceived as action-outside-or-against-the-system, as a potentially destabilising force and a necessary conceptual complement to 'structure'. The ideological dupe appears in such a theoretical context, explaining why individuals act in ways which meet the needs of the order of domination, since the existence of a stable order of domination is *prima facie* evidence that many individuals must be acting against their own interests (must be accepting a kind of 'voluntary servitude' (Rosen, 1995). It is, however, only a *kind* of voluntary servitude, one which is not authentically voluntary but which is contracted under misinformation: through actors' absorption of (nowadays) hegemonic ideological misrepresentations, there is a sense in which the members of society act for reasons that are not genuinely their own reasons.

The 'knowledgeability' clause in Giddens is designed as a corrective to the ideological dupe conception, given as a generalised assumption: the members of society know what they are doing, at least to a greater degree than has been supposed in the structuralist tradition, though the participants' understanding remains only partial, relative to that of the 'structurationist' who has access, presumably, to an aggregated overview of the interconnection between the actions of a plurality of individuals and the further ramifying unintended consequences of these. The repudiation of the 'ideological dupe' is a move that would fall at least partially under Garfinkel's rejection of 'irony' (the sociologist-knows-what-people-are-really-doing), but does not remotely begin to address the cultural dope issue (Garfinkel, 1967: 68). Crudely, this is to do with competences (Giddens calls them 'capabilities'). It is not that society's members have knowledge of institutions as a distinct competence amongst other competences but that they have, through their assorted competences, understanding of how to enact (some) social practices. Understanding how social settings practically operate is integral to the competences that equip people to get on with their everyday affairs. Their 'knowledge of society' is extensively, then, knowledge of, for example, how to work in the taxi business, how to teach elementary maths while maintaining order in the classroom, how to select successful applicants for social security according to the municipal authority's rules and procedures, how to negotiate pre-trial settlements of criminal matters to expedite court work and so on. There is a very strong sense in which these understandings are sociological, but it is practical-sociological: how to act within the relationships and conventions of social settings.

The cultural dope is simply an underspecified typological construct, contrived to represent real persons for sociological purposes. Such constructs should be operated strictly in accord with the procedures that the theorist has explicitly assigned them – 'dopes' have been assigned insufficient competences to carry out the everyday affairs they are meant to replicate. Giddens' 'knowledgeable actors' are not explicitly endowed with any practical competences, because the theorist himself is unable to specify what those competences are or how they are operated. Postulating 'knowledgeable actors' is like writing 'Here be dragons' on a map – it tells us only how much we have not said. 'Social actors' in social theory are rather like those plastic engines that Garfinkel and Sacks describe as mock-ups which represent how an engine works, except that one is expected to use one's finger to turn the wheel. Sociological types are operated by the unregulated deployment of the sociologist's commonsense understandings (Garfinkel and Sacks, 1970: 362).

This point applies not just to social theory's concept of 'agency' but equally to its concept of 'structure', for the acting out of structural demands is conceived in any empirical application through the imagined operations of commonly known social types (employers, workers, rebels etc.). Egon Bittner is incisive on this:

> In general, there is nothing wrong with borrowing a common-sense concept for the purposes of sociological inquiry. Up to a certain point it is, indeed, unavoidable. The warrant for the procedure is the sociologist's interest in exploring the common-sense perspective. The point at which the use of common-sense concepts becomes a transgression is where such concepts are expected to do the analytical work of theoretical concepts. When the actor is treated as a permanent auxiliary to the enterprise of sociological inquiry at the same time as he is the object of that inquiry, there arise ambiguities which defy clarification. (Bittner, 1974: 70)

Again, the main point is about the failure of structuration as a synthetic enterprise, one which evades fundamental dissatisfactions with the whole style of theorising that excludes the determinable capacities that enable the enactment of society's affairs: the invocation of 'knowledgeability' merely references the engagements of SI and EM.

Conclusion

I have not been able to go into the reasons why SI and EM are deeply resistant to the idea of theorising or to why, for understanding their position, there is no substitute for reading the studies (among which, Sudnow, 1965, is exemplary). Not only is there little sense of dialogue between the 'synthesisers' and those whose work they raid for concepts of 'agency' that are to be given subsidiary status within their schemes, but in addition one finds little consideration of the studies themselves – it is as though SI and EM had written only theoretical manifestos, and as if their understanding of social life were to be conveyed by a series of slogans snatched from their argumentative context. However, SI and EM are alienated from the specifics of any given theorist's mix of existing sociological positions; indeed, they distance themselves from that kind of theorising altogether. It is as simple as this: grand theory is empirical only in the sense that it expects or imagines that someone else will carry out the (much more difficult, if even practicable) task of making the orderliness of social organisation researchable in their terms. Structuration is theoreticist, through and through. Theory of that kind speaks generally only because it speaks very vaguely.

8

On the reception of Foucault

Allison Cavanagh and Alex Dennis

Introduction

Much of the energy devoted to 'resolving' the structure–agency 'dispute' derives from particular readings of sociology's founding fathers: Durkheim, Marx and Weber. The contemporary dominance of theorists such as Bourdieu, Giddens and Habermas, however, did not emerge seamlessly. There was no smooth transition in Anglophone sociology between the 'structuralist' Marxism of the early 1970s – as filtered through Antonio Gramsci (by the Birmingham Centre for Contemporary Cultural Studies) and Louis Althusser (in the sociology of education and 'welfare') – and today's theoretical doldrums. Many sociologists used Michel Foucault's ideas to supplement, and then replace, the left-structuralist consensus of the 1970s and 1980s, and, we will suggest, his reception and adaptation over this period allowed for the transition from one perspective to another to be achieved in an apparently less haphazard manner. Foucault, for thinkers like Stuart Hall, complemented and later superseded the works of Althusser and Gramsci, while for others (e.g. Silverman, 1985), his perspective bridged the structure–agency 'dichotomy'.

It is ironic, however, that Foucault was chosen to fill these theoretical holes. As Fox argues, the 'sociological' Foucault was 'largely vapid, except to the extent that philosophy, literary theory and emancipatory politics impinge on the discipline' (Fox, 1998: 429). The problems of 'translation' that Fox highlights were very real, and the unwillingness of sociologists working 'with Foucault' or 'in the Foucauldian tradition' to take them seriously had serious effects.

Firstly, Foucault's ideas were used to both shore up existing positions in sociology and to instantiate (or solve) the 'new' structure–agency 'problem'. Rather than engaging with Foucault's body of work – or, indeed, his individual works as coherent wholes – sociologists tended to treat elements of his work, individual concepts, in isolation, using them for their own theoretical purposes. As with the earlier appropriations of, for instance, Gramsci and Becker by members of the Birmingham Centre for Contemporary Cultural Studies (Hall et al., 1978) and the 'New Criminologists' (Taylor et al., 1973) respectively, concepts and empirical observations were used without reference to their place in systematic theoretical statements. Through such decontextualisation, a mosaic of ideas of the sociologists' own making could be presented as 'Foucauldian'.

Secondly, where Foucault's works were considered as integrated wholes, they were 'adapted' to address specifically sociological problems, rather than examined as possessing their own pre-existing theoretical integrity. Very much like modern sociologists' 'readings' of Marx to 'cover' gender and ethnic inequality (e.g. McRobbie, 2000), such 'readings' of Foucault tended to remove or modify key elements of Foucault's work – to the extent that such elements proved incompatible with the problem at hand – and to misunderstand others as 'speaking to' sociological concerns rather than Foucault's own philosophical project.

Thirdly, sociologists were able to find in Foucault's work instantiations of the kinds of problems their own research was meant to solve. By attributing particular failings to Foucault – whether those were his failings or not – some sociologists could argue that their work 'went beyond' Foucault's, thus giving it the appearance of something new and innovative.

Finally, sociologists found in Foucault a means of bridging theoretical disagreements which, we will argue, had previously dogged the discipline. In this respect Foucault was illegitimately employed less as a theorist than as a conceptual emollient, allowing sociologists to evade the theoretical implications of their previously held positions. Faced with external attacks and disciplinary competition for its topics of enquiry, many sociologists were able to appropriate Foucault to reflexively constitute their work as theoretically homogeneous and united as a community of practitioners.

In short, then, Foucault was misread, misrepresented or rhetorically rejected by many of the sociologists who claimed to be using his ideas. The question we will address here is how these responses allowed sociologists to solve their theoretical problems. Instead of considering his utility for sociology, or examining what kinds of questions his work might provide answers for, we aim to show how a theorist from outside sociology came to be so important to so many sociological thinkers at a particular time. To anticipate our conclusion, we will show that precisely the problems of adapting Foucault's work to a sociological problematic, as elaborated by Fox (1998), were used to loosely support a vague theoretical *status quo*. In other words, Foucault allowed sociologists to conduct 'business as usual' between the demise of structuralism and the contemporary consensus around Bourdieu–Giddens–Habermas and the structure–agency dualisms.

Foucault in the 1980s and 1990s: from 'traditional' theory to structure–agency

Even a cursory review of 'Foucauldian sociology' reveals that his work is treated in a more cavalier manner than that of many other theorists. Typically his name is invoked to allow sociologists to do what they want to do – often despite the fact that this goes against the aims and objectives of his own work. Foucault was uniquely positioned to play this role as his works developed over time, often contradicted earlier positions, and did not form a systematic theoretical framework in the way that, for instance, Parsons' early work might be understood to have done. Fox (1998), for example, argued that the 'earlier' ('deterministic') and 'later' ('reflexive') works of Foucault are mutually incompatible. By trying to incorporate a model of the body that emphasises its passive nature, the site of inscriptions of power/knowledge and a subsequent emphasis on the 'autonomy of the individual' (Fox, 1998: 426), Fox argues, key concepts in Foucault's work become unstable:

> Both Poster and McNay have offered alternative explanations to Foucault's efforts to interpret historical notions of sexuality, such as ancient Greek attitudes to sexual over-indulgence. 'Discourse' has become a moveable feast. (Fox, 1998: 427)

Ultimately, for Fox, Foucault's earlier work is 'structural' and 'determin-istic', and his later work 'individualistic' and 'anti-essentialist'. *Within* Foucault's thought, Fox finds both structure and agency – and the two cannot be reconciled:

> From what might be seen as an over-emphasis on determinism, we now find an over-emphasis on agency. Rorty has suggested that Foucault's dilemma rested on his twin aspirations – to be both a moral citizen concerned with the possibilities for resistance to power, and his refusal to be complicit with power by taking on its own vocabulary of essentialised subjects. While his work on power and truth met the latter objective at the expense of the former, the re-introduction of a self privileges the former but makes his previous ontology untenable. Unfortunately both positions are naive when applied in sociology, and the much-vaunted rapprochement of agency and structure is illusory. (Fox, 1998: 427)

Fox goes on to argue that a '"Foucauldian sociology"' will necessarily be 'underpinned by dubious or unacknowledged theoretical positions' (Fox, 1998: 430). It is just this unacknowledged theoretical confusion that made Foucault so agreeable to many sociologists, however. The appropriation of Foucault's ideas, terms of reference and concepts could not have been under-taken had they been clearly embedded in a sociologically recognisable frame-work (see, for instance, Dennis and Martin, 2005, on how Foucault's work is compatible with a pragmatist understanding of the sociological project). That they were not so embedded facilitated their being used in a loose, impressionistic and vague manner – temporarily shoring up already-existing sociological approaches in the face of *their* theoretical underpinnings no longer being capable of bearing weight.

Earlier sociologists in the 'Foucauldian' period thus tended to emphasise

Foucault's compatibility with existing sociological tropes, and the uses to which his work could be put to 'enhance' other sociological theories. Thus, from 1986:

> It has been argued that Weber's formal theory of bureaucracy needs to be complemented by the history of factory discipline, the latter overlapping with prison discipline and eventually overlaid with bureaucratic discipline. Thus we return to Weber via Foucault and Marx ... [T]he two bureaucracies of state and economy share an interest in depoliticizing the perception of their power and ideology by subordinating them to the neutral image of disciplined technology and expertise. With this strategy, the two bureaucracies seek to manufacture public docility and in this way have citizens support the state which in turn supports them with a modicum of legal force exercised against their occasional disobedience. (O'Neill, 1986: 57–58)

For O'Neill, 'problems' with existing theorists – in this case an alleged limitation of Weber's concept of bureaucracy which prevents it from being applied to prison or factory discipline – can be resolved by 'broadening' their theories with reference to others' ideas and concepts. In this case, Foucault and 'the social historians', in particular Thompson (1967), can be used to 'supplement' Weber's account and allow for its extension to other fields. What is also interesting here is the way in which Foucault is introduced to support very conventional notions of power and domination: Weber's concept of bureaucratic domination is subtly reconfigured into domination by bureaucrats, and Thompson's theoretically radical ideas about the organisation and perception of time become subsumed under a flabby sociological notion of 'embodied strategies of industrial power'. Foucault, Thompson and Weber are combined to produce something less radical or coherent than any one of them.

By 1998, however, Foucault's adoption by sociologists reflected much more closely their preoccupations with 'reconciling' structure and agency – and so their appropriation of his ideas reflected this new theoretical project. Again, though, the uses to which Foucault was put tended to index how well he could be pushed into existing categories rather than how he could inform or develop theoretical preconceptions. Hence, for example, Flyvbjerg (1998) praises Foucault for 'situating' norms and values in social context, finding his work to be compatible with, and covering similar sociological ground to, that of Habermas:

> Distancing himself from foundationalism and metaphysics does not leave Foucault normless, however ... Foucault's norms are based on historical and personal context, and they are shared with many people around the world. The norms cannot be given a universal grounding independent of those people and that context, according to Foucault. (Flyvbjerg, 1998: 221)

Given the problems Fox (1998) identifies – Foucault's limited utility in shoring up existing sociological theories and his ambiguous status with respect to the structure–agency 'debate' – one might legitimately ask why his work has proved so popular among sociologists. We would argue that *these problems themselves* provide the main reason: Foucault's limited utility for conventional sociological purposes means he can be 'used' in loose and impressionistic ways. In short, by careless references to an author whose work has an ambiguous sociological status, sociologists can avoid having their own theoretical presuppositions subjected to critical scrutiny.

Name-checking Foucault

The ways in which many sociologists have 'used' Foucault, however, lack even this level of theoretical rigour. As with many developments in the 1980s and 1990s, the tendency was to push ahead with what you wanted to do anyway. Thus, for example, Bottero (1998) is able to 'demonstrate' that the 'socially constructed' nature of economics allows one to replace class theory with a theory based on gender inequality:

> The problematic paternalism of male employers (in not uniformly employing women to undercut male wages they are not maximising profit as capitalists should) is only a contradiction in terms of the initial assumptions of class theory ... Once we accept that all considerations of profit, productivity or skill are socially constructed (which does not mean that they have no material basis), then the apparent theoretical contradiction is resolved. Of course, this means that we do not have two systems but one, and that system does not appear to be capitalist as it has been conventionally understood. (Bottero, 1998: 474)

The weasel words here come towards the end. Why should we accept that 'all considerations of profit, productivity or skill are socially constructed', and what does accepting such a proposition entail? If such things are socially constructed, does that mean that others are not, and – if so – which and why? If, however, *every* social phenomenon is 'constructed', surely that means that we cannot treat *some* as 'merely' constructs – as if others were 'real'. Furthermore, and more damagingly, Bottero claims that the fact that all such considerations 'are socially constructed' 'does not mean they have no material basis'. If this is the case, what *does* their being socially constructed mean? Do some things that are socially constructed have a material basis whereas others do not? If so, surely that means the former are 'less' socially constructed than the latter – in which case one should have criteria for distinguishing between the two.

Of course, it is uncharitable to ask such questions. The invocation of 'social construction' does not represent adherence to a theoretical position or show that a category or criterion has been applied to a set of social phenomena. Instead, it allows the writer to carry on with business as usual:

because (in 1998 at least) 'social construction' did not require definition, it could be used to facilitate evidence-free assertions. A putative 'theoretical contradiction' – 'discovered' and described by the author – is 'solved' by claiming that a category of social phenomena are 'socially constructed'. It is our claim that the use of Foucault by sociologists in the 1980s and 1990s both facilitated and acted as a warrant for such vague, loose and impressionistic 'theory'.

An early example of such a use of Foucault can be found in Dobash's (1983) paper on the history of Scottish and English prisons. Opening up his invocation of Foucault, he correctly points out that Foucault's understanding of power did not depend on 'economic or structural considerations' as means of ultimate explanation:

> Foucault has emphasised the moral, social and institutional basis of confinement ... Since we cannot assume that macro political and economic structures and processes automatically produce corresponding and concomitant micro technologies of power, each site or location of discipline and punishment must be investigated in its own right. (Dobash, 1983: 2)

In the very next paragraph, however, he goes on to assert the exact opposite:

> It should not be assumed, however, as some have done that Foucault rejects the significance of the economic and structural basis of society. For him the transformation in the technologies of responding to crime, disorder and mendicancy must be located relative to the rise of capitalism ... Thus, according to Foucault, the social and material changes accompanying the rise of capitalism produced the carceral or panopticon society with the penitentiary at its centre. (Dobash, 1983: 2)

This latter series of claims reads as a much more conventional structuralist–Marxian explanation of power and domination. Technologies were developed to 'alter the minds and bodies of the labouring poor' – presumably by other classes and social groups. This manner of approaching Foucault's work opens up two questions.

Firstly, and most obviously, what is Dobash's actual position on power? He simultaneously, we are led to understand, argues that there is 'no necessary or direct correspondence between global strategies of domination, economic forces, policies of the state and any specific form of coercion and punishment' *and* that 'the social and material changes accompanying the rise of capitalism produced the carceral or panopticon society with the penitentiary at its centre' – both of which, he asserts, derive from Foucault. Unless there are inconsistencies in Foucault's theoretical framework – which must require elaboration for this framework to be used – or two different phases of Foucault's theoretical development are being inappropriately juxtaposed, *at most* one of these statements can be true.

Secondly, and more to our purposes in this chapter, why is Foucault invoked at all? The second paragraph quoted provides Dobash with the framework he needs to undertake his study, which turns out to be a mainstream narrative history of Scottish and English prisons interspersed with odd quotes to demonstrate the compatibility of the account with some of Foucault's empirical observations. By removing the references to Foucault nothing analytical is removed from this account, but its aura of newness is removed: it becomes just another history of the prison. Foucault is used, then, to provide a patina of newness to established approaches. His invocation stands proxy for a theoretical basis for empirical work, and – in the case of Dobash (1983) at least – for empirical work that would not be regarded as original were it not for a 'Foucauldian' flavour.

Foucault doesn't work

Most commonly, Foucault's work is used so as to provide for a distinction between the ideal and the material – often by demonstrating his theoretical 'weakness'. Thus, Anchor (1983) criticised Foucault for 'denying' the reality of 'crime':

> Foucault's work has the merit of demystifying these practices and serving as a conduit for a new discourse of and by prisoners *against* these practices. But a literary work, which proceeds as if crime were *nothing more than* a product of the discursive practices about crime, must surely be suspect. (Anchor, 1983: 114)

This begs every possible question. By arguing that crime is 'nothing more than a product of the discursive practices about crime' – if that is what he is arguing – Foucault is not denying that people do things which are classified as criminal, or that such people might well re-offend on a regular basis. His activism is not directed towards arguing that prisoners are innocent of the offences for which they have been convicted, but towards questioning the way 'crime' is socially constituted and used.

Anchor's argument reflects a more general 'realist' critique of Foucault's theories, which is often rooted in sociologists' desire to change – usually 'improve' – the social phenomena they are studying. Foucault is found wanting by such sociologists because his work seems to undermine their desire to categorise social groups, individuals and practices as morally right or morally wrong. (The idea that social science could or should have such a reformist agenda is, of course, just the kind of concatenation of ideas Foucault sought to excavate and criticise.) Thus, Porter (1996: 59) argues that 'there are weaknesses in Foucauldian notions of power' because 'Foucault places the exercise of power within extremely wide parameters ... A word which covers everything possesses no explanatory usefulness. If power is found in all interactions, it becomes impossible to differentiate between different instances of the application of power' (Porter, 1996: 60).

What is significant here is that Foucault's ideas are not *theoretically* challenged. Porter's concern is not with whether Foucault is right or not but with what the implications of Foucault being right might be for his own agenda – working out how power is distributed structurally:

> rather than seeing power as some sort of Nietzschean monolith, it is possible to differentiate between various instances of its exercise ... [P]ower is something that is possessed ... as a function of their social structural position, some groups possess more power than others. Maintaining the more traditional concept of power means that it is possible to compare the amount of power enjoyed (or suffered) by different groups within society. (Porter, 1996: 61)

According to Porter, Foucault is arguing that instances of the exercise of power are indistinguishable, and no one is more powerful than anyone else (since power cannot be possessed). Furthermore, Foucault's *philosophical* arguments about the *concept* of power can be shown to be deficient through an empirical investigation. Porter fears that if Foucault's conceptions of power/knowledge are valid, the kind of sociology Porter seeks to undertake cannot be 'scientifically' or 'philosophically' underwritten. This is a form of reading backwards, evaluating the utility of premises on the basis of the conclusions they would require to be drawn. In this sense Porter's arguments are no different from the kinds of assertions that any member of society might make about power and so cannot be understood to rest on any analytically privileged position.

Central to these debates, significantly, was the concept of power as articulated both by Foucault and by sociologists who understood themselves to be part of an ongoing critical tradition. We have already touched upon two problematic areas that we feel such sociologists evaded with respect to their use of Foucault's ideas. Firstly, how could they reconcile Foucault's articulation of the concept of power with their own commitments to understanding power as a stable entity subject to contestation within and between pre-constituted social entities? This becomes the more general problem of how to render Foucault's articulation of power commensurable with the approaches to power such sociologists *really* wanted to espouse. In order to achieve this, commentators were forced to grapple with the question of how Foucault's work could be used to shore up a division between the ideal and the material, which *is* central to such understandings of power. Holding together incompatible statements on the nature, forms and operations of power, however, is a perilous enterprise, as the example of Stuart Hall amply demonstrates.

That Hall appropriates eclectic elements of different theories is well observed within commentaries upon his work. Chris Rojek, Hall's primary critical expositor, has coined the term 'syncretic narrative fusion' to refer to the 'welding of interdisciplinary components from dispersed and, in some cases, mutually incommensurate intellectual traditions' (Rojek, 2003: 16) seen in his writings. For Hall, such academic *bricollage* is part and parcel of his overarching commitment to hybridity, to anti-essentialist theories of the subject and of identity that emphasise fluidity and process, and of his belief that 'the future belongs to the impure' (cited in Rojek, 2003: 186). Hall brings into his own theorising his epistemological commitments and laudably practices what he preaches. For Hall, the act of theorising is:

> a process ... that always operates by deconstructing existing paradigms and at the same time snatching important insights from what is tossing out [*sic*] ... [Y]ou recover things that stand in the wrong place in the old conceptual matrix but that nevertheless give you insights into aspects of society and culture you did not have before. You have to reposition them. (Hall, 1988: 69)

However, this is not without its dangers for, as Rojek further argues, it produces a 'strained eclecticism' in Hall's corpus of work, such that 'the attribution of consistency becomes an act of authorial fiat' (Rojek, 2003: 19).

This is never more the case than in relation to Hall's appropriation of Foucault. For Hall, Foucault's utility lies in the way in which he directs attention towards the circulation of power and moves away from what Hall understands as monolithic Marxian notions of the origins of power. However, Hall is scathing about Foucault's refusal to discuss power in terms of generalised authorities or institutions. 'The toad in the garden' finds Hall arguing that in Foucault's work power is theorised

> utterly without reference to any point of condensation or articulation as *the state* ... The problem with Foucault, to put it brusquely, is a conception of difference without a conception of articulation, that is a conception of power without a conception of hegemony. (Hall, 1988: 53)

In a later discussion he goes on to argue:

> I object to [Foucault's] theoretical proviso against recuperating complex notions of articulation ... I want to insist that there *are* centres that operate directly on the formation and constitution of discourse. The media are in that business. Political parties are in that business. When you set the terms in which the debate proceeds, that is an exercise of symbolic power ... So power is already in circulation. But it circulates between constituted points of condensation. In that sense I do borrow the Foucaultian notion but refuse his absolute dispersion. (Hall, 1988: 70–71)

At first glance this is an odd position to take, for it raises the question as to why Hall wants to appropriate Foucault to begin with since his objection appears to be precisely to what makes Foucault unique in the first place. The answer to this conundrum lies in Hall's take on Foucault's approach to discourse. For Hall, it is essential to note that he does not

> in any way refuse the advances made by the development of the analysis of *the discursive*. No social practice exists outside the domain of the semiotic, the practices and production of meaning. (Hall, 1988: 51)

Hall goes on to argue that

> many of Foucault's insights into the operation of the discursive deeply refresh and inform our understanding of how ideological formations work, even where he positively refuses the concept of ideology itself. (Hall, 1988: 51)

For Hall, then, Foucault's chief virtue is the extent to which he can be interpreted as supporting an approach to culture in which the semiotic is primary – exactly the 'failing' Porter (1996) castigated him for. It is this that is the basis of his understanding that power is primarily exercised through the symbolic. When he identifies the circulation of power with the circulation/control of symbols (as in Hall, 1988: 70–71, cited above), Hall explicitly reads Foucault through particular models of language and ideology. However, as Kendall and Wickham have argued, this is close to a *wilful* misreading of Foucault. Hall, they argue,

> does not treat Foucault seriously, using him only up to the point where he might frighten the children – that is, up to the point where he might disturb the obviousness of culture as meaning ... Culture here remains the a repository of those meanings accepted and promoted by the powerful ... The concept of power is used only as a synonym for membership of the board of the Culture Meaning-Bank – the powerful help to stock the bank with those meanings which suit them; the powerless have no choice but to withdraw these meanings and eventually come to accept them as their own. (Kendall and Wickham, 1999: 119)

Thus we can see that the problems Hall faces in using Foucault are largely a consequence of his magpie eclecticism. Trying to bring Foucault's conception of discourse to bear on a theoretical apparatus which is dominated by the notion of pre-existing loci of power requires Hall to firstly ignore Foucault's injunction to see points of enunciation as co-emergent with discourse and secondly to privilege some meanings over others. In short, bringing together incommensurable schema produces a confused notion of power and its nature, to which we now turn.

Strategic essentialism

Ostensibly, Hall's justification for rejecting Foucault's approach to power is an eminently practical one:

> Having refused the binarism which is intrinsic to essentialism, you have to remind yourself that binaries persist. You've questioned them theoretically, but you haven't removed their historical efficiency ... The binary is the form of the operation of power, the attempt at closure: power suturing language. (Hall, 1997, cited in Rojek, 2003: 6)

Thus Hall calls for the use of a little 'strategic essentialism', endeavouring by so doing to retain a critical capacity to undo the sutures of language, whilst at the same time maintaining a scholarly distance from them. Or, put less charitably, Hall both deconstructs and argues against the reality of binaries and then enjoys analytic recourse to them. It is this more critical approach to his work that is taken by Rojek, who argues that it is tantamount to endeavouring 'at one and the same time to pursue the structuralist thesis that meaning is arbitrary, and to defend the orthodox position of the Left, that some meanings are more important than others' (2003: 7).

We can see how this contradictory stance dogs Hall when we consider his seminal 'encoding/decoding' model. This model sought to move away from purely semiotic readings and to relate them within their environments of production. Hall isolated 'determinate moments' in production and consumption; 'differentiated moments within the totality formed by the communicative process as a whole' (Hall, 1973: 3). Insofar as texts are produced within certain institutional and material confines, their encoding can properly be considered as a product of this environment and the key 'structures of knowledge' which they engender. Decoding is another, symmetrical determinate moment in the cycle. When the message, realised through the formal rules of discourse and language, leaves the producer it passes on to the audience/decoder. At this point the structure, encoded within the text, 'employs a code and yields a "message": at another determinate moment, the "message", via its decodings, issues into a structure' (Hall, 1973: 5). Hence the encoding/decoding model, for Hall, allows the analyst to track the progress of the message from structure back into structure, the twist in the tale being that monolithic readings of texts are always qualified in practice. Messages are regarded as subject to systematic misreadings and misunderstandings which Hall understands as a product of the asymmetry between the social locations of the producers and receivers (1973: 6).

The logic of the encoding/decoding model appears on the surface as a move away from both semiotic formalism and structural determinism. However, whilst the model gestures towards these ends, it is critically flawed by its importation of alien conceptual articulations. On the decoding side, in Hall's system of structured readings, of the possible decodings – dominant, negotiated and oppositional – the latter two are mere products of the identification of the former, which is itself identifiable only from the point of view of the analyst. Thus we see again the retention of the binary of power–resistance, given a post-modern Gaussian blur by the addition of a woolly third way – a negotiated reading.

This is problematic, however, insofar as Hall walks a narrow path. On the one hand, as Jennifer Slack has argued, the conceptualisation of the communicative process as merely articulations of structure, without meaning or essential identities, if considered in pure and abstract terms, leads to the conclusion that there is a 'necessary non-correspondence' between moments, as no single moment can act upon another (Slack, 1996: 124). Thus the relative autonomy of decodings is central to Hall's analysis insofar as it acts as a guarantor of meaning, a means of securing the analyst's perspective. However, in order to allow for relative autonomy of readings, a master reading, the dominant reading encoded by and in the interests of 'constituted points of condensation' (1988: 71), must be secured. The result, as Sparks has noted, is an 'increasingly baroque structure (which) has less and less internal stability' (Sparks, 1996: 88).

This problem was anticipated by Foucault. As Chen explains:

> to place resistance in binary opposition to domination is to effect a reproduction of the dominant, of the binary logic set up by the 'strong' party; unless the resisting forces are strong enough to explode the logic itself, it will infinitely reproduce the original dominance. (Chen, 1996: 313)

Thus, whereas Foucault requires resistance and power to be contingently related in order to avoid precisely this trap, Hall, by tying the two together, entrenches and recapitulates the problems he sought to deconstruct.

Moreover, Hall's identification of power and resistance as directly related causes him to misrepresent the nature of regimes of knowledge, which he understands in terms closer to a *Weltanschauung* than a *Zeitgeist*. For Hall, Foucault's failure to recognise the dual nature of power leads him to an inadequate understanding of relations of power. Thus Hall argues that

> [i]f Foucault is to prevent the regime of truth from collapsing into a synonym for the dominant ideology, he has to recognise that there are different regimes of truth in the social formation. And these are not simply 'plural' – they define an ideological field of force ... [A]s soon as you begin to look at a discursive formation, not just as a single discipline but as *a formation*, then you have to look at the relations of power which structure the inter-discursivity, or the inter-textuality of the field of knowledge. (Hall, 1996 [1986]: 136)

Hall's call for Foucault to recognise the deep structures at work organising 'regimes of truth' into opposing positions, however, fails to recognise that Foucault's definition of discourse precludes this approach. In the first instance, Foucauldian discourse cannot be so used since it cannot be merely collapsed into the notion of representation or used as a synonym for ideology. As Chen has argued,

> Hall's reading of Foucault is not so much incorrect as unproductive: it misses Foucault's formulation in accounting for the non-discursive (non-ideological) forms of power, and it fails to understand that, indeed, with Foucault, 'there are different regimes of truth in the social formation' (Hall, 1996[1986]; 48), of which the ideological is only one. In not recognising these points Hall has 'let himself off the hook' of having to theorise the ideological without the asignifying and non-representational dimensions. (Chen, 1996: 313–314)

In the second instance it is illegitimate because, for Foucault, discourse has no 'outside'. This means that there are no external boundaries against which rival discourses can be massed; neither can rival regimes of truth contesting around stable material objects be posited. Rather, contestation is within discourse, creating the material, the visible, the objects of knowledge, and thus forming relations between words and things. Therefore there cannot be a rival way of ordering discourse in the sense that Hall means it, since there is not a rival which has an entirely different material and social location. What Hall is trying to do here is reconstitute Foucault's focus on the relation between power and knowledge in order to be able to advance claims concerning the situatedness of knowledge without falling into a relativist trap of asserting incommensurability.

Conclusion

To try to bring some of these strands together, a question which has recurred within our analysis has been just *what* sociologists might obtain through their use of Foucault. As we suggested in our introduction, we did not seek to privilege a particular reading of Foucault or to engage in Foucauldian scholarship ourselves. Rather, we sought to situate the reading of Foucault within a particular problematic and arena of scholarship. In so doing, the question 'who has accurately represented Foucault?' has been replaced with a broader question concerning utility: 'what does the use of Foucault *do* for those sociologists who invoke him?'

In the first instance, then, we have found that Foucault answers the problems raised by the theoretical impasse in which sociology found itself in the 1980s with the decline of left structuralism. This decline, however, occurred at the same time that sociology's position in the academy and more broadly was under increasingly concentrated scrutiny. Sociology attracted less central funding, and the political engagement of many sociologists was questioned by university and government bodies – those who ultimately employed and funded them. A sense of simultaneously needing to 'man the barricades' and pull together emerged among sociologists, cultural analysts, and all those engaged in hermeneutic, social and political investigation. The Thatcher regime found many sociologists cowering, Anne Frank-like, in the attic of cultural studies. Thus, sociology's theoretical impasse was exacerbated by a crisis of integration in the discipline itself, as previously workable disciplinary boundaries were breached and the integrity of separate disciplines compromised.

Against this backdrop it is not surprising to find that sociology and cognate disciplines found in Foucault a theorist to rally around and a theoretical sticking-plaster to cover their wounds. Hall's theoretical assertions, in particular, reveal how deeply many needed a theorist like Foucault at the time. Hall's appropriation of Foucault – like Bourdieu's of Mauss, or Giddens' of Weber – simultaneously obscures and facilitates. In many ways Foucault himself is to blame in this. His work is notoriously flirtatious. At times it opens up generously to multiple interpretations. At others, though, it is a rarefied elaboration of methods, in which the precise way of operationalising concepts into analysis constitute a shining horizon which constantly eludes capture. Against this background his invitation to understand his empirical work as a 'toolbox' is little more than incitement. The understanding that there was not a proscribed indexical range for these 'tools' allowed those sociologists already committed to particular theoretical positions to employ Foucault's ideas to downplay the extent to which their commitments might not be shared by others. This has had two consequences. In the first instance, at the level of theory it addressed the theoretical impasse, sidestepping around the question of structure/agency and ensuring a continuity in views of power that allowed sociologists to retain a focus on power as domination. This in turn warranted sociology's cherished self-image as the discipline of the left, providing a coherence and a sense of mission which British sociology's recent experiences had badly eroded. Secondly, in terms of institutional needs Foucault provided a means of smoothing tensions between apparently warring factions, pouring oil on waters which were increasingly being troubled by those previously regarded as neutral paymasters.

The reception of Foucault, then, reveals something about sociological misrepresentation that is concealed in the use of other theorists in the structure–agency milieu. It certainly reveals much about the material foundations of sociology and cultural studies in the later part of the twentieth century. To recognise the misreadings of Foucault is not point to an error as much as it is to point to the urgent cultural, political and social conditions which privileged a certain reading of this, often infuriatingly, cryptic theorist. When the definitive history of sociology in the United Kingdom is written, the influence of cultural studies, and the theoretical and institutional *necessity* of Foucault must be two key elements.

PART THREE

After the debate

9

Beyond social structure
Richard Jenkins

The 'structure–action' debate focuses on the persistent difficulty experienced by social theorists in reconciling, within a coherent framework that might serve the purposes of empirical research, what are arguably – other than T. S. Eliot's bare facts of 'birth, copulation and death' – the two most elementary observable realities of the human world.[1] The first of these is that human individuals are able to exercise a substantial degree of agency. We can reflect upon our own and others' behaviour, remember and manipulate huge amounts of information, formulate preferences and choose among alternatives, improvise, innovate, and imagine and plan beyond the immediate here-and-now. The second is the collective dimension of human experience: the 'more-than-the-sum-of-the-parts' that is something other than the mere co-presence of human beings in relationships with each other. Among other things, this is manifest as constraints upon individual agency which, often taken-for-granted to the point of invisibility, are bound up with collective resources such as language and the organisation of the environment.

Marx captured these, apparently paradoxical, realities when, in *The Eighteenth Brumaire of Louis Bonaparte*, he said that although humans make their own histories, they necessarily do so in circumstances that they do not choose (Marx, 1977[1852]: 300). I refer to them as the *most* elementary human realities because, to a greater or lesser degree, they hold good for humans regardless of gender, ethnicity, status or wealth. This does not, however, mean that they are true for every individual human. Much depends, for example, on how individual 'normality' is locally understood, in particular how impairments or psychological difficulties are treated: the capacity to exercise agency and inclusion in collective life are opposite sides of the same coin, and both require acceptance by others.

Most recently incarnated as the 'structuration' debate (Parker, 2000; Stones, 2005), the conversation between social theorists about the relationship between 'structure' and 'action' shows no sign of resolution, although war weariness may have set in. In this chapter I will argue – with no claim to novelty[2] – that this debate and its predecessors have been inconclusive because of a fundamental misconception. The concept of 'social structure', upon which they depend, is vague, does not correspond to observable realities, and imports into social science a set of assumptions that are inappropriate if we want to understand the human world. The notion of social structure has dispatched many social theorists on wild goose chases from which they could never return with anything useful. In short, social structure is a concept without which we can, and should, learn to live.

The vagueness of social structure

'Social structure' is not a concept that can be employed analytically with rigour or clarity. At best, it is a colloquial expression of sorts, part of the social science vernacular. One of the rare attempts to illuminate this notion begins by acknowledging that, despite being 'one of the central concepts in sociological theory and analysis',

> social structure is usually treated as a taken-for-granted concept that is not
> in need of any definition or discussion. Actual uses of the concept ... are
> strikingly nebulous and diverse. As a result, there is little consensus over
> what the word means, and it is all too easy for sociologists to be talking
> at cross purposes, because they rely on different, and generally implicit,
> conceptions of social structure. (López and Scott, 2000: 1)

That López and Scott do not exaggerate can be illustrated by dipping into some recent authoritative overviews of sociology and social theory (chosen simply as what was ready to hand in my office). In *The International Handbook of Sociology*, sponsored by the International Sociological Association, the editors begin promisingly, highlighting, as one of the three 'compelling issues' in contemporary sociology, 'the nature of social structure, with the discussion centered on randomness versus coherence and asymmetry versus equilibrium' (Quah and Sales, 2000: 4). Having thus emphasised its significance, and its status as a contested concept, the nearest they get to defining social structure subsequently is when they gloss 'structural conditions' as 'historical events and socio-economic and political changes' (ibid.: 7). You will search the rest of the *Handbook* in vain for anything better, or, indeed, for anything on the subject at all.

Ritzer's two-volume *Encyclopaedia of Social Theory* includes a brief entry devoted to 'social structure', written by the editor himself. Ritzer offers the following definition, with an explicit acknowledgement to Durkheim:

> social structures can be defined as real material social facts that are external
> to and coercive over actors. For example, the state is such a social struc-
> ture, as is the market in the realm of the economy. (Ritzer, 2005: 764)

Ritzer identifies social structure as one of four 'levels' of social analysis, with social institutions, social interaction, and the internal mental lives of individuals. Although there is something to be salvaged from this scheme, to which I will return later, Ritzer's vision of social structure, with its contradictory mixture of remote externality and proximate effects (coercion), begs more difficult questions than it answers. Finally, in the third edition of the Kupers' *The Social Science Encyclopedia* Sharrock's entry about 'Structure and agency' defines 'structures', simply and economically, as '"large-scale" social arrangements' (2004: 1014). To return to where this section began, and to an argument developed further in Chapter 2 of this book, Sharrock concludes that:

> There is ... little sign of clarity or agreement about what the idea of 'structure' is supposed to do, and how it is to play the role in sociological thought that some nevertheless consider to be indispensable. (Ibid.: 1015)

Allowing for vagueness and lack of 'clarity or agreement', what do social theorists and sociologists mean when they talk about this 'indispensable' concept, social structure? There appear to be three distinct constellations of ideas:

First, social structure is a concise way of discussing extensive (large-scale) and/or established (long-term) patterns of organised human activity. In other words, social structure amounts to institutions and patterns of institutions.

Second, the many varieties of structuralism, from Lévi-Strauss to Chomsky, presume that species-specific cognitive structures generate universal patterns of human behaviour, such as the 'incest taboo', which, in their local versions – preferential marriage arrangements, for example – count as social structures.

Third, social structure refers to any patterns of human life that are revealed by aggregate data. While these might be institutional patterns, they also include demographic or epidemiological trends, for example, or distributions of resources. While it is an article of structural faith that these large-scale patterns shape individual behaviour – and Ritzer's reference to coercion suggests something stronger than 'shaping' – just *how* this happens is generally unclear.

The three versions of social structure do not conflict with each other. The third, for example, clearly encompasses the first and second, adding to them and making explicit the theme of causality. There is, however, a division of labour. Mirroring a broader dualism within social science, the first version approximates to 'society', the second to 'culture'. As I have argued elsewhere, however, society and culture are themselves ideas that we should if possible avoid, other than as social science colloquialisms: neither can be defined with sufficient clarity to be analytically useful; they are difficult to distinguish from each other; they reify everyday life and portray the world produced and experienced by humans as an objectified reality; they are inconsonant with, and oversimplify, the complexities of the human world; and they encourage to us to treat human individuality as more clear-cut and straightforward than it is (Jenkins, 2002a: 39–62).

The observable realities of social structure

A concept that is as vague as social structure is unlikely to correspond to the observable realities of the human world.[3] Everyday human life, whether viewed in the short or long term, is anything but vague. It may be strikingly complex, it is frequently difficult to understand, it may even be elusive, it is often inconsistent, and it may be conveniently discussed in terms of greater or lesser abstraction, but the everyday human world is a matter of the observable practices of real flesh-and-blood individuals.

It is in exactly this sense, however, that social structure – in its sense as institutionalised patterns of behaviour and/or patterns of institutions – might be thought to have a reasonably straightforward relationship to everyday reality. Institutions can be defined simply as established ways of doing things and notions of how things should be done, which people know about and can identify (Jenkins, 2008b: 157–163). They can be understood as part of the axiomatic abstraction that helps to render the complexities of the human world cognitively manageable. In Britain, for example, instead of having to describe and negotiate from scratch, whenever the issue arises, the norms attaching to how one should wait to gain access to a desired good that is in limited supply, we can mobilise the appropriate institutional abstraction and talk about 'forming a queue'. Often we don't even have to talk about it. The queue is no less a British institution than the monarchy, and anyone with the correct local knowledge can, with others, organise a queue.

While the abstraction of institutionalisation is fundamental to human cognition, and indeed to language, institutions are exemplified and embodied by individuals during interaction. As normative patterns of human practice, they are concrete, observably real. So, isn't social structure *in this sense* surely among the observable realities of the human world? However, even if our answer to this question is affirmative – and, as will become clear, I don't believe that it can be – we are entitled to ask why we need the concept 'social structure'. What added value does it bring to social theory and analysis? If 'social structure' simply means the institutionalised aspects of human life – from informal everyday conventions to multi-national organisations – then talking about institutions and patterns of institutions should be sufficient. It is difficult to see how the concept of social structure contributes anything useful to our discussions.

There is, however, more at stake here than conceptual redundancy. There is also the *general* inappropriateness of applying notions of structure to the human world, which brings into play the second and third meanings of social structure listed above. In any of its meanings, social structure is a concept originally coined to allow us to talk in a shorthand fashion about the broad, 'macro' patterns of human life without perpetually having to return to conceptual first principles or resort to detailed micro-description. I don't imagine that anyone reading this needs to be convinced that there is pattern in the human world, or that we need to be able to talk about it concisely, without perpetual resort to ontological fundamentals.

Given this need, where did the notion of social structure come from? The most obvious and influential source is the 'organic analogy', which in this context derives from Spencer and Durkheim. It is a theoretical version of the, probably universal, human use of bodily imagery in order to think about social relationships and the more-than-the-sum-of-the-parts of human collectivity (Bourdieu, 1977: 87–95; Douglas, 1973: 93–112; Johnson, 1978). Bodily structure comprises the bone, muscles, blood vessels and other tissue that lie beneath outward appearances, and their shape and arrangement: it is what enables bodies to stand and to move. The other source of the concept of social structure is a well-established way of thinking in post-Enlightenment, and certainly post-Industrial Revolution, Western thought, which draws on architecture to model complexity and pattern. Architectural structure consists of foundations, girders, stanchions, flying buttresses, load-bearing arches and walls, and whatever else prevents buildings and bridges from collapsing. So on the one hand there are organisms, and on the other buildings. In each case, structure is intimately bound up with function and purpose. Nor are the organic and architectural options necessarily alternatives: modern architecture drew on, and developed through, the use of organic analogies (Steadman, 1979).

Why are these images unhelpful, and why do they not even approximate to the realities of human lives? We can begin to answer these questions by looking at the conventional meanings of 'structure': it denotes, first, a system of connected parts forming a whole, and second, a unitary construction. Used as a verb, the word refers, third, to the act of creating system and pattern, and it is imbued with an unmistakeable implication of intentionality. The verb is perhaps the easiest to deal with, in that there is no design – intelligent or otherwise – and no designer. Above all, there is no *purpose*. This is not to deny the usefulness of a non-teleological notion of 'function', in the limited sense of the consequences of practices and institutions. Nor is it to ignore the fact that institutions have architects; they clearly often do, especially if we are talking about those institutions that we call organisations (although whether organisations conform to the intentions of their architects is another matter). However, even in the strongest versions of structural realism that we might be able to formulate, the enduring patterns of institutions and their interconnections, and of human behaviour more generally, are *at least* as much emergent unintended consequences of countless unrelated and unconnected practices as they are the products of intentional organising.

What's more, the human world, as an observable 'macro' reality, is neither a *unitary construction* nor a *system* of connected parts. The objections to the notion of unitary construction are, in part, those that I have already rehearsed with respect to the verb 'to structure'. In addition, however, we need to ask what is unitary – in the sense of exhibiting a unified integrity –

about the human world? The answer is, not a lot: the human world is insti-
tutionally diverse and individually diverse, constituted in and by a myriad
of overlapping groups, organised by different membership criteria, to which
heterogeneous spectra of individuals belong. The human experience is of a
multitude of human worlds, of different kinds, standing in relationships to
each other of greater or lesser similarity and difference, proximity and distance, in and out of many of which individuals may move in the course of a
day or a week or a lifetime.

The obvious response to this objection invokes the notion, or at least
a notion, of 'society'. According to this perspective on the human world,
humans live together in large groups, collectivities called 'societies' (which
are, indeed, internally differentiated in a similar manner to that which I have
just suggested). Being, apparently, definitely bounded and characterised
by shared institutions that operate within the boundary, these 'societies',
when viewed at the appropriate scale – the 'macro level' – are, in this view,
'unitary'. They may, therefore, appropriately be characterised in terms of
macro-level social structure(s). Invoking the notion of 'society' recalls my
earlier comment that the concept is insufficiently distinct from 'culture' to
be analytically useful and, more unhelpfully, reifies the everyday business of
human lives. This still leaves, however, the more specific question of boundedness. I have discussed this matter in greater detail elsewhere (Jenkins,
2002a: 73–76, 2002c: 23–29), and I will return to it later in this chapter, so
I will be brief here. The basic point is that human groups do not typically
have clear, unambiguous boundaries. First, even in the very short term, the
membership of *any* human collectivity is indefinite: who is considered to
belong is, to some extent, negotiable and manipulable, depending on situ-
ational contingencies and who is deciding. Second, collectivities persist over
time despite the coming and going of individual members, for whatever
reasons: not even a complete change of membership prevents a group's continued existence.

Although these are old arguments (see Barth, 1969, for example) they
are worth reiterating, given their implications for the organic and architectural analogies. For example, the boundary of an organism or a building is
a fairly straightforward thing: each, in its way, has a 'skin'. Collectivities,
however, do not have definite boundaries in this sense (or anything *like*
this sense). Additionally, under the right circumstances 'dead' collectivities
can be re-animated: by mobilising the symbolic devices that have in the
past constituted them, by the return of old members, or by the recruitment
of new. Witness the potential re-emergence of Scotland as a nation-state,
the post-1989 return to the map of nation-states in the Balkans that had
vanished decades earlier, or the reunions of rock bands such as Cream.
Organisms' life spans are, however, unitary and irreversible, and a building or a bridge, once rebuilt, is not the 'original'. Human collectivities, a
category that includes 'societies', are not unitary in any of the senses that
organisms and buildings are.

That human collectivities may endure in ways that their individual members do not – and cannot – suggests that there is something specific, and definitively non-unitary, about collectivities and their production and reproduction. They are 'symbolically constructed' (Cohen, 1985), conjured up and imagined in processes that can be thought of as 'collective enchantment' or 'the enchantment of collectivity' (and Martin is referring to something similar when he discusses 'representation' in Chapter 3). In this sense, all collectivities are 'imagined communities' (Anderson, 2006), 'imaginary institutions' (Castoriadis, 1987), or 'social imaginaries' (Taylor, 2004). However, the fact that collective symbolism – and collectivity more broadly – is imagined does not mean it is imaginary. It is tangible and material: a product of work, in the first instance, which, if it is to endure, requires maintenance, in the second. And although symbols do endure – sometimes to a remarkable degree – they are not set in stone: collective symbolism transcends, survives, and undergoes change. Nor is symbolic construction hegemonic or homogeneous: collective enchantment accommodates internal diversity in that members can share collective symbols without having to agree about their significance. And, although group leaders and ritual specialists control some collective symbolism, much is demotic, vernacular and un-policed (or un-policeable). None of this can be described as 'unitary'.

To return to macro-sociological theory, there is a final point to be made about why unitary images of 'society' cannot rescue the notion of social structure. Urry (2000a, 2000b, 2007) has usefully argued that the impacts of globalisation and technological development mean that it no longer makes sense for the basic unit of sociological analysis to be the spatially and socially bounded set of locally focused institutions that we call 'a society'. He argues, instead, that we are entering a new epoch in which the old rules no longer apply. We must shift our focus away from boundaries and towards individual and collective patterns of spatial and social 'mobilities'. He is, in effect, arguing that there are no more societies.

Despite this argument – which is a major signpost towards the way out of the present impasse – Urry remains trammelled by the misconceived sociological conventional wisdom that overstates the unitary solidity and boundedness of human collectivities and, in the process, misunderstands them. His argument about the novelty of the coming epoch of mobilities only makes sense if 'societies', as he understands them – as largely self-regulating, possessing definite boundaries, culturally unified if not uniform, different in important respects from other societies, and self-reproducing – have in the long run of human history been the norm of human collective organisation. Unfortunately for his argument, when viewed within that long run the 'formal organisation' or 'nation-state' model of human collectivity doesn't correspond well to the observable realities of the human world. It has probably never been the only, or even the dominant, form of collective human organisation. That the last two or three centuries or so have seen increasingly determined *efforts*, over extensive swathes of the human world, to formalise and exert control over the boundaries of collective identification and territory, and the cultural stuff 'contained' within them, doesn't mean that fixed, definite boundaries or cultural homogeneity are the human collective norm. Had they been, less determination and effort might have been required to maintain and police them, and they might not seem, as in Urry's characterisation of the present state of the human world, to be in decline today.

Fortunately, there is a minority analytical tradition to which we may usefully attend. Reaching back through interactionism to Weber and Simmel and emerging – long before post-modernist forays in the same general direction – in the anthropology of Barth (1966, 1969), Boissevain (1968), Cohen (1985), Leach (1954) and others, this tradition problematises the solidity and fixity of collectivities by focusing on processes of boundary maintenance during interaction between members of different groups. These authors, and others, suggest that the boundaries of human collectivities are, and have always been, permeable, shifting, and at least somewhat indefinite, and that collectivity is an ongoing practical achievement that requires constant making and remaking. What's more, this tradition suggests that heterogeneity within the fuzzy boundaries of collectivity is not new – certainly not post-modern, however we define that notion – and that 'internal' pluralism and diversity are the historical human norm (Barth, 1989; Cohen, 1985; Jenkins, 2008a).

Recognising that the organisation of collectivity is generically untidy allows us to recast Urry's argument in a different light: collectivities – call them 'societies' if you will – have *never* been clearly bounded or homogeneous. This may explain why, during recent centuries of human population growth, characterised by increasingly extensive and complex human worlds, the collective projects of states and corporations have become ever more organising and controlling; why all of this work to establish and maintain the integrity of states and organisations has apparently been necessary. The contemporary collective fluidity identified by Urry may challenge national and corporate imaginings of security, predictability and posterity, but, if so, it is merely a contemporary variation on a historically routine theme.

As Friedmann argues (1999), 'society' is an historical, *not* an objective concept. Rooted in Eurocentric Enlightenment thinking, and specifically in the linked political projects of the nation-state and civil society, the dominant social theoretical notion of society privileges as universal what is actually a historically particular way of organising the complexities of human collectivity. Rooted in the nation-state, it should be understood as reflecting merely one aspect of the contemporary organisation of collectivity. Paradoxically, this may suggest that societies of the kind that Urry describes as increasingly obsolete are probably not, in fact, about to become less significant or visible. Nor is 'society' likely to vanish from the social theoretical toolkit. Simply in the interests of attending to observable realities, however, mainstream social theory and empirical social science should always have recognised and attended to mobility as well as stability, to fluidity as well as solidity, and should always have problematised the ontology of collectivity, instead of taking it for granted in the image of the dominant European geopolitical forms and concerns of the day.

If actually existing collectivities lack the unitary character that the notion of structure implies, what about the connectedness that the notion of structure as a system of linked parts also implies? Some of the comments made above are relevant here. In particular, if collective boundaries are somewhat indefinite, then where a system 'begins' and 'ends' will also be unclear. Nor, if heterogeneity and diversity are routine within boundaries, are systems likely to be comprehensive. In other words, a model in which one system approximates to one collectivity is implausible.

If we focus on the internal connectedness that is a defining characteristic of systems, even modern nation-states and formal organisations – which have been shaped by cumulative planning and design processes that have attempted, in the pursuit of predictability and efficiency, to produce 'joined-up' institutions – are, as the most casual observation of their workings suggests, as much the disjointed and piecemeal evolutionary products of long-term unintended consequences as they are anything else. If it were not so, government and management would be more straightforward enterprises than they are. Although there is no space for it here, there is a discussion to be had about the inadequacy of sociological accounts of overweening rational modernity that derive loosely from Weber. Suffice it to say that, because humans can and do exercise agency, control is likely to generate resistance, formalisation to produce informality, and systematisation to create its own unanticipated feedback and change (e.g. Jenkins, 2008b: 201–205). The notion of system *may* have some social theoretical application – not least because it is an influential modern normative concept – but the complex and contingent observable realities suggest that its value as a theoretical model of the human world is, at best, limited. That world may well include various systems – and this is something to which I shall return – but there is no 'social system'.

Considerations of fact aside, the idea of 'system' demands further interrogation, anyway, and the closer we examine it the less helpful to social theory it seems. For example, the convection currents in a heated fluid can easily and accurately be described as a system, as can the circulation of mammalian blood, the complex flight patterns of starlings *en masse*, the migration patterns of wildebeest, the natural events that we call 'weather', or the movements of planets around a star. None of these inspires the extension of the term's application to human affairs, however, not least because their components are fundamentally different from those of human beings, and the processes that produce the phenomena that can be understood as systems have few or no analogues in human life. In applying the word 'system' indiscriminately to the natural and the human worlds we run the risk of, first, stretching its meaning to breaking point and, second, smuggling from one domain notions – particularly about ontology and causality – that belong in another. Just as anthropomorphism obstructs our understanding of non-human organisms, notions of system may encourage us to tell the wrong story about humans. I will return to this matter briefly in closing.

To approach the issue from yet another direction, perhaps much – or even most – of what the notion of system conveys about pattern and connectedness is in the eye of the beholder. This is not to deny the reality of patterns, or to suggest that the relationships that can be identified between their constituent components are necessarily illusory, but simply to recognise that 'system' is a product of analysis and theory. Different theoretical frameworks are apt to produce different patterns, connections and systems.[4] This also suggests the ultra-rationalist conclusion that 'social structure' is the product of the pattern- and sense-making activities of social scientists. The only way out of this particular cul-de-sac is to prioritise theory's role as the servant of empirical research. We need a pragmatic conceptual toolbox that is grounded in the individual and collective observable realities of the human world and continuously reviewed in the light of its fit with our – theoretically conditioned – data. Neither blunt empiricism nor mandarin rationalism will do.

How structure works

The final reason for rejecting 'structure' as a social theoretical concept is that it imports into social science, probably inevitably, a set of notions about how the human world works that are inappropriate if we wish to understand that world. In particular, in conjuring up a human domain that is somehow external to, or other than, the face-to-face world of everyday life, 'social structure' offers an image of powerful invisible influences on our everyday business, operating above our heads or behind our backs. It is a perspective on the human world that discourages a model of human beings as capable of agency. Determinism, if not inevitable – not least because notions of inevitability sit uncomfortably beside my own insistence upon human agency – is an ever-present temptation. In order to prove this point, it would be easy to line up an array of soft structuralist targets for selective quotation and rhetorical execution: Parsons or Althusser would be fairly obvious candidates. To do so, however, would not prove the point. Instead, it may be better to look at two theorists who have tried harder than most to avoid the problems that I have outlined so far: Bourdieu, to whom I shall attend only briefly, having already discussed him in Chapter 6, and Giddens.

The cornerstone of Bourdieu's theoretical project was his attempt to move beyond a realist model of the regularities and patterns of human life and the determinism that it encourages, towards an understanding of the principles and processes that produce them. He wanted neither an objectivism that modelled structure as aloof from actors' lives but acting on them, nor a subjectivism that dismissed anything but the conscious intentionality of individuals. His solution was the concept of *habitus*, an embodied site where objective external structures and internalised structures produce and reproduce each other. Despite his best efforts, here is where he ended up:

> The structures constitutive of a particular type of environment (e.g. the material conditions of existence characteristic of a class condition) produce *habitus*, systems of durable, transposable dispositions, structured structures predisposed to function as structuring structures. (Bourdieu, 1977: 72)

Here are all of the meanings and connotations of structure that I have described above, not least the notion that 'structures' constitute and produce – note the use of the verb 'structuring' – the human world. Unable to abandon the notion of structure, perhaps because he was still in mild thrall to the 'blissful' structuralism of his early career (Jenkins, 2002b: 32), Bourdieu could not escape the determinism and denial of human agency that accompanied it.

Giddens, while insisting that a concept of 'structure' remains indispensable, has made a thorough attempt to avoid the problems that I have identified. *Inter alia*, after criticising the tendency for 'structure' to be taken for granted as a 'received notion' (Giddens, 1984: 16), he acknowledges that conventional uses of the concept incline to determinism because they focus almost exclusively on constraint, that societies are not unitary, and that social systems transcend collective boundaries and are not comprehensively co-ordinated. Most strikingly, he insists that

> there is no such entity as a distinctive type of 'structural explanation' in the social sciences: all explanations will involve at least implicit reference both to the purposive, reasoning behaviour of agents and to its intersection with constraining and enabling features of the social and material context of that behaviour. (Ibid.: 179)

These are strong words, and sufficiently central to his theory of structuration that he paraphrases them on page 213 of the same book.

Giddens, conceptualising structure as produced in and through the meaningful practices of agents, and as both constraining and enabling, defines it as:

> structuring properties allowing the 'binding' of time-space in social systems, the properties which make it possible for discernibly similar social practices to exist across varying spans of time and space and which lend them 'systemic form'. To say that structure is a 'virtual order' of transformative relations means that social systems, as reproduced social practices, do not have 'structures' but rather exhibit 'structural properties' and that structure exists, as time-space presence, only in its instantiations in such practices and as memory traces orienting the conduct of knowledgeable human agents. (Ibid.: 17)

Giddens distinguishes between 'structural principles', 'structures' and 'structural properties' (ibid.: 180–193). 'Structural principles' are the characteristic principles of organisation that allow us, for example, to distinguish a 'tribal society' (tradition, kinship, group sanctions) from a 'class society' (routinisation, family, surveillance, military power and economic interdependence). 'Structures' – and he is probably more concerned with concrete structures than the arguably more abstract and distant 'structure' – are combinations of rules and resources that reproduce practices *and* reproduce the system; this what he means by the 'duality of structure' (ibid.: 19). Rules include procedures and techniques that reproduce practices and institutions, while resources are everything, from raw materials and technology, to patterned spatial and social organisation (ibid.: 258–262). Structures are also conceived as 'major aspects of the transformation/mediation relations which influence social and system integration' (ibid.: 377). Finally, 'structural properties' appear, simply put, to be established institutions.

We cannot accuse Giddens of taking the concept of 'structure' for granted. However, his elaborations on the theme, even where they don't engender greater obscurity, don't clarify much either. What, for example, are 'transformation/mediation relations'? It isn't easy to be sure. Two things that are germane to this discussion can, however, be said with some confidence. First, throughout Giddens' *The Constitution of Society* (1984), the definitive statement of structuration theory that I have concentrated on here, the emphasis, despite the consistent *leitmotif* of human agency and discussions of transformation, conflict and contradiction, is overwhelmingly on systemic reproduction and integration. Mild determinism, at least – and perhaps a functionalist impulse, too – seems to be integral to Giddens' theory of structuration.

Second, traces of stronger versions of structural determinism can also be found. For example, whereas conflict, for Giddens, involves struggles between actual individuals or groups, structural contradiction is defined – and here he seems to oscillate between Marx and Lévi-Strauss – as a disjuncture between, or mutual contravention of, structural principles which has real effects on individuals (ibid.: 193–199, 310–319). It is obvious that individuals or groups can contradict each other and be in conflict, and how. However, if we rule out 'structural explanation' and remember that Giddens is careful about his use of language, it is not obvious how structural *principles* can *contravene* each other. Outside of formal logic – which is a human practice after all, and one which he explicitly does not have in mind (ibid.: 193) – only people can, in any sense that has anything to do with observable realities, contravene each other. The implication, about which Giddens was less reticent in earlier publications (1976: 118–126, 1979: 141–145), is that 'structural principles' exist on a different 'plane' or 'level' than the practices and memory traces of individuals. If nothing else, there is an implicit ontological distinction between structure and action, and implicit structural determinism.

This is the baggage with which the concept of structure, probably inevitably, travels. Social structure, whether incarnated as principles or properties, is always seen as removed and/or different from the immediate realities of human interaction. It always invites unhelpful images of different 'levels' (or something similar). It is nearly always, in some sense, seen to be real; otherwise it could not have the effects that it is believed to have and would not be worth bothering with. Why, after all, would Giddens spend so much time defining and elaborating the concept – and differentiating it from everyday practices – if he doesn't believe that it refers to something real? Something that is different from, yet which shapes or effects, practices? Once we accept that structure has, if you like, its own agency in the human world, determinism, whether weak or strong, enters the field and the reality of human agency is compromised, if not completely negated.

Towards alternatives

I have argued that the concept of social structure, in all its varieties, is too vague to be useful; that it does not correspond to the observable individual and collective realities of the human world; and that it is too tainted with determinism to accommodate a view of human beings as reasoning agents. Thus we still have a problem: how to reconcile individual human agency with the constraints produced by human collectivity?

One place to begin to move away from the present impasse is by recognising that, criticisms notwithstanding, there is much in Giddens, for example, to help us. His insistence on the constraining *and* enabling nature of 'structure' can, for example, be translated into an even-handed general principle that human collectivity is no more constraining that it is enabling. In particular, his detailed discussion of constraint (1984: 169–185) is a useful contribution to how we might begin to think about the matter more creatively (although, for a less positive view of Giddens' views on constraint, see Chapter 7). Moving beyond Giddens – or, indeed, Archer, Bourdieu or Habermas, any of whom might offer useful points of departure – there are three directions in which we need to travel if we are to escape the dead hand of 'structure' without lapsing into the subjectivism that is widely believed to be inevitable if we abandon the concept altogether (e.g. Giddens, 1996: 100). First, we need a model of the human world that comprehends the individual and the collective without reifying either, and is firmly grounded in observable realities. Second, the nature of human collectivity needs to be re-thought, rather than taken-for-granted. Third, we need to explore non-structural approaches to capturing and understanding the patterns that characterise the human world.

With respect to the first of these, I have elsewhere proposed a model of the human world that starts with the proposition that embodied individuals are as central to a sociological understanding of the human world as collectivities (Jenkins, 2002a: 68–76). This model sees the human world as three 'orders': the *individual order*, the human world understood as made up of embodied individuals and what-goes-on-in-their-heads; the *interaction order*, the human world understood as constituted in the relationships between individuals, in what-goes-on-between-people; and the *institutional order*, the human world understood as pattern and organisation, established-ways-of-doing-things.

These are analytical orders only, epistemological devices. They are not different 'levels'; they are merely different points of view, complementary perspectives on the observable complexities of what people do.

Encouragingly, this scheme resembles the responses of others to the issues with which I am concerned here. Ritzer (2005), for example, in his account of 'social structure', discussed above, argues that there are four 'levels' of social analysis: social structure, social institutions, social interaction, and the internal lives of individuals. If we sidestep for the moment the vocabulary of 'levels', and, as we should, remove 'structure' from the picture, we are left with institutions, interaction and individuals. Similarly, López and Scott distinguish between 'institutional structure', 'relational structure' and 'embodied structure'. Ignoring, once again, their discussion of 'levels' – although it is sophisticated and critical (2000: 65–88) – and deleting the word 'structure', we are left with what appears to be a similar tripartite scheme. Finally – and setting aside once again images of 'structure' and 'levels' – the 'circle of emergence' of Sawyer's 'emergence paradigm' (2005: 219–223) seems to be broadly homologous, distinguishing as it does between individuals, interaction and 'emergents' (which are groups and institutions).

The pervasive and problematic architectural imagery of 'levels' suggests that I should be as clear as possible about what I mean by 'orders'. Borrowed directly from Goffman (1983), the notion of the 'order' insists, first, that the human world is ordered even if it is not necessarily always orderly. Pattern is part of the observable reality of the human world (although not all pattern is immediately observable). Second, the word 'order' also indicates that these are classificatory notions, epistemological devices which should not be confused with the stuff of the human world to which they refer. They are different ways of apprehending the same observable realities and are an act of ordering in their own right. They exist only in the eye of the beholder; only by sticking to this position can we hope to avoid carelessly reconstituting them as the kind of reifications that I have criticised earlier.

The observable realities in question are not mysterious and are the sources of the convergence, such as it is, between Ritzer, López and Scott, Sawyer, and me: there are embodied individuals, interaction happens between those individuals, and the institutions that they produce and reproduce persist and have a presence in the world. The individual, interactional and institutional *orders* do not exist in any of these senses, however; they are neither *things* nor *spaces*. They are not observable realities. They are 'ways of talking', 'ways of knowing' or 'ways of seeing' – nothing else. In observable reality, individuals, interaction, and institutions necessarily co-exist, they are not easily separated, and they do not make sense without each other.

The embodied simultaneity of individuals, interaction and institutions creates what López and Scott call the 'ontological depth of social organization', 'the layering, nesting or embedding of aspects of social structure one in relation to another' (2000: 66). To rephrase this, ontological depth is the somewhat intangible, more-than-the-sum-of-the-parts character of human collectivity and the human world. Although the three 'orders' I have identified can, for analytical purposes, be treated as distinct, in observable reality the phenomena about which they help us to think are not so easily separated. They are not different 'levels'. They are a trinity, one-in-three and three-in-one, necessarily and simultaneously occupying the same physical and social spaces: each is a matter of (the same) real, embodied individuals, their actual behaviour, and their products.

This tells us that it is only possible, or sensible, to separate the individual and the collective – the particular and the general, the biographical and the historical – for analytical and presentational purposes. The observable and experiential realities of the human world suggest that individuals and the collective 'more-than-the-sum-of-the-parts' co-habit, in some sense that has thus far proved to be sociologically elusive; and for which it is certainly difficult to find adequate words. They may not be as separate, or even perhaps as different, as they are commonly presumed to be. To say this should not, however, lead us into the mistake of imagining that the individual and the collective can simply be collapsed into each other. In any consideration of the relationship between the individual and the collective, it is, for example, immediately striking that individuals are obvious or visible in a way that collectivities are not. Embodied humans are 'here' or 'there', breathing, moving and occupying a fairly definite space. Collectivities are not always either 'here' or 'there'; even when they *appear* to be, appearances are not straightforward.

Which brings me to the second direction in which we need to travel: an exploration of collectivity, in the spirit of Peter Martin's call, in Chapter 3, to recast, rather than retreat from, collective concepts. More precisely, we need to think about collectivities, in the concrete plural that is an observable reality of the human world. We need to ask, with appropriately authentic naïveté, 'What *are* collectivities?' Once we take this question seriously, the problem becomes clear. In our everyday lives we participate in a world populated by embodied individuals, who are tangible, three-dimensional, distinct from each other, and very material. They possess agency, they act. Collectivities, by contrast, are less visible or tangible – certainly visible and tangible in different ways – and they do not 'act', other than in the actions of their members. Collectivities have a distinctive ontological status: they do not exist in the same way that individual humans can be said to exist.

So, *how* can collectivities be said to exist? To allow for a manageable discussion, I will focus on groups: other kinds of human collectivity
– categories, for example (Jenkins, 2000, 2008a: 54–76, 2008b: 102–117)
– would require a different treatment. A group is a human collectivity, the
members of which recognise its existence, recognise their membership of
it, and share some representations or symbolic constructions of their 'col-
lectivity-in-common'. This minimal definition covers an enormous range of
actual groups, from the most transient and informal to formal organisations
and nation-states. Most obviously, with the exception of small face-to-face
groups, a group's individual members hardly ever, and in many cases never,
gather together at the same time. For very large groups such a gathering is
impossible: there are too many members to assemble in the same place at
the same time. Even if one could muster in one place all of the members
of the Sony Corporation or the United States, for example, the logistics of
communication and co-ordination would militate against the mobilisation
of meaningful collectivity, and, simply in terms of area, the concept of 'one
place' would be problematic.

Nor are size and observable presence the only difficulties. The mere co-
presence of all the individuals that constitute its membership is not 'all
there is' to a group. There are bodies of knowledge and tradition, rules and
customs, collective symbols, hierarchies of authority and status, artefacts,
constitutions and charters, and so on, all of which must also be in place,
and in use – because enactment is crucial – in order for the collectivity of the
group to be 'here' or 'there'. These are at least as significant as the actual
membership at any point in time and, in many cases, a lot less immediately
visible.

Furthermore, who counts as a member is never straightforward: the
boundaries of group membership are always at least a little fuzzy, due
to the availability of differing avenues of recruitment (descent or various
forms of selection), depletion as members die or leave, and, in many cases,
uncertainty or vagueness about the criteria of inclusion and exclusion and
the procedures for resolving contested cases. As I have already suggested,
human individuals are embodied in ways that human groups are not. The
individual, in a definite *physical* fashion, stops at the skin; where, however,
is the 'skin' of a group? To repeat an earlier point, this suggests something
else that must be taken into account when conceptualising collectivity. As
organisms, human individuals have a definite and relatively brief, if somewhat unpredictable, lifespan. In contrast, groups – and, indeed, other collectivities – may routinely persist in the very long term, sometimes surviving
many complete turnovers in their membership. It is a defining ontological
characteristic of collectivities that they can continue – albeit changing all the
time – despite the coming and going of their constituents.

To summarise a long discussion that is available elsewhere (Jenkins,
2002c), a generic model of groups as emergent products of what people do
in everyday life might comprise a number of related propositions, thus:

- Although group identification is arguably part of the human species-specific repertoire, human collectivity is neither primordial nor 'natural' in the sense, for example, of a 'herd instinct'.
- Human groups emerge as a consequence of individuals doing things together in mutually meaningful and co-ordinated ways.
- Individual behaviour is thus not *determined* by group membership (although the constraints and enablements attendant upon membership are relevant for the understanding of behaviour).
- The boundaries of groups are neither fixed nor clear and are continually produced and reproduced during social interaction between members and non-members.
- Groups exist in, and as, symbolic constructs and complexes, which are known about, understood, and manipulated by individuals.
- Groups are more than their individual constituent parts; they are products rather than sums, geometric rather than arithmetic constructs.

The collective and the individual may not be 'the same', but they are not in any sense opposites either. Each conditions, and is inconceivable without, the other.

Nor is this discussion of 'the group' the last word about this well-worn and sometimes taken-for-granted concept. In addition to Urry's work, discussed earlier, there has been a recent resurrection of debate about the conceptual and ontological status of groups, and the possibility of meaningful collective identification without groups (Brubaker, 2003, 2004; Brubaker et al., 2006; Calhoun, 2003a, 2003b; Jenkins, 2002c, 2006). Following arguments that I have sketched out earlier, suffice it to say that groups, although they are 'real' enough for all everyday practical purposes, are, ontologically speaking, not as straightforward as complacent sociologists and anthropologists seem to assume.

Finally, there is the third move that we need to make: the exploration of 'non-structural' approaches to the identification, investigation and interpretation of the patterns of the human world. These patterns are not necessarily self-evident – although local everyday lay models are often a good guide – which is why we require theoretical models to apprehend them. The 'group model' of collectivity that I have just discussed does not begin to exhaust the possibilities in this respect. Here I can only offer some suggestions, because the options are many; a lengthy work of synthesis remains to be done.

Simmel's formal sociology is a good place to start looking for inspiration. His discussion of how incremental increases in the *number* of individuals interacting with each other – from two to three to four, for example (Simmel, 1950: 87–177) – transform completely the *nature* of what is going on, is underestimated and underexplored. Not least, Simmel's dyads and triads challenge conventional distinctions between the quantitative and the qualitative. Similar themes appear to be present in recent discussions of networks and their properties (Barabási, 2003; Buchanan, 2002; Watts, 1999, 2003). Other recent arguments about how collectivities work and what makes collective human life distinctive, which attend to scale and relational density, are also relevant (Ball, 2004; Surowiecki, 2004).

The study of networks may, therefore, be the most obvious route to a non-structural model of pattern and collectivity. A conventional notion of structure has, depressingly, colonised research in this field (López and Scott, 2000: 57–61), hand-in-hand perhaps with a fascination with increasingly sophisticated quantitative methods (Scott, 2000). There is, however, another – earlier – theme in social network analysis that explores alternatives to structural models of 'the social' and problematises human collectivity (Boissevain, 1968, 1974; Boissevain and Mitchell, 1973; Mayer, 1966; Mitchell, 1969). More recently, useful insights into the relationship between networks and the nature and variable qualities of collective human life can be mined from policy-driven debates about 'social capital' (Field, 2003: 44–70; Lin, 2001; Phillips, 2006: 132–157). The network image may also help us to understand better the new patterns and new scales of IT-driven globalisation (Castells, 2000; Wellman, 1999). And, with respect to scale, an earlier literature remains worthy of attention (Barth, 1978).

The specialist study of networks aside, the broader issue remains: how are large-scale and enduring patterns – what I call the institutional order – produced and reproduced during small-scale interactions between individuals? Intriguing work in this respect is being done using game-theory, and drawing on economics and psychology, to address questions about human co-operation that few sociologists and anthropologists have yet begun to broach (Gintis et al., 2005; Henrich et al., 2004). This is assimilable to the literature, so far largely the domain of economists, which addresses relationships between individual decision-making and emergent macro-patterns (Schelling, 2006). In approximately the same ball park, the anthropologist Barth argued more than forty years ago for 'generative' models of social organisation, in which *form* – which is a stronger notion than pattern, in that, like the notion of 'order', it suggests something other than the human equivalent of Brownian motion or fractal pattern emergence – is an emergent product of interaction between individuals (Barth, 1966; 1981: 32–104). Sawyer's discussion of 'emergence' (2005) seems to be addressing many of the same issues.

To take these matters a little further in closing, whether we are talking about Simmel's dyads and triads, networks, or Barth's forms, we are talking about aspects of the human world – recurrent patterns with implications for what people can do and how they can do it – that are independent of human planning and decision-making. They are *at most* unintended, and possibly unattended to, consequences of plans and decisions. We are back to the more-than-the-sum-of-the-parts discussed in the opening paragraphs.

At which point it is time to reconsider whether 'system' is an appropriate concept to apply to the human world. Discussions of the sociological applicability of systems theory and complexity theory (Byrne, 1998; Luhmann, 1995: Smith and Jenks, 2006) argue forcefully for the continued usefulness of the notion of 'system'. To refer to a well-known example, road traffic flows and jams can be modelled using the mathematics of complexity. However – and this is not an original observation (cf. Spruill et al., 2001) – doing so says very little about the planned and institutionalised environment, created by strategic human intentionality, through which traffic flows and jams, and which in some senses generates those flows and jams. Road traffic is not the same as, or even similar to, thousands of starlings in flight. What is stubbornly challenging, however, is that complexity models can tell us *something* useful about how traffic flows emerge and work. This suggests that 'system' may, after all, have some defensible applications to the human world; to return to an earlier observation, while there is no unitary system, there may be some systems.

The above is a speculative shopping list, not a theoretical agenda, and leaves much work to be done. To begin to address this list will require interdisciplinary working, not least the power of mathematics. It will demand that we abandon an approach to social theory that seems to see theory as an end in itself, rather than as a tool that enables empirical research, and embrace a renewed theoretical engagement with the observable realities of the human world. It may also mean that we move towards what Smith and Jenks (2006) call 'post-humanist social theory', in which self-conscious human actors, while neither vanishing nor becoming insignificant, are no longer the axiom and centre of our sociological compass.

Acknowledgements

Without Peter Martin's comments this would have been a much worse chapter.

Notes

1   My expression 'the human world' – the world as produced and experienced by humans – is discussed systematically elsewhere (Jenkins, 2002a). It resembles Blumer's 'the empirical social world in the case of human beings' (1969: 35) and Bauman's 'the human-made world' (1990: 3).

2   'Since the early 1970s, social theorists have been more apt to identify a "structure" problem than an "agency" one' (Sharrock, 2004: 1014).

3   This is 'everyday realism', which insists that there are observable realities in the human world, that they are in principle knowable via systematic inquiry, and that it is possible to defend, as more or less plausible, a claim to know them (see Jenkins, 2002a: 7–8).

4   Which doesn't mean that all interpretations and analyses are equal defensible: the fit between analysis, theory and the observable realities, documented in the most systematic and epistemologically objective fashion, is the only arbiter (Jenkins, 2002a: 85–110). It is why we do empirical research; it also why so much contemporary social theory, which is undisciplined by systematic inquiry, is frivolous.

10

Two kinds of social theory: the myth and reality of social existence

Anthony King

Introduction

The structure and agency debate in one form or another has been a periodic feature of sociology since the origins of the discipline. Since the debate deals with the question of what fundamentally a society is, this is unsurprising – for the way sociologists conceive of society determines how they study it. In the last decade, it has once again become a topic of intense struggle. Given the seemingly eternal return of the debate, it is probably unwise to believe that it will stop, or that adherents of structure and agency will be converted as a result of the latest interventions. However, it is perhaps possible to persuade the non-aligned to reject the conceptual framework of structure and agency. To this end, in the art of persuasion, rhetoric rather than argument may be more effective. In the last instance, satire may consequently be most effective means of breaking off the debate and encouraging at least the non-aligned to an interactionist or hermeneutic viewpoint.

Since its publication in 1954, J. R. R. Tolkien's *The Lord of the Rings* has remained a bestselling book in the history of Western publishing. Reflecting its consistently high sales, it is regularly cited as the most popular book in a variety of readers' polls. Although drawing heavily on Wagner and on various other well-known Anglo-Saxon and Early English sources, *The Lord of the Rings* is a seminal piece of fiction which has given rise to a fantasy literary genre. Peter Jackson's recent *Lord of the Rings* film trilogy has been internationally successful, converting a twentieth-century bestseller into a new medium, raising the profile of the books once again and introducing Tolkien to a new and much wider audience. Jackson's film alters some of the plot and excludes other parts; nevertheless, the film remains generally close to the novel in structure and in meaning. In this, the film has served a useful purpose in demonstrating why the novel has had such an enduring fascination for readers in the five decades since its publication. The film affirms that *The Lord of the Rings* is a modern myth, a fantasy which temporarily brackets the profane and mechanical experience of modern existence and introduces readers and, now, audiences to a terrible and yet sublime reality. *The Lord of the Rings* is a communal idyll which transcends the mundane.

Yet, although Tolkien's novel is certainly a fantasy, its power as a myth resides not in the fact that it is fantastical. On the contrary, *The Lord of the Rings* is a predominant myth in modern culture precisely because it illuminates contemporary reality. Modernity is not erased in *The Lord of the Rings*. It has maintained a powerful hold over public imagination precisely because it is always situated in contemporary realities, which it only distorts and exaggerates into monsters and wizards in order to illustrate that reality all the more clearly. In this *The Lord of the Rings* performs the universal service of myths, widely noted by anthropologists. Thus, famously, Lévi-Strauss prioritised the study of myth in anthropology: although the myths of tribal peoples could not be said to be historically accurate, for Lévi-Strauss they represented a reality which could not be ignored. Myths formed a systematic order of knowledge through which cultures understood and organised the world and their activities within it. Myths were ultimately the equivalent of a primitive science. There, often in grotesque forms, fundamental classification systems were articulated and vindicated. There, the fundamental existential problems of life were examined.

It is, perhaps, no coincidence that Richard Wagner, whose *Ring of the Nibelung* was an evidently important source for Tolkien's own Ring cycle, understood myth in a similar way. For Wagner, myths – and for him a particular kind of Teutonic myth – had the ability to express fundamental truths about contemporary existence which a more 'realistic' account could never suggest: from this perspective, myth expressed the essential truth of a culture. As Bernard Shaw noted (1923), the first three operas of the Ring cycle involve a critique of industrial capitalism and the state which, although less technical, are no less perceptive than Marx's own analysis. Precisely because myths are fantastic, separating audiences temporarily from their everyday existence, they are able to illustrate that reality with prodigious power. They are able to estrange the familiar, to illuminate the unacknowledged and to demonstrate the fundamental social understandings and practices which comprise everyday existence. Myths can often legitimate these activities – and stories of national origin normally serve such a purpose. However, the greatest myths, those which constitute great art, transcend this purely functional purpose: they illuminate in order to question and to criticise. Wagner's Ring cycle unquestionably reaches this status.

It is less clear that Tolkien's *Lord of the Rings* can be given the status of a literary masterpiece, although it does serve the mythic purpose which Lévi-Strauss, and Wagner, emphasised, creating a fantasy the better to illustrate modern social reality. Consequently, although perhaps an unusual strategy, the myth of *The Lord of the Rings* might be drawn upon for sociological and more specifically social theoretical insights. As a mythical representation of the everyday, *The Lord of the Rings* can be used in the current debates about structure and agency. Famously, Adorno and Horkheimer drew on the myth of Odysseus to reject the hegemony of Instrumental Reason in industrial society (1979). Similarly, *The Lord of the Rings* can be employed so that it, too, contributes to contemporary debates in social theory. Certainly, this myth cannot resolve the technical issues of those debates – it cannot demonstrate the shortcomings of the concepts of structure and agency – but it does usefully symbolise the major positions in this debate. Thus, the work operates around two visions of social order, symbolised by the Ring and the Fellowship. Each represents alternative social ontologies: while the Ring signifies a dualistic society of autonomous individuals, unified only by a centralised, all-seeing power, the Fellowship represents society based on collaborative social interaction. *The Lord of the Rings* can thus serve as a myth exaggerating the positions in this debate, all the better that participants can understand what is actually at issue.

The Ring

Drawing on Wagner's idea of a Ring of Power, the One Ring of *The Lord of the Rings* represents pure individualism and the pursuit of personal gratification. As its name suggests, 'only one hand at a time can wield the One' (Tolkien, 1977: 249). The One Ring cannot be shared. It can be used only by a single person, who is bent on exerting their will and pursuing their own self-interest. The individualism of the Ring is demonstrated most graphically in the novel by the character Smeagol, who finds the Ring after it has been lost. Having killed his friend to take possession of the Ring, Smeagol's behaviour changes so that 'he became very unpopular and was shunned' (Tolkien, 1977a: 60). Eventually, he was expelled from his family and 'he wandered in loneliness' (ibid.). Under the influence of the Ring, he becomes incapable of normal social interaction and becomes a pure individualist. He becomes a 'ghost that drank blood', killing and eating young animals and babies (Tolkien, 1977a: 64). Thus Smeagol is transformed from a social being with friends and family into a purely self-interested actor who rationally and remorselessly pursues his own private ends. The Ring represents pure individualism and, when worn by Sauron, the dark wizard of the novel and creator of the Ring, it represents the expression of pure tyranny, bent only on the increase of power and wealth.

However, as a symbol of individualism, the Ring demands a distinctive kind of social order, and it is precisely at this point that the novel becomes deeply relevant to current debates in social theory. The Ring represents the individual pursuit of reward and all its followers are individualists – but this creates a problem for the Ring, since it is very difficult to create a political order out of self-interested individuals. Selfish individuals will always seek their own return, to the detriment of the group: ultimately social coherence and group action are vitiated by the existence of individual reward-seekers. At any moment, they might turn on each other to achieve their own private ends, at a cost to the group of which they are part. The orcs, Sauron's misshapen servants and warriors, ultimately demonstrate the impossibility of creating a social regime on the basis of independent individuals, since at decisive points the orcs descend into random selfish action. It seems to be impossible to create social order on the basis of independent individuals.

Significantly, the transformation of Smeagol into Gollum, under the influence of the Ring, demonstrates how social order is produced out of a multitude of independent agents. As he uses the Ring, Smeagol becomes an individualist for whom all others are but the means to his private ends. However, he also comes under thrall of the Ring and ultimately of Sauron. Tolkien describes how Smeagol becomes known as Gollum, as a result of the curious way he speaks and the gulping sounds he makes, but it is clear that he chooses the name Gollum as a homonym. Gollum, under the power of the Ring, becomes a golem. He is controlled no longer by himself but by the higher power of the Ring. He becomes an extension of Ring's will. As Tolkien notes, as a result of his long ownership of the Ring, 'he had no will left in the matter' (Tolkien, 1977a: 61). It is interesting that at the moment of the Ring's destruction, all its individualist servants resort to random action; 'the creatures of Sauron, orc or troll or beast spell-enslaved, ran hither and thither mindless; and some slew themselves, or cast themselves in pits, or fled wailing' (Tolkien, 1977b: 200). Although the Ring's minions naturally follow their own self-interest, they are dominated and unified by a single central source. They all ultimately become golems, their selfish interests unified to a single purpose by a higher centralising authority.

The Ring represents a very particular vision of social order, often seen as the Hobbesian problem of social order. Sauron's society consists of independent beings who rationally pursue their self-interests. It consists of creatures like Gollum, or the orcs, which steal and kill to further their own ends and which actively reject the moral obligations of social ties. This is a utilitarian social order comprised of self-seekers. For Hobbes, the only way of making an ordered society out of self-interested individuals is by creating a supreme sovereign, a Leviathan, who is able to enforce order by denying individual autonomy. In every case, subjects must subordinate their own will and interest to that of the sovereign, for it is only in this way that the diverse wills of a self-interested multitude can be unified and ordered. The Ring represents the only social order possible on the basis of independent, rational individuals. On this account, order can be attained only by means of a higher power, which subordinates selfish individual interests to a single goal. Individuals in this order must be determined or they will inevitably pursue random ends. The Ring represents a dualistic social order. It consists of individuals, but in order for these individuals to form a coherent political regime – a social order – they must be directed by a separate and superior entity. They must be directed by a higher, objective force, structured by this inexorable and unseen determining power. Tolkien's account is fantastical, yet philosophically it traverses the same contours as many contemporary social theorists who explain coherent action by reference to rules or structures – often unrecognised – which direct individuals. The Ring represents vertical social order in terms of structure and agency.

The Fellowship

The Ring represents one bleak vision of social order. Crucially, there is a second account of social order proffered by *The Lord of the Rings*: the Fellowship – the group who dedicate themselves to helping the central character of the novel, Frodo, destroy the Ring. As a social order, the Fellowship differs markedly from the Ring's regime. This social order is represented most clearly by the relationship between Frodo, the hero, and his friend and helper, Sam. With the exception of the moment when he thinks that Frodo is dead, Sam remains with Frodo throughout the novel, and it is precisely because Sam is always with Frodo that Frodo does not become corrupted by the Ring. Frodo's individualism is constantly checked by his interactions with Sam. Frodo is never portrayed as an individual but always as a member of group. Even though he personally bears the Ring, his quest is a social one. As he says to Sam when they separate from their companions, '*We* will go, and may the others find a safe road! (Tolkien, 1977a: 385, emphasis added). Frodo is always part of a 'we', never an 'I'. Crucially, their relationship is founded on voluntary consent: Frodo does not give orders to Sam, nor is Sam a mere minion. They are bound together by the joint pursuit of a collective goal, the destruction of the Ring, and they co-operate with each other to achieve this, willingly obligating themselves to each other. They are bound by honour, where neither will betray the other for fear of shame. Tolkien illustrates the importance of honour in binding voluntary fellowship together in an early passage in the book, when Frodo is trapped in a barrow with Sam, Merry and Pippin (two other companions) by a wight which is about to kill them. Frodo contemplates saving himself – but then 'he thought of himself running free over the grass, grieving for Merry, and Sam and Pippin but free and alive himself' (Tolkien, 1977a: 142). The members of the Fellowship, and above all Sam and Frodo, are bound to help each other, even to the point of self-sacrifice, by a sense of honour; they will be shamed if they betray their friendship. Consequently, they are capable of feats which would be quite impossible for a lone individual. As a co-operative partnership, the social group they form is, consequently, extremely robust. Indeed, despite the extraordinary pressure which their quest places upon them, together they are able to achieve their end. Together they strive to pursue a single collective goal out of a desire to assist and protect each other.

The grander alliance against the Ring demonstrates the same voluntary commitment to collective goals, but it usefully illustrates the potent mechanisms of honour and shame more clearly. Significantly, once these diverse people, animals and, indeed, plants have committed themselves to this group, they are bound to act collectively – their honour demands it. If they fail to contribute to the group, they will be shamed and will feel guilty, but, more importantly, they will be excluded from the benefits of group membership. Symbolically, those who renege on the alliance die alone and unaided. The alliance consists therefore not of rational individuals pursuing private goals, coerced by a higher power, but of beings who are able to commit them-selves voluntarily to each other and to collective goals; once so committed, they are obliged to achieve them by the powerful sanctions of honour and shame. *The Lord of the Rings* stands as a metaphor for social theory today; it counterposes the fantastical ontology of structure and agency against an interactional account of social existence.

1930s social theory

As an independent text, *The Lord of the Rings* provides a useful analogy for contemporary debates in social theory. However, when Tolkien's work is sit-uated in a wider historical context, it becomes even more pertinent to current structure–agency debates. *The Lord of the Rings*, although eventually pub-lished in 1954, was originally conceived much earlier; Tolkien worked on it from the late 1930s, after the publication of *The Hobbit*. This is historically interesting, for it situates *The Lord of the Rings* with a series of other great works published at a similar time which amount to a critique of individual-ism. Particularly in the 1920s and 1930s a series of books were published which all rejected individualism – and specifically economic utilitarianism – as the philosophical basis of the social sciences and the legitimate basis of Western political democracy. In economics, Karl Polanyi (1957) and John Maynard Keynes (1936) rejected classical theories, founded on the rational, self-interested actor, as the legitimate basis for national economic policy. In its place, they promoted a concept of the nation as a co-operative, consen-sual and unified entity nurtured by the state. In anthropology, Malinowski (1922) and Mauss (1967[1929]) rejected rational economic transactions as the basis of social order. Instead, they argued that societies were formed through exchange, in which dense social relations were formed on the basis of honour and shame. Indeed, Wittgenstein's *Philosophical Investigations*, also originally conceived in the 1930s, replaced the individualistic accounts of language use favoured by analytic philosophers with the concept of the 'form of life', in which participants co-operate with each other in specific forms of practice. However, perhaps the work that resonates most obviously with the *Lord of the Rings* in this period is Talcott Parsons' *The Structure of Social Action* (1937).

Like Tolkien's Ring trilogy, the starting point of *The Structure of Social Action* is utilitarian individualism, which Parsons regarded as the dominant philosophy in the social sciences in the early twentieth century. Since its original formulation by Thomas Hobbes, utilitarianism understood social order as the product of the interaction of rational and independent indi-viduals. However, although utilitarianism was elegant as a social theory, Parsons demonstrated its total inadequacy as an explanation of social order.

In particular, he claimed that utilitarianism was trapped in an unavoidable dilemma. Parsons brilliantly noticed that the attempt to explain social order from the premise of the rational, autonomous actor led to two unacceptable theoretical positions, which he called the 'utilitarian dilemma' (Parsons, 1968[1937]: 64).

For Parsons, utilitarians were forced to oscillate between individualism and objectivism in order to explain social order:

> Either the active agency of the actor in the choice of ends is an independent factor in action, and the end element must be random; or the objectionable implication of randomness is denied, but then their independence disappears and they are assimilated to the conditions of the situation, that is to elements analyzable in terms of nonsubjective categories, principally heredity and environment. (Parsons, 1968[1937]: 64)

If individuals really were rational and free as utilitarianism claimed, then the action of diverse individuals could never be co-ordinated. Their choices would remain random and no regular social intercourse could take place. Social order would be impossible as each individual randomly pursued now this end and now that. In order to explain the co-ordination of ends, utilitarianism has, therefore, to postulate the existence of some external factor – a Leviathan – which impresses itself upon individuals directing their choices. Parsons argued that utilitarianism typically appealed to biology (heredity) or the environment to explain the convergence of individual choice. Once determined in this way, individuals no longer choose randomly; their choices are co-ordinated to the same ends. Social order was then possible – but only at the cost of individual autonomy. Utilitarianism must assume either that rational individuals are themselves determined by objective factors, and therefore not independent, or that the autonomy of individuals is maintained and their choices are random – in which case social order remains inexplicable. Thus, on a utilitarian account, social order cannot be explained. The parallel with Tolkien's Ring trilogy is clear; the only way to unify self-interested individuals is to submit them to a higher power which eliminates their independence.

Parsons' solution to the utilitarian dilemma matches Tolkien's own fictional account:

> A society can only be subject to a legitimate order, and therefore can be on a non-biological level something other than a balance of power of interests, only in so far as there are *common* value attitudes in the society. (Parsons, 1968[1937]: 670; see also 392)

Social order is possible only once humans knowingly and voluntarily orient themselves to these common values and consequently form social groups. His 'value attitudes' were not merely normative in nature. For Parsons, social order was not a matter simply of passively believing the same values. On the contrary, in *The Structure of Social Action* – at least, if not in his later work – common value attitudes were always grounded in action, and specifically in collective, social action. Crucially, common value attitudes are an organic and indivisible part of the unit-act in the action frame of reference, unifying ends and means. Common-value attitudes refer to the shared goals and means to which the participants in any collective endeavour agree. Social order arises for Parsons not because people share the same value dispositions but, on the contrary, because they do things together. They orient themselves consciously towards the same goal and, in this way, are able to co-operate with each other, to their mutual benefit. Against an individualistic, utilitarian account, Parsons proposes a quite different view of social life. By agreeing to common values (to shared goals and means), therefore, humans are able to co-operate with each other in concrete projects. All direct their activities towards the common and shared ends upon which they have agreed.

Although the establishment of common values and goals requires a conscious act of understanding – it must be voluntary – shared norms imply moral obligation; adherence to them is not an individual matter of choice (Parsons, 1968[1937]: 383–384). Once participants have committed themselves to a collective goal, they are obliged to contribute to the group on pain of serious sanctions. Human groups have powerful means of sustaining co-operation through the very dynamics of interaction. In his discussion of Durkheim, Parsons demonstrates the efficacy of collective understandings in social life:

> A moral rule is not moral unless it is accepted as obligatory, unless the attitude towards it is quite different from that of expedience. But at the same time it is also not truly moral unless obedience to it is held to be desirable, unless the individual's happiness and self-fulfillment are bound up with it. Only the combination of these two elements gives a complete account of the nature of morality. (Parsons, 1968[1937]: 387)

Members of social groups gain manifest collective benefits from their participation in the group. However, with these collective benefits come enforceable obligations on those who would be group members. Co-operation induces a sense of moral obligation in and of itself. When individuals publicly consent to co-operate, they are committing themselves to the other members of the group and to the collective practices of the group. They are mutually accepting the obligation of group membership and are understood by their fellow members to be doing this. Moreover, every group has an effective mechanism of encouraging co-operation. As Parsons notes, the 'happiness and self-fulfillment' of individuals are dependent on their abiding by these shared understandings; it is not an internal good which is produced independently. Individuals feel happy and fulfilled insofar as they abide by the values which are regarded as honourable by their fellow group members and can thus contribute to the goals of the group. Humans feel fulfilled insofar as they are held in esteem by the group. Self-esteem arises from the honour which individuals receive from the group, even if that honour is given only implicitly. Thus, people commit themselves to the shared values of their group and are held to those values by the desire for honour and the fear of shame.

Parsons does not explore this further point sufficiently, focusing only on the individual motivation to adhere to the collective goals of the group. However, the desire for honour and aversion to shame play a fundamental role in social interaction. Group members' access to the collective goods of the group is substantially a function of the esteem in which they are held by the group. Consequently, the more honour in which people are held, the greater their access to the collective benefits produced by co-operation, while shame will lead to limited access and finally to exclusion; group members will not co-operate with a shamed individual. This is not to say that social actors are not interested in tangible material rewards. Typically, they are. However, concrete material rewards, such as money, economic opportunities, housing, goods and services, are collective goods, created and sustained by groups and institutions. In order to gain access to these material goods, it is necessary to participate in the institutions which monopolise these resources. It is only possible to do that if a participant is seen as contributing to these groups and institutions by co-operating with others. Even then, there are huge internal debates about who deserves what. The honour of group members – and hence their access to collective goods – is contested. The concepts of honour and shame do not imply a consensual view of society in which participants are not interested in material reward – it notes rather that the rapacious pursuit of collective goods which is the norm cannot be understood in individualistic terms.

For Parsons, the voluntaristic theory of action offered great prospects for the social sciences in the twentieth century: 'It is hoped, in transcending the positivist–idealist dilemma, to show a way of transcending also the old individualism–society or, as it is often called, social nominalism–realism dilemma which has plagued social theory to so little purpose for so long' (Parsons, 1968[1937]: 74). *The Structure of Social Action* and the utilitarian dilemma, in particular, endure as penetrating refutations of dualistic social theory. In the form of myth, *The Lord of the Rings* similarly attempts to reject individualism and the dualistic account of social order which individualism implies. So in an age very different from the 1930s, the book can still find its place in a wider constellation of works which together reject individualism and which understand society in terms of the co-operation of group members. Within this constellation, *The Lord of the Rings* has a direct bearing on the structure–agency debate in sociology today, illustrating in mythic terms the shortcomings of ontological dualism. Humans do not act as individuals pursuing random private goals, only to be controlled and co-ordinated by a higher force. Humans are not golems. On the contrary, the ontological reality of human social life is represented by the specifically social parts of this myth and above all by the interactions of Sam and Frodo.

Their relationship represents how humans actually orient themselves to common goals – even when many humans draw themselves into very large social groups and institutions. Even in the largest institutions, face-to-face interaction and the power of mutual obligation underpin human existence, not obedience to a transcendental authority by independent agents.

Contemporary social theory

For Tolkien, the Ring involves a social order of individuals who pursue their own interests constrained and directed only by means of a higher force, a Leviathan. He calls this higher force the Ring, but his solution as to how evil individuals are unified reflects in mythical form the solution at which some social theorists have also arrived. In contemporary social theory, the ontological landscape is very similar, although the starting point is usually different. Social theorists normally begin with the premise that social order exists and with the fact that individuals are manifestly confronted by potent social institutions which are not of their making. Habermas conceives of modern society as a system of state bureaucracies and economic institutions. In his structuration theory, Giddens also proposes the existence of an objective system, consisting of institutions and organisations. 'Critical Realists', like Bhaskar and Archer, have forcefully promoted the idea of a prior structural reality: 'There is more to coping with social reality than coping with other people. There is coping with a whole host of social entities, including institutions, traditions, networks of relations and the like – which are irreducible to people' (Bhaskar, 1991: 71). Similarly, Archer proposes 'that it is fully justifiable to refer to structures (being irreducible to individuals or groups) as pre-existing them both' (Archer, 1995: 75). Bourdieu (1984) asserts the existence of prior economic conditions which determine class formation, while for Foucault modern society is a total institution in which individuals are subject to constant surveillance from a central authority; in this he echoes Tolkien's novel. For all these social theorists, modern society consists of objective structures which surpass individual understanding and activity and which have a determining force over individuals.

At the same time, drawing closer to Tolkien's description of the order of the Ring, all these social theorists assert the existence, or at least the possibility, of autonomous individual freedom. Thus, there is a broad consensus in contemporary social theory that humans have agency, which is emphasised most obviously in the work of Giddens, Bhaskar and Archer. The last of these demonstrates this individualism at its most extreme. Against Durkheim's claim that identity is given to the individual by society, Archer insists that certain elements of the self are prior to and separate from society. 'I will use three arguments to rebut the contrary view that our humanity itself is a social gift, in order to maintain that the sense of the self, which has been shown to be essential to social life, cannot be derived from life in society' (Archer, 1995: 285). Archer explicitly returns to the philosophical traditions

of the seventeenth and eighteenth century and, in particular, to the philosophies of Locke and Kant (Archer, 1995: 289) by positing a notion of an
individual subject who exists prior to social interaction. Archer's individualism is not unusual. Giddens and Bhaskar have adopted a similar position, as
when both insist that 'a person could have acted otherwise' (Giddens, 1976:
75; Bhaskar, 1989: 114). The individual is at a certain point free and independent. Although less obvious, the autonomy of the agent is also implicit
in the works of Foucault and Bourdieu. Despite his (often unfortunate)
descriptions of the habitus, Bourdieu evidently sees it as allowing room for
slippage, so that the habitus constrains social action without finally determining it (Bourdieu and Wacquant, 1992: 134). Individuals have agency
even under the habitus, because they choose how to follow it. Foucault
similarly celebrates certain individuals who have liberated themselves from
discourse, such as the nineteenth-century peasant, Jouy, who engaged in free
and apparently un-socialised sexual practices with local children (Foucault,
1990: 32). Moreover, while (the early) Foucault regarded modern discourses
as absolutely determining, he believed that his own writing offers the possibility of overcoming their tyranny. If he personally is able to escape discourse, then it is logical to assume that other individuals are also capable
of freeing themselves from it. Thus the individual *can* resist and subvert
modern discourses and the modern class structure. In Habermas' work, too,
the individual becomes autonomous: for him, the central problem of modern
society is that individuals pursue their own rational interests unconstrained
by communicative action.

Consonant with Tolkien, therefore, all these theorists understand social
reality in terms of a dualism: a pre-existing and objective system, or structure, on the one hand, and potentially free individuals or agents, on the
other. Significantly, echoing Tolkien, the only way to explain social order
on these assumptions is to posit the existence of determining mechanisms
which direct individual action; individual will and agency are subverted
as humans become golems to a structuring force. Habermas claims that in
modern society, individuals act on the basis of unseen purposive-rational
codes. Similarly, Giddens maintains that the social system is reproduced
when individuals instantiate the virtual rules of structure: 'One of the main
propositions of structuration theory is that the rules and resources drawn
upon in the production and reproduction of social action are at the same
time the means of system reproduction (duality of structure)' (Giddens,
1984: 19). Giddens is ambiguous about the status of these rules. He refers
to them as 'memory traces' (Giddens, 1984: 17), implying that they are
known, but at the same time, like Habermas, he suggests that individuals
are not fully conscious of them. He emphasises that they are like linguistic
structures (which language users do not normally know) and are 'marked
by the absence of a subject' (Giddens, 1984: 25). They seem therefore to be
applied independently of the actor's conscious understanding; these rules
are not understood and applied collectively but automatically by the indi-

vidual. Similarly, Bourdieu maintains that the economic reality of a society – and its class structure – is maintained insofar as individuals internalise the appropriate habitus for their class position: 'the cognitive structures which social agents implement in their practical knowledge of the social world are internalized, "embodied" social structures' (Bourdieu, 1984: 468). Although operating from a quite different political perspective, Foucault makes a similar argument, envisaging modern society as an order in which individuals are totally dominated by discourse, abstract codes, which constitute fields of knowledge and practice:

> I would like to show with precise examples that in analysing discourses themselves, one sees the loosening of the embrace, apparently so tight, of words and things, and the emergence of a group of rules proper to discursive practice. These rules define not the dumb existence of a reality, nor the canonical use of vocabulary, but the ordering of objects ... Of course, discourses are composed of signs; but what they do is more than use these signs to designate things. It is this *more* that renders them irreducible to language (*langue*) and to speech. It is 'this' more that we must reveal and describe (Foucault, 1972: 48–49).

Archer and Bhaskar maintain that individuals are constrained by structures which they can at best only modify and transform. Consequently, 'if society is always already made, then any concrete praxis or, if you like, act of objectivation can only modify it' (Bhaskar, 1995[1979]: 42). Structure frames and constrains individual action. Of course, at every point, social theorists – especially politically liberal ones like Habermas or Giddens – gloss their accounts so that the bleak regime of the Ring is obscured in their work. However, despite these caveats, they share Tolkien's ontological presumptions. Indeed, once society has been understood in terms of an autonomous structure and isolated individuals, it becomes theoretically necessary to invoke determining mechanisms which connect the two.

Fortunately, in all the works of contemporary social theory, there is an alternative ontology: a Fellowship is recognisable. Thus Habermas describes how people actually live in lifeworlds, and in the work of Giddens the concept of 'practical consciousness' refers to the taken-for-granted understandings which underpin social interaction at every point (Giddens, 1984: 7). Although the habitus has attained a position of priority in Bourdieu's work and its interpretation, he developed a practical theory in which human interaction is primary (Bourdieu, 1977: 1–15). Gift exchange is not then determined by logic but arises out of the dynamics of social interaction:

> All experience of practice contradicts these paradoxes, and affirms that cycles of reciprocity are not the irresistible gearing of obligatory practices found only in ancient tragedy: a gift may remain unrequited, if it meets with ingratitude; it may be spurned as an insult. (Bourdieu, 1977: 9)

Similarly, Foucault himself ultimately rejected the notion of the discourse and presented an idea of power as a capillary process. Power was not the product of monolithic discourses which imposed upon individuals. On the contrary, power emerged precisely from the myriad of social interactions between humans in any regime (Foucault, 1982: 217; Dennis and Martin, 2005). Realists such as Archer and Bhaskar also emphasise the importance of social interaction (Archer, 1995: 157); Bhaskar, in particular, has insisted that there is a meaningful dimension to human social life which cannot be ignored. Thus, although humans are confronted by a prior structure, they act in the present on the basis of shared understandings to reproduce and transform this structure. For both Bhaskar and Archer, this moment of transformational activity is central to their social theory. Although Bhaskar and Archer ontologise interaction in the present into structure, they presuppose the existence of structure. What they presume to be structure can be reduced to interactions and collective activities in other times and places by other participants and groups. Ultimately, they too cannot explain social order without drawing on a concept of collective human practice. The illusion of structure and agency is replaced by the genuine basis of human society, interaction.

The mirage of structure and agency can be overcome as soon as social reality is comprehended in terms of interacting participants engaged in collective forms of practice. Then, a vertical image of isolated individuals organised around a centralising authority is replaced by a picture of a dynamic constellation of human gatherings, dispersals and re-gatherings at each of which actors co-ordinate themselves in relation to shared goals, sometimes fleeting, sometimes enduring. Social reality consists not of a dull interface of structure and agency but spirals of interaction ritual chains (Collins, 1994: 232ff.). The unifying feature of human existence is social interaction and the collective practices which arise from it. *The Lord of the Rings*, with its Ring and Fellowship, represents the current predicament of contemporary social theory, but in fantastical form.

Conclusion: what is to be done?

In one sense, we have not come very far since the 1930s. Contemporary social theory is still trapped in a dualistic account of social life comprehended in terms of agency and structure. The pernicious individual–society dualism is still prevalent, despite its refutation in the works of those like Parsons or its mythical representation in Tolkien's novel. Given the failure of Parsons and others to uproot ontological dualism, it seems unlikely that interventions today will be any more successful – however apparently decisive. Perhaps the best way of transcending the structure–agency dualism is not to argue with it but, on the contrary, merely do something different. Instead of engaging in debate which ultimately drags social theorists around the same totem, those sociologists oriented to an interactionist approach might engage in a practice which has always been central to sociology: the empirical study of human activity in all its rich diversity. Instead of discussing structure and agency, sociologists might simply turn to human lifeworlds themselves and, through a process of collaboration and co-operation, exchanging ideas and criticisms, build upon the excellent work which sociology has done since its origins on the lives which people actually lead. Instead of worrying about structure and agency, sociologists should focus on the terrible and fascinating things which people are, in fact, doing in the world today. While structure and agency prevent them from doing that, an interactive approach demanding above all else immersion in the reality of contemporary social practices could at least set them on the correct course. This approach could begin at least to unify sociologists around a collective endeavour to which they hold each other through mechanisms of shame and honour.

At the end of Wagner's Ring cycle, the Rhinemaidens take back the Ring forged from their gold. The Rhine floods and sweeps away the pyre on which Brünnhilde has immolated herself, with the Ring on her finger. As the Ring disappears, Hagen, the son of Albrecht, cries at the Rhinemaidens, 'Zurück vom Ring [Stay away from the Ring]'. He wants it for himself, but, of course, the phrase has an ironic secondary meaning which summarises the underlying motif of the entire cycle. As a metaphor for structure and agency, social theorists might usefully take this advice about the Ring. Stay away from structure and agency.

Bibliography

Adorno, Theodor, and Horkheimer, Max (1979[1944]) *The Dialectic of Enlightenment*. London: Verso.

Alexander, Jeffrey C., and Giesen, Bernhard (1987) 'From reduction to linkage: the long view of the micro–macro debate', pp. 1–42 in Jeffrey C. Alexander et al. (eds) *The Micro–Macro Link: Problems and Prospects*. Berkeley: University of California Press.

Althusser, Louis (1969[1965]) *For Marx*. Harmondsworth: Allen Lane.

Anchor, Robert (1983) 'Realism and ideology: the question of order', pp. 107–119 in *History and Theory* (22/2).

Anderson, Benedict (2006[1983]) *Imagined Communities: Reflections on the Origins and Spread of Nationalism* (3rd edn). London: Verso.

Anderson, R. J., Hughes, J. A., and Sharrock, W. W. (eds) (1987) *Classic Disputes in Sociology*. London: Allen and Unwin.

Andreski, Stanislav (1983) 'Introduction', pp. 1–12 in Andreski (ed.) *Max Weber on Capitalism, Bureaucracy and Religion*. London: Allen and Unwin.

Archer, Margaret S. (2000a) *Being Human: The Problems of Agency*. Cambridge: Cambridge University Press.

Archer, Margaret S. (2000b) 'For structure: its reality, properties and powers: a reply to Anthony King', pp. 464–472 in *Sociological Review* (48).

Archer, Margaret S. (1996a) *Culture and Agency*. Cambridge: Cambridge University Press.

Archer, Margaret S. (1996b) 'Social integration and system integration: developing the distinction', pp. 679–699 in *Sociology* (30/4).

Archer, Margaret S. (1995) *Realist Social Theory: The Morphogenetic Approach*. Cambridge: Cambridge University Press.

Archer, Margaret S. (1988) *Culture and Agency: The Place of Culture in Social Theory*. Cambridge: Cambridge University Press.

Archer, Margaret S. (1983) 'Process without system', pp. 196–221 in *Archives Européennes de Sociologie* (24/1).

Archer, Margaret S. (1982) 'Morphogenesis versus structuration: on combining structure and action', pp. 455–483 in *British Journal of Sociology* (33/4).

Archer, Margaret S. (1979) *Social Origins of Educational Systems*. London: Sage.

Atkinson, Paul and Housley, William (2003) *Interactionism*. London: Sage.

Baldamus, W. (1976) *The Structure of Sociological Inference*. London: Martin Robertson.

Baldwin, John D. (1986) *George Herbert Mead: A Unifying Theory for Sociology*. Newbury Park, CA: Sage.

Ball, P. (2004) *Critical Mass: How One Thing Leads to Another*. London: Heinemann.

Barabasi, A-L. (2003) *Linked: How Everything Is Connected to Everything Else and What it Means for Business, Science and Everyday Life*. New York: Plume.

Bargava, Rajeev (1992) *Individualism in Social Science*. Oxford: Oxford University Press.

Barth, Frederik (1989) 'The analysis of culture in complex societies', pp. 120–142 in *Ethnos* (54/3–4).

Barth, Frederik (1981) *Process and Form in Social Life: Selected Essays of Frederik Barth, Vol. I*. London: Routledge and Kegan Paul.

Barth, Frederik (ed.) (1978) *Scale and Social Organization*. Oslo: Universitetsforlaget.

Barth, Frederik (1969) 'Introduction' in F. Barth (ed.) *Ethnic Groups and Boundaries: The Social Organisation of Cultural Difference*. Oslo: Universitetsforlaget.

Barth, Frederik (1966) *Models of Social Organisation*. Occasional Paper No. 23. London: Royal Anthropological Institute.

Bauman, Zigmund (1990) *Thinking Sociologically*. Oxford: Blackwell.

Becker, Howard S. (1982) *Art Worlds*. Berkeley: University of California Press.

Becker, Howard S. (1963) *Outsiders: Studies in the Sociology of Deviance*. New York: The Free Press.

Bell, Daniel (1974) *The Coming of Post-Industrial Society*. New York: Harper Colophon.

Bendix, Reinhard (1966[1959]) *Max Weber: An Intellectual Portrait*. London: Methuen.

Berger, Peter, and Luckmann, Thomas (1991[1966]) *The Social Construction of Reality*. London: Penguin.

Berry, Christopher J. (1997) *Social Theory of the Scottish Enlightenment*. Edinburgh: Edinburgh University Press.

Bhaskar, Roy (1989) *Reclaiming Reality*. London: Verso.

Bhaskar, Roy (1995[1979]) *The Possibility of Naturalism*. Sussex: Harvester.

Bittner, Egon (1974) 'The concept of organisation', pp. 69–81 in R. Turner (ed.) *Ethnomethodology*. Harmondsworth: Penguin.

Blau, Peter M. (1977) 'A macrosociological theory of social structure', pp. 26–54 in the *American Journal of Sociology* (83).

Blau, Peter M., and Duncan, Otis D. (1967) *The American Occupational Structure*. New York: Wiley.

Bloor, David (2000) 'Institutions as collective representations', pp. 157–176 in W. S. F. Pickering (ed.) *Durkheim and Representations*. London: Routledge.

Blumer, Herbert (2004) *George Herbert Mead and Human Conduct*. Walnut Creek, CA: Alta Mira Press.

Blumer, Herbert (1981) Review of David L. Miller *George Herbert Mead: Self,*

Language and the World, pp. 902–904 in *American Journal of Sociology* (86).

Blumer, Herbert (1969) *Symbolic Interactionism: Perspective and Method.* Englewood Cliffs, NJ: Prentice-Hall.

Blumer, Herbert (1966) 'Sociological implications of the thought of G. H. Mead', pp. 61–77 in Blumer (1969).

Boissevain, J. (1974) *Friends of Friends: Networks, Manipulators and Coalitions.* Oxford: Basil Blackwell.

Boissevain, J. (1968) 'The place of non-groups in the social sciences', pp. 542–546 in *Man* (3).

Boissevain, J., and Mitchell, J. Clyde (eds) (1973) *Network Analysis: Studies in Human Interaction.* The Hague: Mouton.

Bottero, Wendy (1998) 'Clinging to the wreckage? Gender and the legacy of class', pp. 469–490 in *Sociology* (32/3).

Bourdieu, Pierre (1990a) *In Other Words: Essays Towards a Reflexive Sociology.* Cambridge: Polity.

Bourdieu, Pierre (1990b) *The Logic of Practice.* Cambridge: Polity.

Bourdieu, Pierre (1984) *Distinction: A Social Critique of the Judgement of Taste.* London: Routledge and Kegan Paul.

Bourdieu, Pierre (1977) *Outline of a Theory of Practice.* Cambridge: Cambridge University Press.

Bourdieu, Pierre, and Passeron, J-C. (1977) *Reproduction: In Education, Society and Culture.* London: Sage.

Bourdieu, Pierre, and Wacquant, L. J. D. (1992) *An Invitation to Reflexive Sociology.* Cambridge: Polity.

Brubaker, Rogers (2004) *Ethnicity Without Groups.* Cambridge, MA: Harvard University Press.

Brubaker, Rogers (2003) 'Neither individualism nor "groupism": a reply to Craig Calhoun', pp. 553–557 in *Ethnicities* (3).

Brubaker, Rogers, Feischmidt, M., Fox, J., and Grancea, L. (2006) *Nationalist Politics and Everyday Ethnicity in a Transylvanian Town.* Princeton: Princeton University Press.

Buchanan, M. (2002) *Small World: Uncovering Nature's Hidden Networks.* London: Weidenfeld and Nicolson.

Bucher, Rue, and Strauss, Anselm (1961) 'Professions in process', pp. 325–334 in *American Journal of Sociology* (66/4).

Byrne, D. (1998) *Complexity Theory and the Social Sciences.* London: Routledge.

Calhoun, Craig (2003a) ' "Belonging" in the cosmopolitan imaginary', pp. 531–553 in *Ethnicities* (3).

Calhoun, Craig (2003b) 'The variability of belonging: a reply to Rogers Brubaker', pp. 558–568 in *Ethnicities* (3).

Calhoun, Craig (2003c) 'Pierre Bourdieu' in G. Ritzer (ed.) *The Blackwell Companion to the Major Social Theorists* (Rev. edn). Cambridge, MA: Blackwell.

Calhoun, Craig, LiPuma, Edward, and Postone, Moishe (eds) (1993) *Bourdieu: Critical Perspectives.* Cambridge: Polity.

Campbell, Colin (1996) *The Myth of Social Action*. Cambridge: Cambridge University Press.

Castells, Manuel (2000) *The Rise of the Network Society* (2nd edn). Malden: Blackwell.

Castoriadis, C. (1987) *The Imaginary Institution of Society*. Cambridge: Polity.

Chen, Kuan-Hsing (1996) 'Post-Marxism: between/beyond critical postmodernism and cultural studies', pp. 309–325 in Morley and Chen (eds.) (1996).

Cicourel, Aaron V. (1993) 'Aspects of structural and processual theories of knowledge', pp. 89–115 in Calhoun et al. (eds) (1993).

Cicourel, Aaron V. (1967) *The Social Organisation of Juvenile Justice*. New York: John Wiley.

Cohen, Anthony P. (1985) *The Symbolic Construction of Community*. London: Harwood/Tavistock.

Cohen, G. A. (2000) *Karl Marx's Theory of History: A Defence* (Expanded edn). Oxford: Oxford University Press.

Cohen, Percy S. (1968) *Modern Social Theory*. London: Heinemann.

Collier, Andrew (1994) *Critical Realism: An Introduction to Roy Bhaskar's Philosophy*. London and New York: Verso.

Collin, F. (1997) *Social Reality*. London: Routledge.

Collins, Randall (1994) *Four Sociological Traditions*. New York and Oxford: Oxford University Press.

Collins, Randall (1988) 'Theoretical continuities in Goffman's work', pp. 41–63 in P. Drew and A. Wooton (Eds.) *Erving Goffman: Exploring the Interaction Order*. Cambridge: Polity.

Collins, Randall (1981) 'On the microfoundations of macrosociology', pp. 984–1014 in the *American Journal of Sociology* (86).

Crews, F. (1986) 'In the big house of theory', pp. 36–42 in *New York Review of Books* (33/9).

Crossley, Nick (2008) 'Small-world networks, complex systems and sociology', pp. 261–277 in *Sociology* (42).

Crossley, Nick (2005) 'The new social physics and the science of small-world networks', pp. 351–358 in *Sociological Review* (53).

Davey, N. (1985) 'Habermas' contribution to hermeneutical theory', pp. 109–131 in *Journal of the British Society for Phenomenology* (16/2).

Dawe, Alan (1970) 'The two sociologies', pp. 207–218 in *British Journal of Sociology* (21).

Demerath, Neil J., and Peterson, Richard A. (eds) (1967) *System, Change and Conflict*. New York: Free Press.

Dennis, Alex, and Martin, Peter J. (2007) 'Symbolic interactionism and the concept of social structure', pp. 287–305 in *Sociological Focus* (40/3).

Dennis, Alex, and Martin, Peter J. (2005) 'Symbolic interactionism and the concept of power', pp. 191–213 in *British Journal of Sociology* (56/2).

Denzin, Norman K. (1992) *Symbolic Interactionism and Cultural Studies: The Politics of Interpretation*. Cambridge, MA, and Oxford: Blackwell.

Descartes, René (1994) Selected Philosophical Writings. Cambridge: Cambridge University Press.

Bibliography

Dobash, Russell P. (1983) 'Labour and discipline in Scottish and English prisons: moral correction, punishment and useful toil', pp. 1–27 in *Sociology* (17/1).

Douglas, Mary (1973) *Natural Symbols: Explorations in Cosmology.* Harmondsworth: Pelican.

Durkheim, Emile (1982 [1895]) *The Rules of Sociological Method.* London: Macmillan.

Durkheim, Emile (1952 [1897]) *Suicide.* London: Routledge and Kegan Paul.

Eagleton, Terry (2000) *The Idea of Culture.* Oxford: Basil Blackwell.

Eglin, Peter (1987) 'The meaning and use of official statistics in the explanation of deviance', pp. 184–212 in Anderson et al. (eds) (1987).

Elster, Jon (1985) *Making Sense of Marx.* Cambridge: Cambridge University Press.

Elster, Jon (1982) 'Marxism, functionalism and game theory: the case for methodological individualism', pp. 453–482 in *Theory and Society* (11/4).

Ferguson, Harvie (2006) *Phenomenological Sociology.* London: Sage.

Field, J. (2003) *Social Capital.* London: Routledge.

Fine, Gary Alan (1993) 'The sad demise, mysterious disappearance and glorious triumph of symbolic interactionism', pp. 61–87 in *Annual Review of Sociology* (19).

Fine, Gary Alan (1991) 'On the macrofoundations of microsociology: constraint and the exterior reality of structure', pp. 161–177 in *Sociological Quarterly* (32/2).

Finnegan, Ruth (1989) *The Hidden Musicians.* Cambridge: Cambridge University Press.

Flyvbjerg, Bent (1998) 'Habermas and Foucault: thinkers for civil society?', pp. 210–233 in *British Journal of Sociology* (49/2).

Foucault, Michel (1990) *The History of Sexuality, Vol. 1.* Harmondsworth: Penguin.

Foucault, Michel (1982) 'Afterword: The subject and power' in H. Dreyfus and P. Rabinow (eds) *Michel Foucault: Beyond Structure and Hemeneutics.* Sussex: Harvester.

Foucault, Michel (1972) *The Archaeology of Knowledge.* London: Tavistock.

Fox, Nick J. (1998) 'Foucault, Foucaldians and sociology', pp. 415–433 in *British Journal of Sociology* (49/3).

Frayn, Michael (2006) *The Human Touch: Our Part In the Creation of a Universe.* London: Faber and Faber.

Friedmann, H. (1999) 'The social terrain: the history and future of sociology's project' in J. L. Abu-Lughod (ed.) *Sociology for the Twenty-First Century: Continuities and Cutting Edges.* Chicago: University of Chicago Press.

Frisby, David (1997) 'Introduction to the Texts', pp. 1–28 in Frisby and Featherstone (eds) (1997).

Frisby, David, and Featherstone, Mike (eds) (1997) *Simmel on Culture.* London: Sage.

Gadamer, Hans-Georg (1990) 'Reply to my critics' in G. Ormiston and A. Schrift (eds) *The Hermeneutic Tradition: From Ast to Ricouer.* Albany, NY: State University of New York Press.

Gadamer, Hans-Georg (1986) 'Rhetoric, hermeneutics and the critique of ideology' in K. Mueller-Vollmer (ed.) *The Hermeneutic Reader*. Oxford: Blackwell.

Gadamer, Hans-Georg (1977) 'On the scope and function of hermeneutical reflection' in *Philosophical Hermeneutics*. London: University of California Press.

Gadamer, Hans-Georg (1975) *Truth and Method*. London: Sheed and Ward.

Garfinkel, Harold (1967) *Studies in Ethnomethodology*. Englewood Cliffs, NJ: Prentice-Hall.

Garfinkel, Harold, and Sacks, Harvey (1970) 'Formal structures of practical action', pp. 337–366 in E. McKinney and E. Tiryakian (eds) *Theoretical Sociology: Perspectives and Developments*. New York: Appleton-Century-Crofts.

Geras, Norman (1991) 'Louis Althusser', pp. 16–19 in Tom Bottomore (ed.) *A Dictionary of Marxist Thought* (2nd edn). Oxford: Basil Blackwell.

Geras, Norman (1983) *Marx and Human Nature*. London: Verso.

Giddens, Anthony (1996) *In Defence of Sociology*. Cambridge: Polity.

Giddens, Anthony (1994) *The Consequences of Modernity*. Stanford: Stanford University Press

Giddens, Anthony (1987) 'Structuralism, post-structuralism and the production of culture' in A. Giddens and J. H. Turner (eds) *Social Theory Today*. Cambridge: Polity.

Giddens, Anthony (1984/1995) *The Constitution of Society*. Cambridge: Polity.

Giddens, Anthony (1981[1973]) *The Class Structure of the Advanced Societies*. London: Hutchinson.

Giddens, Anthony (1979/1988) *Central Problems in Social Theory*. London: Macmillan.

Giddens, Anthony (1976) *New Rules of Sociological Method*. London: Hutchinson.

Gimenez, Martha E. (2001) 'Marxism and class, gender and race: rethinking the trilogy', pp. 23–33 in *Race, Gender and Class* (8/2).

Gintis, Herbert, Bowles, S., Boyd, R., and Fehr, E. (eds) (2005) *Moral Sentiments and Material Interests: The Foundations of Cooperation in Economic Life*. Cambridge, Mass: MIT Press.

Goffman, Erving (1983) 'The interaction order', pp. 1–17 in *American Sociological Review* (48).

Greiffenhagen, Christian, and Sharrock, W. W. (2008) 'Where do the limits of experience lie? Abandoning the dualism of objectivity and subjectivity', pp. 70–83 in *History of the Human Sciences* (21).

Habermas, Jürgen (1996[1962]) *The Structural Transformation of the Public Sphere*. Cambridge: Polity.

Habermas, Jürgen (1995a) *Justification and Application*. Cambridge: Polity.

Habermas, Jürgen (1995b) *Postmetaphysical Thinking*. Cambridge: Polity.

Habermas, Jürgen (1993) 'Work and Weltanschauung: the Heidegger controversy from a German perspective' in H. Dreyfus and H. Hall (eds) *Heidegger: A Critical Reader*. Oxford: Blackwell.

Habermas, Jürgen (1991) *The Theory of Communicative Action, Vol. 1*. Cambridge: Polity.

Habermas, Jürgen (1990) *Moral Consciousness and Communicative Action*. Cambridge: Polity.

Habermas, Jürgen (1988) *On the Logic of the Social Sciences*. Cambridge: Polity.

Habermas, Jürgen (1987a) *The Philosophical Discourse of Modernity*. Cambridge: Polity.

Habermas, Jürgen (1987b) *The Theory of Communicative Action, Vol. 2*. London: Polity.

Habermas, Jürgen (1986) 'On hermeneutics' claim to universality' in K. Mueller-Vollmer (ed.) *The Hermeneutics Reader*. Oxford: Blackwell.

Habermas, Jürgen (1979) *Communication and the Evolution of Society*. London: Heinemann.

Habermas, Jürgen (1977) 'A review of Gadamer's *Truth and Method*' in F. Dallmayr and T. McCarthy (eds) *Understanding Social Enquiry*. London: University of Notre Dame Press.

Habermas, Jürgen (1976) *Legitimation Crisis*. London: Heinemann.

Habermas, Jürgen (1974) *Theory and Practice*. London: Heinemann.

Habermas, Jürgen (1971) *Knowledge and Human Interests*. London: Beacon Press.

Habermas, Jürgen (1970) 'On systematically distorted communication', pp. 205–218 in *Inquiry* (13).

Hall, Stuart (1996[1986]) 'On postmodernism and articulation: an interview with Stuart Hall', pp. 131–150 in Morley and Chen (eds) (1996).

Hall, Stuart (1988) 'The toad in the garden: Thatcherism amongst the theorists', pp. 35–73 in C. Nelson and L. Grossberg (eds) *Marxism and the Interpretation of Culture*. London: Macmillan.

Hall, Stuart, Critcher, Chas, Jefferson, Tony, Clarke, John, and Roberts, Brian (1978) *Policing the Crisis: Mugging, the State and Law and Order*. London: Macmillan.

Hall, Stuart (1973) 'Encoding and decoding in the television discourse'. Birmingham: Centre for Contemporary Cultural Studies Occasional Paper.

Healy, Kieran (1998) 'Conceptualising constraint: Mouzelis, Archer, and the concept of social structure', pp. 509–522 in *Sociology* (32/3).

Henrich, J., Boyd, R., Bowles, S., Camerer, C., Fehr, E., and Gintis, H. (eds) (2004) *Foundations of Human Sociality: Economic Experiments and Ethnographic Evidence from Fifteen Small-Scale Societies*. Oxford: Oxford University Press.

Hilbert, Richard A. (1995) 'Garfinkel's recovery of themes in classical sociology', pp. 157–175 in *Human Studies* (18).

Hilbert, Richard A. (1990) 'Ethnomethodology and the micro–macro order', pp. 794–808 in *American Sociological Review* (55/6).

Hobsbawm, Eric, and Ranger, Terence (eds) (1983) *The Invention of Tradition*. Cambridge: Cambridge University Press.

Holmwood, John, and Stewart, Alexander (1991) *Explanation and Social Theory*. London: Macmillan.

How, Alan (1995) *The Habermas–Gadamer Debate and the Nature of the Social: Back to Bedrock*. Aldershot: Avebury.

How, Alan (1985) 'A case of creative misreading: Habermas' evaluation of Gadamer's Hermeneutics', pp. 132–144 in *Journal of the British Society for Phenomenology* (16/2).

How, Alan (1980) 'Dialogue as productive limitation in social theory: the Habermas–Gadamer debate', pp. 131–143 in *Journal of the British Society for Phenomenology* (11/2).

Hughes, John A., Sharrock, W. W., and Martin, P. J. (2003) *Understanding Classical Sociology* (2nd edn). London: Sage.

James, Simon (1999) *The Atlantic Celts: Ancient People or Modern Invention?* London: British Museum Press.

James, Susan (1984) *The Content of Social Explanation*. Cambridge: Cambridge University Press.

Jenkins, Richard (2008a) *Rethinking Ethnicity: Arguments and Explorations* (2nd edn). London: Sage.

Jenkins, Richard (2008b) *Social Identity* (3rd edn). London: Routledge.

Jenkins, Richard (2006) 'When politics and social theory converge: group identification and group rights in Northern Ireland', pp. 389–410 in *Nationalism and Ethnic Politics* (12).

Jenkins, Richard (2002a) *Foundations of Sociology*. London: Palgrave Macmillan.

Jenkins, Richard (2002b) *Pierre Bourdieu* (2nd edn) London: Routledge.

Jenkins, Richard (2002c) 'Different societies? Different cultures? What are human collectivities?' in S. Malesevic and M. Haugaard (eds) *Making Sense of Collectivity: Ethnicity, Nationalism and Globalization*. London: Pluto.

Jenkins, Richard (2000) 'Categorization: identity, social process and epistemology', pp. 7–25 in *Current Sociology* (48/3).

Jessop, Bob (1996) 'Interpretive sociology and the dialectic of structure and agency', pp. 119–128 in *Theory, Culture and Society* (13/1).

Johnson, M. (1978) *The Body in the Mind: The Bodily Basis of Meaning, Imagination and Reason*. Chicago: University of Chicago Press.

Katovich, M. A., and Reese, W. A. (1993) 'Postmodern thought in symbolic interaction: reconstructing social enquiry in light of late-modern concerns', pp. 391–411 in *Sociological Quarterly* (34).

Kendall, Gavin, and Wickham, Gary (1999) *Using Foucault's Methods*. London: Sage.

Keynes, J. Maynard (1936) *The General Theory of Employment, Interest and Money*. London: Macmillan.

King, Anthony (2007) 'Why I am not an individualist', pp. 211–219 in *Journal for The Theory of Social Behaviour* (37/2).

King, Anthony (2006) 'How not to structure a social theory: a reply to a critical Response', pp. 464–479 in *Philosophy of the Social Sciences* (36/4).

King, Anthony (2004) *The Structure of Social Theory*. London: Routledge.

King, Anthony (1999) 'Against structure: a critique of morphogenetic social theory', pp. 199–227 in *Sociological Review* (47/2).

Kiniven, Osmo, and Piiroinen, Tero (2006a) 'On the limits of a realist conception of knowledge: a pragmatist critique of Archerian realism', pp. 224–241 in *Sociological Review* (54/2).

Kiniven, Osmo, and Piiroinen, Tero (2006b) 'Toward pragmatist methodological relationalism: from philosophizing sociology to sociologizing philosophy', pp. 303–329 in *Philosophy of the Social Sciences* (36/3).

Kiniven, Osmo, and Piiroinen, Tero (2004) 'The relevance of ontological commitments in social sciences: realist and pragmatist viewpoints', pp. 231–248 in *Journal for the Theory of Social Behaviour* (34/3).

Kirchberg, Volker (2007) 'Cultural consumption analysis: beyond structure and agency', pp. 115–135 in *Cultural Sociology* (1/1).

Kripke, S. (1982) *Wittgenstein on Rules and Private Language: An Elementary Exposition*. Oxford: Blackwell.

Kuper, Adam (1999) *Culture: The Anthropologists' Account*. Cambridge, MA: Harvard University Press.

Layder, Derek (1994) *Understanding Social Theory*. London: Sage.

Leach, Edmund R. (1954) *Political Systems of Highland Burma*. London: Athlone Press.

Lehmann, Jennifer M. (1993) *Deconstructing Durkheim: A Post-Post Structuralist Critique*. London and New York: Routledge.

Lemert, Edwin M. (1972[1967]) *Human Deviance, Social Problems and Social Control* (2nd edn). Englewood Cliffs, NJ: Prentice-Hall.

Lévi-Strauss, Claude (1968) *Structural Anthropology*. London: Allen Lane/ Penguin.

Lin, N. (2001) *Social Capital: A Theory of Social Structure and Action*. Cambridge: Cambridge University Press.

Lockwood, David (1964) 'System integration and social integration' in G. K. Zollschan and W. Hirsch (eds) *Explorations in Social Change*. London: Routledge.

Lockwood, David (1956) 'Some remarks on "The Social System"', pp. 134–146 in the *British Journal of Sociology* (7/1).

López, J., and Scott, John (2000) *Social Structure*. Buckingham: Open University Press.

Luhmann, Niklas (1995[1984]) *Social Systems*. Palo Alto, CA: Stanford University Press.

Lukes, Steven (1975) *Emile Durkheim: His Life and Work*. Harmondsworth: Penguin Books.

Lynch, Michael (1985) *Art and Artefact in Laboratory Work*. London: Routledge.

McIntyre, Richard (1992) 'Consumption in contemporary capitalism: beyond Marx and Veblen', pp. 40–60 in *Review of Social Economy* (50/1).

McRobbie, Angela (2000) *Feminism and Youth Culture* (2nd edn). London: Palgrave.

Maines, David R. (2001) *The Faultline of Consciousness: A View of Interactionism in Sociology*. New York: Aldine de Gruyter.

Maines, David R. (1982) 'In search of mesostructure: studies in the negotiated order', pp. 267–279 in *Urban Life* (11/3).

Maines, David R. (1978) 'Structural parameters and negotiated orders: comment on Benson, and Day and Day', pp. 491–496 in *Sociological Quarterly* (19).

Malinowski, Bronislaw (1922) *Argonauts of the Western Pacific*. London: Routledge and Kegan Paul.

March, J., and Olsen, J. (1976) *Ambiguity and Choice in Organisations*. Bergen: Universitetsforlaget.

Marshall, Gordon (1988) 'Some remarks on the study of working class consciousness', pp. 98–126 in David Rose (ed.) *Social Stratification and Economic Change*. London: Hutchinson.

Martin, Peter J. (2004) 'Culture, subculture and social organisation', pp. 21–35 in A. Bennett and K. Kahn-Harris (eds) *After Subculture: Critical Studies in Contemporary Youth Culture*. Houndmills and New York: Palgrave Macmillan.

Martin, Peter J. (1987) 'The concept of class', pp. 67–96 in Anderson et al. (eds) (1987).

Marx, Karl (1992[1844]) 'The economic and philosophical manuscripts' in *Early Writings*. Harmondsworth: Penguin.

Marx, Karl (1990[1867]) *Capital: A Critique of Political Economy. Vol. I*. Harmondsworth: Penguin.

Marx, Karl (1977[1852]) 'The Eighteenth Brumaire of Louis Bonaparte', pp. 300–325 in McLellan (1977).

Marx, Karl (1977[1845]) 'Theses on Feuerbach', pp. 156–8 in McLellan (1977).

Marx, Karl (1977[1844]) 'Economic and Philosophical Manuscripts', pp. 75–112 in McLellan (1977).

Marx, Karl, and Engels, Friedrich (1977[1848]) *The Communist Manifesto*, pp. 221–247 in McLellan (1977).

Marx, Karl and Engels, Friedrich (1977[1846]) *The German Ideology*, pp. 159–191 in McLellan (1977).

Mauss, Marcel (1967[1929]) *The Gift*. New York: Norton.

Mayer, A. C. (1966) 'The significance of quasi-groups in the study of complex societies' in Michael Banton (ed.) *The Social Anthropology of Complex Societies*. London: Tavistock.

McLellan, David (ed.) (1977) *Karl Marx: Selected Writings*. Oxford University Press.

Mead, George Herbert (1934) *Mind, Self and Society*. Chicago: University of Chicago Press.

Merton, Robert K. (1968) 'The self-fulfilling prophecy', pp. 421–436 in *Social Theory and Social Structure*. Glencoe: The Free Press.

Mills, C. Wright (1959) *The Sociological Imagination*. London: Oxford University Press.

Misgeld, D. (1977) 'Discourse and conversation: the theory of communicative competence and hermeneutics in the light of the debate between Habermas and Gadamer', pp. 321–344 in *Cultural Hermeneutics* (4/4).

Mitchell, J. Clyde (ed.) (1969) *Social Networks in Urban Situations*. Manchester: Manchester University Press.

Montesquieu, Charles (1748) *The Spirit of the Laws*.

Morgan, David H. J. (2001) 'Family sociology in from the fringe: the three "economies" of family life', pp. 227–247 in R. G. Burgess and Anne Murcott (eds), *Developments in Sociology*. London and New York: Prentice Hall.

Morgan, David H. J. (1996) *Family Connections: An Introduction to Family Studies* Cambridge: Polity Press.

Morley, David, and Chen, Kuan-Hsing (eds.) (1996) *Stuart Hall: Critical Dialogues in Cultural Studies*. London: Routledge.

Morrione, Thomas J. (2004) 'Preface', pp. *ix–xvii* in Blumer (2004).

Mouzelis, Nicos (1995) *Sociological Theory: What Went Wrong?* London: Routledge.

Mouzelis, Nicos (1994) 'Social integration and system integration: reflections on a fundamental distinction', pp. 395–409 in *Sociology* (25).

Mouzelis, Nicos (1993) 'The poverty of sociological theory', pp. 675–695 in *Sociology* (27/4).

Mouzelis, Nicos (1991) *Back to Sociological Theory*. London: Macmillan.

Nisbet, Robert A. (1970[1966]) *The Sociological Tradition*. London: Heinemann.

O'Neill, John (1986) 'The disciplinary society: from Weber to Foucault', pp. 42–60 in *British Journal of Sociology* (37/1).

Pahl, Ray (2005) 'Are all communities in the mind?', pp. 621–640 in *The Sociological Review* (53).

Panek, R. (2004) *The Invisible Century: Einstein, Freud and the Search for Hidden Universes*. New York: Viking.

Parker, J. (2000) *Structuration*. Buckingham: Open University Press.

Parsons, Talcott (1968[1937]) *The Structure of Social Action*. New York: Free Press.

Parsons, Talcott, and Shils, Edward (2001[1951]) *Towards a General Theory of Action*. Edison, NJ: Transaction.

Perkmann, M. (1998) 'Social integration and system integration: reconsidering the classical distinction', pp. 491–508 in *Sociology* (32/3).

Phillips, D. (2006) *Quality of Life: Concept, Policy and Practice*. London: Routledge.

Poggi, Gianfranco (2006) *Weber: A Short Introduction*. Cambridge: Polity Press.

Poggi, Gianfranco (1983) *Calvinism and the Capitalist Spirit*. London: Macmillan.

Polanyi, K. (1957) *The Great Transformation*. New York: Beacon Press.

Popper, Karl (2002[1957]) *The Poverty of Historicism*. London: Routledge.

Poropora, D. (2007) 'On Elder-Vass: Refining a Refinement', pp. 195–200 in *Journal for the Theory of Social Behaviour* (37/2).

Porter, Sam (1996) 'Contra-Foucault: soldiers, nurses and power', pp. 59–78 in *Sociology* (30/1).

Quah, S. R., and Sales, A. (2000) 'Of consensus, tensions and sociology at the dawn of the 21st century' in S. R. Quah and A. Sales (eds) *The International Handbook of Sociology*. London: Sage.

Rawls, Anne Warfield (1987) 'The interaction order sui generis: Goffman's contribution to social theory', pp. 136–149 in *Sociological Theory* (5/2).

Ritzer, George (2005) 'Social structure' in G. Ritzer (ed.) *Encyclopaedia of Social Theory*. Thousand Oaks: Sage.

Rojek, Chris (2003) *Stuart Hall*. Oxford: Polity.

Rosen, M. (1995) *Voluntary Servitude*. Harvard: Harvard University Press.

Rubenstein, David (2001) *Culture, Structure and Agency*. Thousand Oaks, CA, and London: Sage.

Savage, Mike (2000) *Class Analysis and Social Transformation*. Buckingham: Open University Press.

Sawyer, R. Keith (2005) *Social Emergence: Societies as Complex Systems*. Cambridge: Cambridge University Press.

Sawyer, R. Keith (2001) 'Emergence in sociology: contemporary philosophy of mind and some implications for sociological theory', pp. 551–587 in *American Journal of Sociology* (107/3).

Schelling, T. C., (2006) *Micromotives and Macrobehaviour* (2nd edn). New York: W. W. Norton.

Schütz, Alfred (1972[1932]) *The Phenomenology of the Social World*. London: Heinemann.

Schütz, Alfred (1970) *Alfred Schütz on Phenomenology and Social Relations*. Edited by H. R. Wagner. Chicago: University of Chicago Press.

Schütz, Alfred (1964) 'The well-informed citizen', pp. 120–134 in *Collected Papers, Vol. II*. The Hague: Martinus Nijhoff.

Schütz, Alfred (1962) *Collected Papers, Vol. I*. The Hague: Martinus Nijhoff.

Schwalbe, Michael et al. (2000) 'Generic processes in the reproduction of inequality: an interactionist analysis', pp. 419–452 in *Social Forces* (79/2).

Scott, John (2000) *Social Network Analysis: A Handbook* (2nd edn). London: Sage.

Searle, John (1995) *The Construction of Social Reality*. Harmondsworth: Penguin.

Sharrock, W. W. (2004) 'Structure and agency' in Kuper, Adam, and Kuper, J. (eds) *The Social Science Encyclopaedia* (3rd edn). London: Routledge.

Sharrock, W. W. (1987) 'Individual and society', pp. 126–156 in Anderson et al. (eds) (1987).

Sharrock, W. W. and Watson, D. R. (1988) 'Autonomy among social theories', pp. 56–77 in Nigel G. Fielding (ed.) *Actions and Structure: Research Methods and Social Theory*. London: Sage.

Shaw, G. Bernard (1923) *The Perfect Wagnerite*. London: Constable.

Sibeon, R. (1999) 'Anti-reductionist sociology', pp. 317–334 in *Sociology* (33/2).

Silverman, David (1985) *Qualitative Methodology and Sociology*. Aldershot: Gower.

Simmel, Georg (1997[1911]) 'The concept and tragedy of culture', pp. 55–75 in Frisby and Featherstone (eds) (1997).

Simmel, Georg (1997[1907]) 'Sociology of the Senses', pp. 109–120 in Frisby and Featherstone (eds) (1997).

Simmel, Georg (1950) *The Sociology of Georg Simmel*. Translated and edited by Kurt H. Wolff. New York: The Free Press.

Skinner, Quentin (ed.) (1985) *The Return of Grand Theory in the Human*

Sciences. Cambridge: Cambridge University Press.

Slack, Jennifer D. (1996) 'The theory and method of articulation in cultural studies', pp. 112–127 in Morley and Chen (eds) (1996).

Smith, Greg (1999) *Goffman and Social Organisation.* London: Routledge.

Smith, J., and Jenks, C. (2006) *Qualitative Complexity: Ecology, Cognitive Processes and the Re-emergence of Structures in Post-Humanist Social Theory.* London: Routledge.

Sparks, Colin (1996) 'Stuart Hall, cultural studies and Marxism', pp. 71–101 in Morley and Chen (eds) (1996).

Spruill, N., Kenney, C., and Kaplan, L. (2001) 'Community development and systems thinking: theory and practice', pp. 105–116 in *National Civic Review* (90).

Steadman, P. (1979) *The Evolution of Designs: Biological Analogy in Architecture and the Applied Arts.* Cambridge: Cambridge University Press.

Stones, R. (2005) *Structuration Theory.* Basingstoke: Palgrave Macmillan.

Strauss, Anselm (1978) *Negotiations.* San Francisco: Jossey-Bass.

Strauss, Anselm, et al. (1964) *Psychiatric Ideologies and Institutions.* New York: Free Press.

Sudnow, David (1965) 'Normal crimes', pp. 255–276 in *Social Problems* (12/3).

Surowiecki, J. (2004) *The Wisdom of Crowds: Why the Many are Smarter Than the Few.* New York: Doubleday.

Taylor, C. (2004) *Modern Social Imaginaries.* Durham: Duke University Press.

Taylor, Ian, Walton, Paul, and Young, Jock (1973) *The New Criminology: For a Social Theory of Deviance.* London: Routledge and Kegan Paul.

Thompson, E. P. (1967) 'Time, work-discipline and industrial capitalism', pp. 56–97 in *Past and Present* (38/December).

Tolkein, J. (1977[1954]) *The Lord of the Rings.* London: George Allen and Unwin.

Urry, John (2007) *Mobilities.* Cambridge: Polity.

Urry, John (ed.) (2005) 'Complexity', Special Issue of *Theory, Culture and Society* (22/5).

Urry, John (2004) 'Small worlds and the new "Social Physics"', pp. 109–130 in *Global Networks* (4).

Urry, John (2000a) 'Mobile sociology', pp. 185–203 in *British Journal of Sociology* (51).

Urry, John (2000b) *Sociology Beyond Societies: Mobilities for the Twenty-First Century.* London: Routledge. Urry, John (1982) 'Duality of structure: some critical issues', pp. 100–106 in *Theory, Culture and Society* (1).

Vandenberghe, Frédéric (1999) '"The real is relational": an epistemological analysis of Pierre Bourdieu's generative structuralism', pp. 32–67 in *Sociological Theory* (17/1).

Varela, Charles (2007) 'Elder-Vass's Move and Giddens's Call', pp. 201–210 in *Journal for the Theory of Social Behaviour* (37/2).

Walby, Sylvia (2003) 'The myth of the nation-state: theorising society and polities in a global era', pp. 529–546 in *Sociology* (37/3).

Watson, D. R. (1997) 'Prologue', pp. *iv–xii* in *Ethnographic Studies* (1).

Watts, D J. (2003) *Six Degrees: The Science of a Connected Age*. London: Heinemann.

Watts, D J. (1999) *Small Worlds: The Dynamics of Networks Between Order and Randomness*. Princeton: Princeton University Press.

Weber, Max (2001[1905]) *The Protestant Ethic and the Spirit of Capitalism*. Oxford: Blackwell.

Weber, Max (1978[1920]) *Economy and Society, Vols. I and II*. Berkeley: University of California Press.

Wellman, B. (ed.) (1999) *Networks in the Global Village*. Boulder, CO: Westview Press.

Whitehead, Alfred North (1963[1925]) *Science and the Modern World*. New York: Mentor.

Williams, Raymond (1990[1958]) *Culture and Society*. London: The Hogarth Press.

Williams, Robin (2000) *Making Identity Matter: Identity, Society and Social Interaction*. Durham: Sociology Press.

Wittgenstein, Ludwig (1967[1953]) *Philosophical Investigations*. Oxford: Blackwell.

Wrong, Dennis (1961) 'The over-socialised conception of man in modern sociology', pp. 183–193 in *American Sociological Review* (26).

Index

actor-network theory 17
Adorno, T., and Horkheimer, M. 72,
    153–154
agency 18–22, 28, 33, 99, 100,
    102–103, 115, 116, 133, 141, 142,
    144, 161
agency and structure
  issues of, *passim*
alienation 39, 53
Althusser, Louis 55–59, 94, 96, 117,
    142
Anchor, Robert 123
Anderson, Perry 41, 42
Archer, Margaret S. 6, 17, 20, 21, 23,
    24, 145, 161–162, 163, 164
architecture 137

Baldamus, W. 100, 105
Barth, Frederik 140, 150
Bataille, A. 72
Becker, Howard S. 5, 37, 117
Bendix, Reinhard 36
Berger, P., and Luckmann, T. 11, 12
Bhaskar, Roy 5, 6, 71, 161, 162, 163,
    164
Birmingham Centre for Contemporary
    Cultural Studies 117
Bittner, Egon 47, 48, 80–81, 115
Blau, P., and Duncan, O. D. 16
Blumer, Herbert 4, 9, 10, 13, 15, 101
Boissevan, J. 140
Bottero, Wendy 121
Bourdieu, Pierre 14, 18, 71, 86–99,
    100, 117, 118, 129, 142–143, 145,
    161, 162, 163
  habitus 90, 91, 92–93, 94, 96, 98, 99,
    142–143, 162, 163
  misrecognition 96
  practice 91–92, 93

social reproduction 95–96, 99
Bucher, R., and Strauss, A. 48
bureaucracy 120

capitalism 52–53, 62–63, 66, 122
Chen, K-H. 128
Chomsky, Noam 135
class consciousness 36
Cohen, Anthony P. 42, 140
Cohen, G. A. 53–56, 58
collective concepts 7, 24, 34–51, 147
collective understandings 82–84, 85,
    106, 107, 108, 109, 136, 158–159,
    164
collectivities 138–141, 145, 147, 149
Collier, Andrew 8
Collins, Randall 9, 50
  interaction ritual chains 50, 164
commodities 60, 61–62
communicative reason 73, 74
community 41–43, 73, 74
Comte, Auguste 35, 52
conscience collective 36, 37
consciousness 97
constraint 19, 20, 24, 63–64, 89, 95,
    105, 106, 133, 143, 145, 162, 163
conversation analysis 29, 104, 111, 112
crime 123
critical realism 5–7, 8, 161, 164
culture 37, 135

decision-making 81–82, 88, 89, 93, 97,
    150
definition of the situation 30–31, 104,
    105
demographic structures 33
Derrida, Jacques 72
Descartes, René 34, 72
determinism 6, 79, 80, 93, 98–99, 100,

142, 143, 143, 145, 161, 162

Dilthey, Wilhelm 73

Dobash, Russell 122, 123

dualism 4, 6, 7–8, 10, 13, 14, 15, 66, 71–74, 77, 78, 84, 85, 86, 87–91, 98, 100, 101, 102, 135, 154, 160, 162, 164

Duchess of Sutherland 65

Durkheim, Emile 4, 5, 8, 12, 14, 18, 29, 34, 35, 36, 51, 52, 106–107, 117, 134, 135, 137, 159, 161

Durkheim, E., and Mauss, M. 92

economic man 34

education 95

Eliot, T. S. 133

Elster, Jon 23, 54–55, 56, 58–59

emergent properties 6, 26, 27

enactment 38, 41, 45, 48, 49, 50, 105, 112, 148

Engels, Friedrich 23, 44, 45, 54

Enlightenment 34, 140

ethnomethodology 9, 12–13, 29, 101, 103, 104, 105, 109, 110, 111, 112, 113, 114, 116

existentialism 9, 89, 91, 93, 99

family 48–49, 77

feminism 48

Ferguson, Harvie 10

fetishism 53, 60

Fine, Gary Alan 14, 50

Finnegan, Ruth 50

Flyvbjerg, Bent 120

Foucault, Michel 72, 117–130, 161, 162, 163, 164
  discourse 125, 126, 128–129, 162, 163, 164
  power/knowledge 119, 124, 129
  structure and agency 119

Fox, N. J. 117, 118, 119, 121

France 44

free will 89

Friedmann, H. 140

functional analysis 40, 48, 49, 54–55, 58, 65, 94, 113, 137

Gadamer, Hans-Georg 75

Garfinkel, Harold 4, 12, 29, 103, 113, 114–115

Garfinkel, H., and Sacks, H. 115

generic social processes 30, 104

Geras, Norman 56–59

Giddens, Anthony 4, 17, 18, 26, 27, 44, 71, 93, 100–116, 117, 118, 129, 142, 145, 161, 162, 163
  duality of structure 102, 109, 144, 162
  notion of structure 106–109
  social reproduction 102, 109, 110, 144

Goffman, Erving 29, 93, 111, 146

Gramsci, Antonio 117

'grand' theory 103, 104, 116

Habermas, Jurgen 18, 71–85, 101, 117, 118, 120, 145, 161, 162, 163
  concept of system 74–77, 78, 79, 80–84
  ideal speech situation 78, 81–82, 84
  public sphere 83
  purposive codes 78–80, 162

Hall, Stuart 117, 124–129
  'encoding/decoding' 127–128

Healy, Kieran 17, 19

Hegel G. W. H. 52, 72, 92

Heidegger, M. 72

hermeneutics 75, 76, 100, 103, 152

Hilbert, Richard A. 12

Hobbes, Thomas 34, 52, 110, 155

Hobsbawm, E., and Ranger, T. 43

honour 156, 157, 160, 165

Hughes, Everett 29

human world 133ff

Husserl, Edmund 11, 73, 92

idealist philosophy 52, 75

identity 49, 50, 62

ideology 59, 60, 78, 114

inequality 15, 52

individualism 4, 5, 7, 8, 9, 10, 14, 18, 19, 32, 35, 40–41, 66, 72–73, 74, 154, 156, 157, 158, 159, 160, 161, 162

institutions 136, 137, 146, 150, 161

interaction 14, 15, 16, 38, 42, 45, 50, 51, 62, 71, 73, 74, 75, 76, 77, 78, 84, 85, 101, 104, 106, 111, 136, 145, 146, 152, 154, 157, 160, 161, 163, 164, 165

International Sociological Association 134
intersubjectivity 7, 11, 73, 74, 75, 77, 101
invention of tradition 43
'iron cage' of bureaucracy 80

Jackson, Peter 152
James, Simon 42
Jenkins, Richard 5

Kant, Immanuel 162
Kendall, G., and Wickham, G. 126
Keynes, J. M. 157
King, Anthony 5, 6, 14
Kiniven, O., and Piiroinen, T. 7
Kirchberg, Volker 9
Kuper, Adam 135

labour power 63–64, 65
language 27, 75, 107–108, 127, 136, 157
Layder, Derek 102
Leach, Edmund R. 140
Lemert, Edwin 37
Leviathan 155, 158, 161
Lévi-Strauss, Claude 107, 135, 144, 153
lifeworld 71–78, 80–84, 85, 163, 165
Locke, John 162
Lockwood, David 17
Lopez, J., and Scott, J. 134, 146, 147
Lord of the Rings 152ff
Lukes, Steven 8

Maines, David R. 8, 9, 50
Malinowski, Bronislaw 157
March, J., and Olsen, J. 81
Marshall, Gordon 45–46
Martin, Peter J. 4, 139, 147
Marx, Karl 18, 21, 23, 39, 43, 44, 45, 51, 52–67, 72, 117, 118, 133, 144, 153
  and human nature 57–58
Mauss, Marcel 129, 157
Mead, G. H. 9, 12, 38
meritocracy 96
methodological individualism 18, 22–25, 59
micro-sociology 7, 8, 9–13, 14, 18,

19–20, 28, 29, 111
middle-range theory 103, 104
money 82
Montesquieu, Charles 35
moral order 12
Morgan, David 48–49
Mouzelis, Nicos 17, 19, 28–30
myth 153–154, 160

nation-state 41–43
negotiated order 47
'New Criminologists' 117
Nietzsche, Friedrich 72
Nisbet, Robert 8

O'Neill, John 120
organic analogy 137
organisations 46–48, 80–81

Pahl, Raymond E. 43
Parsons, Talcott 4, 18, 77, 83, 94, 101, 110, 119, 142, 157–160, 164
Perkmann, M. 17, 20, 28, 31, 32
phenomenology 9, 10–12, 13, 18, 73, 88
Poggi, Gianfranco 36
Polanyi, Karl 157
Popper, Karl 22, 23
Porter, Sam 123, 124, 126
power 122, 123, 124, 125, 126, 129, 164
primitive accumulation 64–66
professions 48
psychoanalysis 78
psychology 35

quantitative studies 16

rational action theory 89, 91
rationality 47, 58–59, 72–73, 77, 80, 158
reification 7, 11–12, 14, 24, 25, 33, 38, 40, 60, 67, 88, 99, 135, 138, 145
religion 52, 55
Ricardo, David 52
Ritzer, George 134, 146
Rojek, Chris 124, 125, 127
Rubenstein, David 7
rules 47, 79–80, 92, 155, 162–163

Sartre, Jean-Paul 109
Savage, Mike 46
Sawyer, R. Keith 6, 146, 150
Scotland 43
Scottish Enlightenment 35
Sharrock, Wes 5, 15, 135
Schütz, Alfred 4, 5, 11, 73, 93, 105
Schwalbe, Michael *et al.* 45
Searle, John 82
self-fulfilling prophecy 110
Shackle, G. L. S. 109
Shaw, Bernard 153
Sibeon, R. 17, 31–32
Simmel, Georg 3, 39, 140, 149, 150
situations 106, 111
Slack, J. D. 127
Smith, Adam 34, 52
Smith, J., and Jenks, C. 151
social action 13, 18, 30, 101, 103–106, 109ff, 111ff
social boundaries 138–140, 148
social change 97
social class 16, 23, 35, 43–46, 52, 54, 63
social construction 121–122
social contract 34
Social Darwinism 35
social groups 147–149, 156–157, 159–160
social networks 149–150
social order 155, 156, 158, 159
social process 9–10, 14, 15, 46
social structure 5–7, 8, 10, 13, 15, 17–33, 60, 133–151
socialisation 12, 14, 92, 95, 96, 109
society 4, 5, 16, 41–43, 103, 105, 114, 135, 138, 139, 140, 152
sociological imagination 16
Sparks, Colin 128
Spencer, Herbert 137
Stones, R. 105
Strauss, Anselm 29, 47
structuralism 55–56, 65, 66, 94, 99, 100, 103, 106, 109, 117, 118, 122, 129, 135
structuration 17, 18, 44, 100–116, 133, 143, 144, 161, 162
subculture 37
'subjective' meaning 38, 40, 51, 75, 76, 105, 145

survey methodology 45
symbolic interactionism 9–10, 13, 18, 29, 30, 37, 38, 50, 101, 103, 104, 105, 109, 110, 111, 112, 113, 116
symbolic representation 38, 41, 42, 43, 45, 47, 48, 49, 50, 138–139
systems analysis 46, 141–142, 150–151

theoretical fiat 31–32
Thompson, E. P. 120
Tolkein, J. R. R. 152, 153, 155, 162, 163, 164

unified theory 5, 17, 18, 19, 103
unintended consequences 25, 26, 109–110, 112ff, 137, 141, 150
Urry, John 139–140, 149
utilitarianism 35, 155, 157, 158, 159

voluntarism 13, 20, 21, 102, 103, 105, 106, 109
'voluntary servitude' 114

Wagner, Richard 152, 153, 154, 165
Walby, Sylvia 42
Watson, D. R. 3
Weber, Max 4, 12, 23, 34, 36, 38–41, 44, 52, 71, 77, 91, 92, 104, 110, 117, 120, 129, 140, 141
Williams, Raymond 3
Williams, Robin 35
Wittgenstein, Ludwig 80, 157
work 62–64